Outlook® 2007

FOR

DUMMIES®

by Bill Dyszel

BICENTENNIAL
1807
WILEY
2007
BICENTENNIAL

Wiley Publishing, Inc.

Outlook® 2007 For Dummies®

Published by
Wiley Publishing, Inc.
111 River Street
Hoboken, NJ 07030-5774
www.wiley.com

Copyright © 2007 by Wiley Publishing, Inc., Indianapolis, Indiana

Published by Wiley Publishing, Inc., Indianapolis, Indiana

Published simultaneously in Canada

For general information on our other products and services, please contact our Customer Care Department within the U.S. at 800-762-2974, outside the U.S. at 317-572-3993, or fax 317-572-4002.

For technical support, please visit www.wiley.com/techsupport.

Wiley also publishes its books in a variety of electronic formats. Some content that appears in print may not be available in electronic books.

Library of Congress Control Number: 2006934819

ISBN-13: 978-0-470-03830-7

ISBN-10: 0-470-03830-6

Manufactured in the United States of America

10 9 8 7 6 5 4 3 2 1

1B/QY/RR/QW/IN

WILEY

About the Author

Bill Dyszel is a popular speaker and trainer, author of 18 books, and contributor to many leading national magazines, including *PC Magazine*. His speeches and seminars aim to help people simplify their lives by using technology wisely. Bill is also an award-winning filmmaker and an accomplished entertainer. He sang with the New York City Opera for 14 years and still appears regularly on the New York stage. His one-man movie musicals have been seen from coast to coast as part of the 48 Hour Film Project.

Author's Acknowledgments

I'd like to thank all the wonderful people who helped me make this book entertaining and useful to the reader, especially Tonya Cupp, Lee Musick, Greg Croy, and the whole staff of Wiley Publishing, Inc. that makes this series possible. Thanks also to my agent, Laura Lewin of Studio B Productions.

Publisher's Acknowledgments

We're proud of this book; please send us your comments through our online registration form located at www.dummies.com/register/.

Some of the people who helped bring this book to market include the following:

Acquisitions, Editorial, and Media Development

Project Editor: Tonya Maddox Cupp

(Previous Edition: Linda Morris)

Acquisitions Editor: Greg Croy

Technical Editor: Lee Musick

Editorial Manager: Jodi Jensen

Media Development Specialists: Angela Denny, Kate Jenkins, Steven Kudirka, Kit Malone, Travis Silvers

Media Development Manager: Laura VanWinkle

Editorial Assistant: Amanda Foxworth

Sr. Editorial Assistant: Cherie Case

Cartoons: Rich Tennant (www.the5thwave.com)

Composition Services

Project Coordinator: Erin Smith

Layout and Graphics: Carl Byers, Lavonne Cook, Denny Hager, Barbara Moore, Barry Offringa, Lynsey Osborn, Rashell Smith, Alicia South

Proofreaders: Christine Pingleton, Techbooks

Indexer: Sherry Massey

Publishing and Editorial for Technology Dummies

Richard Swadley, Vice President and Executive Group Publisher

Andy Cummings, Vice President and Publisher

Mary Bednarek, Executive Acquisitions Director

Mary C. Corder, Editorial Director

Publishing for Consumer Dummies

Diane Graves Steele, Vice President and Publisher

Joyce Pepple, Acquisitions Director

Composition Services

Gerry Fahey, Vice President of Production Services

Debbie Stailey, Director of Composition Services

Contents at a Glance

Table of Contents

Introduction

- -

*O*ver 200 million people use Outlook every day. If you think they're all sending e-mail to you, you may be right. Ninety percent of those people know less than ten percent of Outlook's features according to the folks at Microsoft. That means that you'll be getting even more messages once everyone reads this book (as I hope everyone does). So you need to know more about Outlook in order to keep up with the fastest rats in the race. Even if that's not your goal, Outlook gives you a fighting chance of finishing your work before you run out of workweek.

Seriously, Microsoft Outlook has been the world's most popular tool for organizing your business, your life, and your communications for over ten years. I've had the pleasure of training literally thousands of people on the power that Outlook can bring to your work and the ways it can simplify your life. People are often amazed when they discover how much they can reduce their daily workload by learning to use Outlook effectively.

Microsoft Outlook was designed to make organizing your daily information easy — almost automatic. You already have sophisticated programs for word processing and number crunching, but Outlook pulls together everything you need to know about your daily tasks, appointments, e-mail messages, and other details. More important, Outlook enables you to use the same methods to deal with many different kinds of information, so you have to understand only one program to deal with the many kinds of details that fill your life, such as

- Finding a customer's phone number
- Remembering that important meeting
- Planning your tasks for the day and checking them off after you're done
- Recording all the work you do so you can find what you did and when you did it

Outlook is a Personal Information Manager (Microsoft calls it a Desktop Information Manager) that can act as your assistant in dealing with the flurry of small-but-important details that stand between you and the work you do. You can just as easily keep track of personal information that isn't business-related and keep both business and personal information in the same convenient location.

About This Book

As you read this book and work with Outlook, you discover how useful Outlook is, as well as new ways to make it more useful for the things you do most. If you fit in any of the following categories, this book is for you:

- ✔ Your company just adopted Outlook as its e-mail program and you need to learn how to use it in a hurry.

- ✔ You've used Outlook for years just because "it was there," but you know you've only used a tenth of its power. Now you're overwhelmed with work and want to plow through that mountain of tasks faster by using Outlook better.

- ✔ You're planning to purchase (or have just purchased) Outlook and want to know what you can do with Outlook — as well as how to do it.

- ✔ You want an easier, more efficient tool for managing tasks, schedules, e-mail, and other details in your working life.

Even if you don't fall into one of these groups, this book gives you simple, clear explanations of how Outlook can work for you. It's hard to imagine any computer user who wouldn't benefit from the features that Outlook offers.

If all you want is a quick, guided tour of Outlook, you can skim this book; it covers everything you need to get you started. Getting a handle on most major Outlook features is fairly easy — that's how the program is designed. (You can also keep the book handy as a reference for the tricks that you may not need every day.)

The first part of this book gives you enough information to make sense of the whole program. Because Outlook is intended to be simple and consistent throughout, when you've got the big picture, the details are fairly simple (usually).

Don't be fooled by Outlook's friendliness, though — you can find a great deal of power in it if you want to dig deeply enough. Outlook links up with your Microsoft Office applications, and it's fully programmable by anyone who wants to tackle a little Visual Basic script writing (I don't get into that in this book). You may not want to do the programming yourself, but finding people who can do that for you isn't hard; just ask around.

Foolish Assumptions

I assume that you know how to turn on your computer and how to use a mouse and keyboard. In case you need a brush up on Windows, I throw in reminders as I go along. If Windows and Microsoft Office are strange to you, I recommend picking up (respectively) Andy Rathbone's *Windows Vista For Dummies* (Wiley) or Wally Wang's *Microsoft Office 2007 For Dummies* (Wiley).

If all you have is a copy of this book and a computer running Outlook, you can certainly do basic, useful things right away, as well as a few fun things. And after some time, you'll be able to do *many* fun and useful things.

How This Book Is Organized

To make it easier to find out how to do what you want to do, this book is divided into parts. Each part covers a different aspect of using Outlook. Because you can use similar methods to do many different jobs with Outlook, the first parts of the book focus on *how* to use Outlook. The later parts concentrate on *what* you can use Outlook to do.

Part 1: Getting the Competitive Edge with Outlook

I learn best by doing, so the first chapter is a quick guide to the things that most people do with Outlook on a typical day. You find out how easy it is to use Outlook for routine tasks such as handling messages, notes, and appointments. You can get quite a lot of mileage out of Outlook even if you do only the things our fictional detective does in the first chapter.

Because Outlook allows you to use similar methods to do many things, I go on to show you the things that stay pretty much the same throughout the program: how to create new items from old ones by using drag-and-drop; ways to view items that make your information easy to understand at a glance; and the features Outlook offers to make it easier to move, copy, and organize your files.

Part 11: Taming the E-Mail Beast

E-mail is now the most popular function of computers. Tens of millions of people are hooked up to the Internet, an office network, or one of the popular online services, such as MSN or AOL.

The problem is that e-mail can still be a little too complicated. As I show you in Part II, however, Outlook makes e-mail easier. Computers are notoriously finicky about the exact spelling of addresses, correctly hooking up to the actual mail service, and making sure that the text and formatting of the message fit the software you're using. Outlook keeps track of the details involved in getting your message to its destination.

Outlook also allows you to receive e-mail from a variety of sources and manage the messages in one place. You can slice and dice your list of incoming and outgoing e-mail messages to help you keep track of what you send, to whom you send it, and the day and time you send it.

Part III: Managing Contacts, Dates, Tasks, and More

Outlook takes advantage of its special relationship with your computer and your office applications (Microsoft Outlook with Microsoft Office, Microsoft Internet Explorer, and Microsoft Windows — notice a pattern emerging here?) to tie your office tasks together more cleanly than other such programs — and make it easier for you to deal with all the stuff you have to do. The chapters in Part III show you how to get the job done with Outlook.

If you've got yellow sticky notes covering your monitor, refrigerator, desktop, or bathroom door, you'll get a great deal of mileage out of Outlook's Notes feature. Notes are little yellow (or blue, or green) squares that look just like those handy paper sticky notes that you stick everywhere as reminders and then lose. About the only thing that you can't do is set your coffee cup on one and mess up what you wrote.

Part IV: Beyond the Basics: Tips and Tricks You Won't Want to Miss

Some parts of Outlook are less famous than others, but no less useful. Part IV guides you through the sections of Outlook that the real power users take advantage of to stay ahead of the pack.

There are parts of Outlook that many people never discover. Some of those parts are obscure but powerful — others aren't part of Outlook at all (technically speaking) — but you'll get a lot of mileage from knowing how to do things like create custom forms and set up Outlook to get e-mail from the Internet. If you use Outlook at home, in your own business, or just want to soup up your copy of Outlook for high-performance work, you'll find useful tips in Part IV.

Part V: Outlook at the Office

Beyond planning and scheduling, you probably spend a great deal of your working time with other people, and you need to coordinate your schedule with theirs (unless you make your living doing something strange and anti-social, like digging graves or writing computer books). Outlook allows you to share schedule and task information with other people and synchronize information with them. You can also assign tasks to other people if you don't want to do them yourself (now *there's* a timesaver). Be careful, though; other people can assign those tasks right back to you.

Part VI: The Part of Tens

Why ten? Why not! If you must have a reason, ten is the highest number you can count to without taking off your shoes. A program as broad as Outlook leaves a great deal of flotsam and jetsam that doesn't quite fit into any category, so I sum up the best of that material in groups of ten.

Conventions Used in This Book

Outlook has many unique features, but it also has lots in common with other Windows programs — dialog boxes, pull-down menus, toolbars, and so on. To be productive with Outlook, you need to understand how these features work — and recognize the conventions I use for describing these features throughout this book.

Dialog boxes

Even if you're not new to Windows, you deal with dialog boxes more in Outlook than you do in many other Microsoft Office programs because so many items in Outlook are created with dialog boxes, which may also be called *forms*. E-mail message forms, appointments, name and address forms, and plenty of other common functions in Outlook use dialog boxes to ask you what you want to do. The following list summarizes the essential parts of a dialog box:

✔ **Title bar:** The title bar tells you the name of the dialog box.

✔ **Text boxes:** Text boxes are blank spaces into which you type information. When you click a text box, you see a blinking I-beam pointer, which means that you can type text there.

✔ **Control buttons:** In the upper-right corner of a dialog box, you find three control buttons:

  • The *Close button* looks like an X and makes the dialog box disappear.

  • The *Size button* toggles between maximizing the dialog box (making it take up the entire screen) and resizing it (making it take up less than the entire screen).

  • The *Minimize button* makes the dialog box seem to go away but really just hides it in the taskbar at the bottom of your screen until you click the taskbar to make the dialog box come back.

✔ **Tabs:** Tabs look like little file-folder tabs. If you click one, you see a new page of the dialog box. Tabs are just like the divider tabs in a ring binder; click one to change sections.

The easiest way to move around a dialog box is to click the part that you want to use. If you're a real whiz on the keyboard, you may prefer to press the Tab key to move around the dialog box; this method is much faster if you're a touch typist. Otherwise, you're fine just mousing around.

Tabs and Ribbons

Some Outlook screens feature a colorful ribbon across the top, adorned with festive-looking buttons. Many of those buttons are labeled with the names of the things that happen if you click them with your mouse, such as Save, Follow Up, or Delete. Sometimes a row of tabs appears just above the ribbon, reading something like Task, Write, Insert. Clicking any of those words reveals an entirely different ribbon full of buttons for a different set of tasks.

This arrangement is a new feature with the release of Microsoft Office 2007, so even if you've used Microsoft Office or Microsoft Outlook for many years, it is new to you. The idea is that people frequently call Microsoft and ask the company to add features to Outlook that don't need to be added because they've been there all along. The ribbon is supposed to make those mysterious, hidden features more obvious. I think a better solution is to get more people to read this book. The best solution is to get everyone to buy this book. As a public service, I'm doing what I can to make that happen. I hope you'll join the cause.

Links

Links are special pictures or pieces of text that you can click to change what you see on-screen. If you're used to surfing the Internet, you're used to clicking blue, underlined text to switch from one Web page to another. Outlook has some links that work just like links on the Internet. When you see underlined text, the text is most likely a link — click that text if you want to see where it leads.

Keyboard shortcuts

Normally, you can choose any Windows command in at least these three ways (and sometimes more):

- ✔ Choose a menu command or click a toolbar button.

- ✔ Press a keyboard combination, such as Ctrl+B, which means holding down the Ctrl key and pressing the letter B (you use this command to make text bold).

- ✔ Press the F10 key or the spacebar to pull down a menu, press an arrow key to choose a command, and press Enter (way too much trouble, but possible for those who love a challenge).

You often tell Outlook what to do by choosing from menus at the top of the screen. I normally simplify menu commands by saying something like "Choose Yeah ⇨ Sure," which means "Choose the Yeah menu; then choose the Sure command."

One rather confusing feature of Outlook is the way each menu appears in two different views. When you first click the name of a menu in the menu bar, a short menu appears to show the most popular choices from that menu. If you leave the menu open for about two seconds, the menu suddenly doubles in length, showing you every command available on that menu. Don't worry, your eyes aren't going bad — that's how the product was designed. Microsoft programmers believe that some people are more comfortable with shorter menus, whereas others prefer longer menus, so this "Jack-in-the-box" scheme will either make everyone equally happy or equally confused.

Icons Used in This Book

Sometimes the fastest way to go through a book is to look at the pictures — in this case, icons that draw your attention to specific types of information that's useful to know. Here are the icons I use in this book:

The Remember icon points out helpful information. (Everything in this book is helpful, but this stuff is even *more* helpful.)

The Tip icon points out a hint or trick for saving time and effort, or something that makes Outlook easier to understand.

The Warning icon points to something that you may want to be careful about in order to prevent problems.

The Technical Stuff icon marks background information that you can skip, although it may make good conversation at a really dull party.

Where to Go from Here

A wise person once said, "The best way to start is by starting." Okay, that's not all that wise, but why quibble? Plunge in!

Part I
Getting the Competitive Edge with Outlook

The 5th Wave   By Rich Tennant

"Your mail program looks fine. I don't know why you're not receiving any personal e-mails. Have you explored the possibility that you may not have any friends?"

In this part . . .

*H*undreds of millions of people spend most of their working life in Outlook, making appointments, sending and reading messages and managing tasks. Many of my consulting clients have learned that a good understanding of the simplest Outlook techniques can speed up their work life and help them reach their goals faster. In this part, I'll give you the "big picture" of how to work more effectively with Outlook.

Chapter 1

Fundamental Features: How Did You Ever Do without Outlook?

In This Chapter

▶ Reading and creating e-mail

▶ Sending files by e-mail

▶ Entering appointments and contacts

▶ Checking your calendar

▶ Entering tasks

▶ Taking notes

*O*utlook is easier to use than you might think; it also does a lot more than you might realize. Even if you use only about 10 percent of Outlook's features, you'll be amazed at how this little program can streamline your life and spiff up your communications. People get pretty excited about Outlook — even if they take advantage of only a tiny fraction of what the package can do. I'm kicking off this book with "Outlook's Greatest Hits," the things you'll want to do with Outlook every single day. The list sounds simple enough: sending e-mail, making appointments, and so on. But there's more here than meets the eye; Outlook does ordinary things extraordinarily well. I know you want to do the same, so read on.

Easy Ways to Do Anything in Outlook

Well, okay, maybe you can't use Outlook to decipher hieroglyphics — but if you learn a little about some basic techniques, you can do a lot in Outlook — click an icon to do something, view something, or complete something.

Using Outlook is so simple, I can sum it up in just a few how-to sentences to cover the most common tasks:

✔ **Open an item and read it:** Double-click the item.

✔ **Create a new item:** Click an icon in the Navigation Pane, click the New button in the toolbar at the top of the screen, and fill out the form that appears. When you're done, click the button labeled Send — or, alternatively, Save and Close.

✔ **Delete an item:** Click the item once to select it, and then click the Delete icon in the toolbar at the top of the screen. The Delete icon contains a black X.

✔ **Move an item:** Use your mouse to drag the item to where you want it.

Does that seem too simple? No problem. If you have an itch to complicate things, you *could* try to use Outlook while hopping on a pogo stick or flying the space shuttle. But why? These four tricks can take you a long way.

Outlook can also do some sophisticated tricks, such as automatically sorting your e-mail or creating automated form letters, but you'll need to learn a few details to take advantage of those tricks. The other 300 pages of this book cover the finer points of Outlook. If you only wanted the basics, I could've sent you a postcard.

The pictures you see in this book and the instructions you read assume you're using Outlook the way it comes out of the box from Microsoft — with all the standard options installed. If you don't like the way the program looks (or what things are named) when you install Outlook, you can change nearly everything. If you change too much, however, some instructions and examples I give you won't make sense, because then the parts of the program that I talk about may have names you gave them, rather than the ones Microsoft originally assigned. The Microsoft people generally did a good job of making Outlook easy to use. I suggest leaving the general arrangement alone until you're comfortable using Outlook.

Reading E-Mail

E-mail is Outlook's most popular feature. I've run across people who didn't know Outlook could do anything but exchange e-mail messages. It's a good thing Outlook makes it so easy to read your e-mail.

When you start Outlook, normally you see a screen with three columns. The center column is your list of messages; the right column (called the Reading Pane) contains the text of one of those messages. If the message is short enough, you may see its entire text in the right column, as shown in Figure 1-1. If the message is longer, you'll have to open it to see the whole thing.

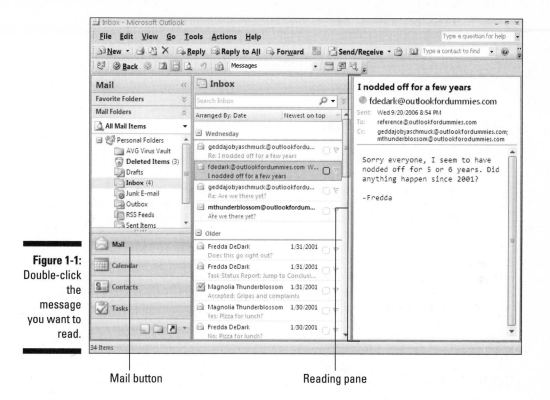

Figure 1-1:
Double-click
the
message
you want to
read.

Mail button   Reading pane

Here's how to see the entire message:

1. **Click the Mail button in the Navigation Pane.**

   You don't need this step if you can already see the messages, but it doesn't hurt.

2. **Double-click the title of the message.**

   Now you can see the entire message.

3. **Press Esc.**

   The message form closes.

A quick way to skim the messages in your Inbox is to click a message, then press the up-arrow or down-arrow key on your keyboard. You can move through your message list as you read the text of your messages in the Reading Pane.

If you feel overwhelmed by the number of e-mail messages you get each day, you're not alone. Billions and billions of e-mail messages fly around the Internet each day, and lots of people are feeling buried in messages. You discover the secrets of sorting and managing your messages in Chapter 6.

Answering E-Mail

When you open an e-mail message in Outlook to read it, buttons labeled Reply and Reply to All appear at the top of the message screen. That's a hint. When you want to reply to a message you're reading, click the Reply button. A new message form opens, already addressed to the person who sent you the message. If you're reading a message sent to several people besides you, you also have the option of sending a reply to everyone involved by clicking the Reply to All button.

When you reply to a message, the text of the message that was sent to you is automatically included. Some people like to include original text in their replies, some don't. In Chapter 5, I show you how to change what Outlook automatically includes in replies.

Creating New E-Mail Messages

At its easiest, the process of creating a new e-mail message in Outlook is ridiculously simple. Even a child can do it. If you can't get a child to create a new e-mail message for you, you can even do it yourself.

To create a new e-mail message, follow these steps:

1. **Click the Mail button in the Navigation Pane.**

   Your message list appears.

2. **Click the New button in the toolbar.**

   The New Message form appears.

3. **Fill out the New Message form.**

   Put the address of your recipient in the To box, a subject in the Subject box, and type a message in the main message box.

4. **Click Send.**

   Your message is on its way.

If you want to send a plain e-mail message, that's all you have to do. If you prefer to send a fancy e-mail, Outlook provides the bells and whistles — some of which are actually useful. You might (for example) send a High

Priority message to impress some big shots, or send a Confidential message about a hush-hush topic. (Discover the mysteries of confidential e-mail in Chapter 4.)

Sending a File

Call me crazy, but I suspect you have more to do than exchange e-mail all day. You probably do lots of daily work in programs other than Outlook. You might create documents in Microsoft Word or build elaborate spreadsheets with Excel. When you want to send a file by e-mail, Outlook gets involved, although sometimes it works in the background.

To e-mail a document you created in Microsoft Word, for example, follow these steps:

1. **Open the document in Microsoft Word.**

   The document appears on-screen.

2. **Click the Office icon in the upper-left corner of the screen and choose Send To ➪ Mail Recipient (as attachment).**

   The New Message form appears with your document listed on the Attachment line (as pictured in Figure 1-2).

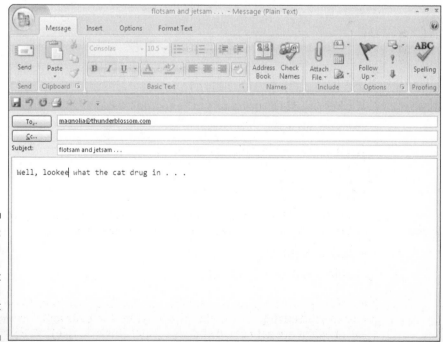

Figure 1-2:
You can
e-mail a
document
right from
Microsoft
Word.

3. **Type the e-mail address of your recipient on the To line.**

   The address you enter appears on the To line.

4. **Click Send.**

   Your file is now en route.

When you're just sending one Word file, these steps are the easiest way to go. If you're sending more than one file, I describe a more powerful way to attach files in Chapter 5.

Entering an Appointment

If you've ever used an old-fashioned paper planner, the Outlook calendar will look familiar to you. When you click the Calendar icon and then click the Day tab, you see a grid in the middle of the screen with lines representing each half hour of the day (as in Figure 1-3). To enter an appointment at a certain time, just click the line next to the time you want your appointment to begin, type a name for your appointment, and press Enter.

If you want to enter more detailed information about your appointment — such as ending time, location, category, and so on; see Chapter 8 for the nitty-gritty about keeping your calendar.

Figure 1-3:
Track your busy schedule in the Outlook calendar.

Checking Your Calendar

Time management involves more than just entering appointments. If you're really busy, you want to manage your time by slicing and dicing your list of appointments to see when you're free enough to add even more appointments. You can choose from several different views of your calendar by clicking the Day, Week, and Month buttons at the top of the Calendar screen. If you need a more elaborate collection of calendar views, choose one of the views listed in the Current View section of the Navigation Pane. To really master time management, see Chapter 8 to see the different ways you can view your Outlook calendar.

Adding a Contact

When it's not *what* you know but *who* you know, you need a good tool for keeping track of who's who. Outlook is a great tool for managing your list of names and addresses, and it's just as easy to use as your Little Black Book. To enter a new contact, click the Contacts button in the Navigation Pane; then click the New button on the toolbar to open the New Contact entry form. Fill in the blanks on the form (an example appears in Figure 1-4), and then click Save and Close. Presto — you have a Contacts list.

Figure 1-4: Keep detailed information about everyone you know in the contacts list.

Outlook does a lot more than your little black book — if you know the ropes. Chapter 7 reveals the secrets of searching, sorting, and grouping the names on your list — and of using e-mail to keep in touch with all the important people in your life.

Entering a Task

Entering a task in Outlook isn't much of a task itself. You can click the Task button see a list of your tasks in a flash. If you see the words Type a New Task, you've got a clue.

To enter a new task, follow these steps:

1. **Click the Tasks button in the Navigation Bar.**

   Your list of tasks appears.

2. **Click the text that says Type a New Task.**

   The words disappear, and you see the insertion point (a blinking line).

3. **Type the name of your task.**

   Your task appears in the block under the Subject line on the Task List (which in turn appears in Figure 1-5).

Figure 1-5:
Entering
your task in
the Task list.

   4. Press the Enter key.

   Your new task moves down to the Task List with your other tasks.

Outlook can help you manage anything from a simple shopping list to a complex business project. In Chapter 9, I show you how to deal with recurring tasks, how to regenerate tasks, and also how to mark tasks as complete (and earn the right to brag about how much you've accomplished). I also show you how to take advantage of a gizmo called the Task Pad to do the job even quicker.

Taking Notes

I have hundreds of little scraps of information that I need to keep somewhere, but until Outlook came along, I didn't have a place to put them. Now all the written flotsam and jetsam I've decided I need goes into my Outlook notes collection — where I can find it all again when I need it.

To create a new note, follow these steps:

   1. Click the Notes button in the Navigation Pane (or press Ctrl+5).

   Your list of notes appears.

   2. Click the New button in the toolbar.

   A blank note appears.

   3. Type the text you want to save.

   The text you type appears in the note (see Figure 1-6).

   4. Press Esc.

   The note you created appears in your list of notes.

An even quicker way to enter a note is to press Ctrl+Shift+N and type your note text. You can see how easy it is to amass a large collection of small notes. Chapter 10 tells you everything you need to know about notes, including how to find the notes you've saved, as well as how to sort, categorize, and organize your collection of notes and even how to delete the ones you don't need anymore.

After you're in the habit of using Outlook to organize your life, I'm sure you'll want to move beyond the basics. That's what the rest of this book shows you. When you're ready to share your work with other people, send e-mail like a pro, or just finish your workday by 5:00 p.m. and get home, you'll find ways to use Outlook to make your job — and your life — easier to manage.

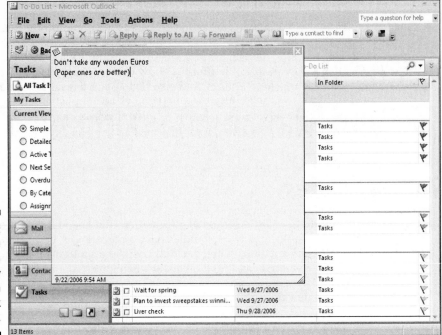

Figure 1-6:
Preserve
your prose
for posterity
in an
Outlook
note.

Chapter 2

Inside Outlook: Mixing, Matching, and Managing Information

. . . .

In This Chapter

▶ Examining the many faces of Outlook

▶ Choosing menus

▶ Using the tools of the trade

▶ Getting the big picture from the Information Viewer

▶ Fine-tuning with the Folder List

. . . .

*Y*ou have too much to do. I know that even if I've never even met you. It's now the 21st century, and if you can read this book, there's a good chance you have more things to do than time to do them. Welcome to the future — it's already here and it's already booked solid.

When I wrote the first edition of this book in 1996, few people had either sent or received an e-mail message. Now many people are slaves to e-mail messages, online appointments, and other electronically generated demands. That means we have more stuff to do than we ever imagined possible — even in the 1990s.

Fortunately, we all get more done now than we did in the past, partly because of tools like Microsoft Outlook. In fact, over 250 million people worldwide use Outlook to get more done every day. But most of those people only use a fraction of Outlook's power, so they work harder than necessary while getting less done. The people I've trained find that knowing even a tiny fraction more about what the program can do for them makes their lives noticeably easier. Let's hear it for making your life easier!

Outlook and Other Programs

Outlook is a part of Microsoft Office. It's called an Office *suite,* which means it's a collection of programs that includes everything you need to complete most office tasks. Ideally, the programs in a suite work together, enabling you to create documents that you couldn't create as easily with any of the individual programs. For example, you can copy a chart from a spreadsheet and paste it into a sales letter that you're creating in your word processor. You can also keep a list of mailing addresses in Outlook and use the list as a mailing list to address form letters (see Chapter 18).

Microsoft Office includes a group of programs that cost less to buy together than you would pay to buy them separately. The concept is a little like buying an encyclopedia; it's cheaper to buy the entire set than it is to buy one book at a time. Besides, who wants just one volume of an encyclopedia (unless you're interested only in aardvarks)?

Outlook turns up in connection with several other Microsoft products, as well. Microsoft Exchange Server is the backbone of the e-mail system in many corporations, and Outlook is often the program that employees of those corporations use to read their company e-mail. Another program, called SharePoint, connects to Outlook to help streamline the work of a group the way Outlook speeds up the work of an individual. Outlook's first cousin, Outlook Express (a.k.a. *Windows Mail*), is included free when you install Internet Explorer and as a part of all versions of Windows. Outlook is also linked strongly to Internet Explorer, although technically they're separate programs. You don't need to worry about all this, though. You can start Outlook and use it the same way no matter which other programs it's bundled with.

About Personal Information Management

When it comes to the basic work of managing names, addresses, appointments, and e-mail, the word processing and spreadsheet programs just don't get it. If you're planning a meeting, you need to know with whom you're meeting, what the other person's phone number is, and when you can find time to meet.

In designing Outlook, Microsoft took advantage of the fact that many people use Microsoft products for most of the work they do. The company created something called a *Personal Information Management (PIM)* program that speaks a common language with Microsoft Word, Excel, and the rest of the Microsoft Office suite. Microsoft also studied what kind of information people use most often, and tried to make sure that Outlook could handle most of it. The program also has scads of *customizability* (a tongue-twister of a buzzword that just means you can set it up however you need, after you know what you're doing).

Whatever the terminology, Outlook is — above all — easy to understand and hard to mess up. If you've used any version of Windows, you can just look at the screen and click a few icons to see what Outlook does. You won't break anything. If you get lost, going back to where you came from is easy. Even if you have no experience with Windows, Outlook is fairly straightforward to use.

There's No Place Like Home: Outlook's Main Screen

Outlook's appearance is very different from the other Microsoft Office applications. Instead of confronting you with a blank screen and a few menus and toolbars, Outlook begins by offering you large icons with simple names and a screen with information that's easy to use and understand. If you've spent much time surfing the Web, you'll find the Outlook layout pretty similar to many pages on the Web. Just select what you want to see by clicking an icon on the left side of the screen, and the information you selected appears on the right side of the screen.

Feeling at home when you work is nice. (Sometimes, when I'm at work, I'd rather *be* at home, but that's something else entirely.) Outlook makes a home for all your different types of information: names, addresses, schedules, to-do lists, and even a list to remind you of all the stuff you have to do today (or didn't get done yesterday). You can customize the main screen as easily as you rearrange your home furnishings. Even so, to make it easier to find your way around at first, I recommend waiting until you feel entirely at home with Outlook before you start rearranging the screen.

The Outlook main screen — which looks remarkably like Figure 2-1 — has all the usual parts of a Windows screen (see the Introduction if you're not used to the Windows screen), with a few important additions. At the left side of the screen, you see the Navigation Pane. Next to the Navigation Pane is the Information Viewer, the part of the screen that takes up most of the space.

Looking at modules

All the work you do in Outlook is organized into *modules,* or sections. Each module performs a specific job for you: The calendar stores and manages your schedule, the Tasks module stores and manages your To-Do list, and so on. Outlook is always showing you one of its modules in the main screen (also known as the Information Viewer). Whenever you're running Outlook, you're always using a module, even if the module contains no information — the same way your television can be tuned to a channel even if nothing is showing on that channel. The name of the module you're currently using is displayed in large type at the top of the Information Viewer, so you can easily tell which module is showing.

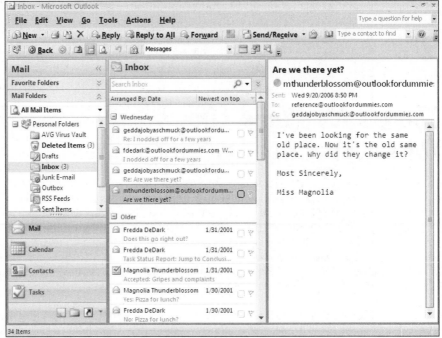

Each module is represented by a button in the Navigation Pane on the left side of the screen. Clicking any button takes you to a different module of Outlook:

- ✔ The **Mail button** takes you to the Inbox, which collects your incoming e-mail.

- ✔ The **Calendar button** shows you your schedule and all your appointments.

- ✔ The **Contacts button** calls up a module that stores names and addresses for you.

- ✔ The **Tasks button** displays your To-Do list.

- ✔ The **Notes button** takes you to a module you can use to keep track of random tidbits of information that don't quite fit anywhere else.

- ✔ The **Folder List button** displays the entire collection of Outlook folders, allowing you to click to see contents.

To change Outlook modules, do either of the following things:

- ✔ Click Go in the menu bar, and then choose the module you want from the menu that appears (as in Figure 2-2).

- ✔ For faster action, simply click the module's button in the Navigation Pane.

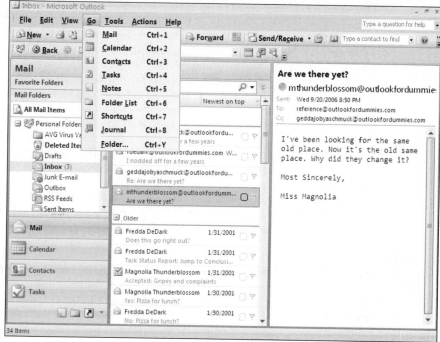

Figure 2-2:
Click Go and choose from the menu if you want to see a new module.

If you're using Outlook on your company network, your network's system administrator may have created a different set of buttons for you to work with. You may have a few more (or a few less) than you see in this book, but the buttons should work the same way.

Finding your way with the Navigation Pane

Navigating your way through some computer programs can be a pain, but Outlook can ease your discomfort somewhat with the help of the Navigation Pane. This part of the Outlook screen was formerly called the Outlook Bar, but to prevent anybody from committing EWI (E-mailing While Intoxicated), Microsoft changed the name of this critter to the Navigation Pane. Now you'll have to do your tippling in some other program.

The column on the left side of the Outlook screen is the one called the Navigation Pane. It contains several buttons with names such as Mail, Calendar, Contacts, Tasks, and Notes — the basic Outlook modules. I explain these modules later, but the names alone already tell you the story.

The Navigation Pane is made up of two sections: an upper window section and a bottom section made up of buttons. Each button in the bottom section is connected to one of Outlook's main modules — Mail, Calendar, Contacts, Tasks, and so on. Just click a button, any button, and you'll see what it sets in motion. Clicking the button changes the stuff on the main screen to fit what that button describes. Click the Calendar button, for example, and a Calendar screen shows up. Click Contacts, and you get a screen for names and addresses. The process is like changing the channels on the TV set. If you switch to a channel you don't want, switch to another — no problem.

The top section of the Navigation Pane displays different kinds of information at different times. Sometimes the top half of the Navigation Pane shows the Folder List, sometimes it shows a list of available views, and sometimes it contains phrases in blue lettering. You can click a phrase, such as Open a Shared Calendar, to do something. If you want to make the Folder List appear in this top window section, choose Go ⇨ Folder List.

Just above the Mail icon in the Navigation Pane, there's a gray border separating buttons on the bottom from the top part of the bar. If you drag that gray borderline downward with your mouse, the buttons in the Navigation Pane disappear one by one. That's something you might want to do to get a better view of your Folder List. You can make those buttons reappear by simply dragging the gray border upward again.

The Information Viewer: Outlook's hotspot

The Information Viewer is where most of the action happens in Outlook. If the Navigation Pane is like the channel selector on your TV set, the Information Viewer is like the TV screen. When you're reading e-mail, you look in the Information Viewer to read your messages; if you're adding or searching for contacts, you see contact names here. The Information Viewer is also where you can do all sorts of fancy sorting tricks that each module in Outlook lets you perform. (I talk about sorting Contacts, Tasks, and so forth in the chapters that apply to those modules.)

Because you can store more information in Outlook than you want to see at any one time, the Information Viewer shows you only a slice of the information available. The calendar, for example, can store dates as far back as the year 1601 and as far ahead as 4500. That might be so you can see the day when your credit card bills will finally be paid off; I'm not sure. That's a lot of time, but the Information Viewer shows it to you in manageable slices. The smallest calendar slice you can look at is one day; the largest slice is a month.

The Information Viewer organizes the items it shows you into units called *views*. You can use the views that are included with Outlook when you install it, or you can create your own views and save them. (I go into more details about views in Chapter 16.)

You can navigate among the slices of information that Outlook shows you by clicking different parts of the Information Viewer. Some people use the word *browsing* for the process of moving around the Information Viewer — it's a little like thumbing through the pages of your pocket datebook (that is, if you have a million-page datebook). To see an example of how to use the Information Viewer, look at the Calendar module in Figure 2-3.

To browse the calendar data in the Information Viewer, follow these steps:

1. **Click the Calendar button in the Navigation Pane (or press Ctrl+2).**

   The calendar appears.

2. **Click the word Week at the top of the Calendar screen.**

   The weekly view of the calendar appears.

Figure 2-3:
A calendar
in the
Information
Viewer.

Try these tricks to see how the Information Viewer behaves:

- ✔ Click a date in the small calendar in the upper-left corner. The large calendar changes to a one-day view.
- ✔ Click the W for Wednesday at the top of one of the small calendars in the To-Do Bar. The large calendar changes to a monthly view.

You can change the appearance of the Information Viewer an infinite number of ways to make the work you do in Outlook make sense to you. For example, you may need to see the appointments for a single day, or only the items you've assigned to a certain category. Views can help you get a quick look at exactly the slice of information you need.

When you choose the Day or Week view, a row at the bottom of the Calendar screen shows all the tasks scheduled for completion that day, as well as any e-mail messages you've flagged for that day. That's to help you manage your time better. After all, if you have too many meetings on a certain day, you may not have time to finish a lot of tasks; the Outlook calendar makes that easy to see. You can drag a task from one day to another to balance your schedule a bit.

The To-Do Bar

Outlook 2007 features a revamped region called the To-Do Bar, the place to go to manage everything you need to do; see Figure 2-4. Outlook's always had a Task List, which offers a tool for tracking all the projects and errands that you think to enter. But now that we all live and work in a 24-by-7 world of e-mail and instant digital communications, you probably have things to do that you don't think to add to your Task List — particularly items that come to you via e-mail.

When fully displayed, the To-Do Bar takes up the rightmost column of the Outlook screen. Clicking the double arrows next to the words To-Do Bar collapses the bar against the side of the screen; clicking the black X makes the To-Do Bar disappear entirely. The To-Do Bar ties together your tasks, flagged e-mail messages, and calendar appointments so that you can see what you need to do at a glance.

Productivity experts say that a well-organized Task List can help you get more done with less effort and even make more money in less time. Who doesn't want that? To find out more about using the To-Do Bar and the Task List, see Chapter 9.

Figure 2-4:
The To-Do
Bar.

Navigating the Folder List

If you want to navigate Outlook in a more detailed way than you can with the Navigation Pane, you can use the Folder List. If you think of the Navigation Pane buttons as being like a car's radio buttons for picking favorite stations, then the Folder List is like the fine-tuning button that tunes in the stations between your favorite ones. The Folder List simply shows you the folders — your Windows folders or your Outlook folders — where your files and Outlook items are stored.

A tale of two folders

Folders can seem more confusing than they need to be because, once again, Microsoft gave two different things the same name. Just as two kinds of Explorer (Windows and Internet) exist, more than two kinds of Outlook exist, and way too many kinds of Windows exist. You may run across two different kinds of folders when you use Outlook — and each behaves differently.

You may be used to folders in Windows 95, XP, or Vista, which are the things you use to organize files. You can copy, move, and delete files to and from folders on your disk drive. Outlook doesn't deal with that kind of folder. If you need to manage the files you've created on your computer, click the Windows Start button, and then choose Documents.

Outlook has its own special folders for storing items (calendar items, contact names, tasks, and so on) that you create in the various Outlook modules. Each module has its own folder, and the Folder List gives you immediate access to any of them.

If you're looking at an Outlook module, such as the Inbox, for example, and you turn on the Folder List by choosing Go ➪ Folder List, you see a list of folders that represent the other standard Outlook modules, such as the Task List, contacts, calendar, and so on.

Using the Folder List

The only time you absolutely must use the Folder List is when you want to create a new folder for a separate type of item (such as a special Contacts List or a folder for filing e-mail) or find that folder again to use the items you've stored there.

You may quite possibly never use the Folder List at all. The Navigation Pane includes the folder choices that most people use most of the time. You may never need to get a different one. Fortunately, the Folder List appears all by itself when you're likely to need it.

If you don't see the Folder List but want to, choose Go ➪ Folder List (or press Ctrl+6). It's a matter of taste, so take your pick.

Clicking Once: Toolbars

Tools are those little boxes with pictures in them all lined up in a row just below the menu bar. Together, they're called a *toolbar,* and they're even more popular than menus when it comes to running Windows programs. Outlook has three toolbars to choose from: the Standard toolbar, the Advanced toolbar, and the Web toolbar. If you don't do anything special, the Standard toolbar is the one you see, and it will probably do everything you need. If you want to get fancy and open another toolbar (or customize any toolbar), see Chapter 20. Toolbars are great timesavers; one little click on a little picture, and voilà — your wish is granted and you're off to lunch.

Viewing ToolTips

Like menus, tools in Microsoft Office programs get a little drop shadow when you hover the mouse pointer over them. The shadow tells you that if you click there, the tool will do what it's there to do: paste, save, launch missiles (just kidding) — whatever.

Another slick thing about tools is that when you rest the mouse pointer on any of them for a second or so, a little tag pops up to tell you the tool's name (see Figure 2-5). Tags of this sort, called *ToolTips,* are very handy for deciphering the hieroglyphics on those tool buttons.

To view a ToolTip, follow these steps:

1. **Place the mouse pointer on the word File in the menu bar (but don't click).**

2. **Slide the mouse pointer straight down until it rests on the New icon, directly below the word File.**

   After about half a second, you see a little tab that says New Office Document or New *Something-or-Other.* (The text changes, depending on what section of Outlook you're in.)

Some tools have a little triangle to their right. This triangle means the tool has a pull-down menu. The first tool at the left end of any Outlook toolbar is the New tool. Click the triangle to pull down its menu and see all the glorious new stuff you can create — a new appointment, a new e-mail message, or even a new Office document.

Figure 2-5: A ToolTip tells you the name of the tool you're using.

Using the New tool

You can use the New tool, which is available in any module of Outlook, to create an item in any other module. Perhaps you're entering the name and address of a new customer who is also mentioned in an interesting article in today's paper. You want to remember the article, but it doesn't belong in the customer's address record. Although you're still in the Calendar module (see Figure 2-6), you can pull down the New button's menu and create a quick note, which gets filed in the Notes section. Using the New tool to create a new note when you're looking at the Calendar screen can get confusing. At first, you may think the note isn't entered, but it is. Outlook just files it in the Notes module, where it belongs.

Figure 2-6:
Use the
New tool to
create a
note,
request a
meeting, or
perform a
variety of
new tasks
without
switching to
another
Outlook
module.

Finding Things in a Flash with Instant Search

Outlook makes it incredibly easy to accumulate dribs and drabs of data. That quickly becomes a problem because it's tough finding things when there is so much to find. Outlook has always had a search feature, but it was painfully slow. By the time it found what you were looking for, you no longer needed what it found. Fortunately, the people at Google scared Microsoft by inventing a tool that could search Outlook data in a jiffy. After ten years of offering the same crummy search tool, the people at Microsoft cooked up a search tool for Outlook that was worth using. The new tool is called Instant Search and it's pretty slick. I hope Google scares Microsoft this way more often.

Near the top of the Information Viewer Pane, in the center of the screen, you see the Instant Search box (see Figure 2-7). Click that box and type the first few letters of a word that you want to find. Almost immediately, the Information Viewer screen goes blank, then shows only the items containing the text you entered. For example, if you're in the Contacts module and you type jon, you see only the records containing names like Jones, Jonas, Jonquil — any word containing the letters jon. While Outlook is displaying the items it found, the magnifying glass is replaced by an X. Clear the search results by clicking the X.

Figure 2-7:
The Instant Search box is marked with a tiny magnifying glass.

In some cases, searching for a certain group of letters isn't specific enough. For example, you may want Outlook to just show the people named Jones *and* who work for XYX Company. You can create a more detailed search by clicking the double arrow just to the right of the magnifying glass. That reveals a group of labeled boxes in which you can search for specific types of information (see Figure 2-8). The exact collection of boxes varies according to which Outlook module you're searching. If you're in the Contacts module, you have choices such as Name, Company, Business Phone, and so on. To find all the Joneses at XYZ Corporation, type Jones in the Name box and XYZ in the Company box; instantly you'll be keeping up with the Joneses at XYZ.

If the items Outlook offers don't meet your needs, you can make different choices by clicking the label for each type of information; then you can see a list of other kinds of information to search for (see Figure 2-9). For example, when you're searching your Contacts List, you can pick City or State to find people in a certain location.

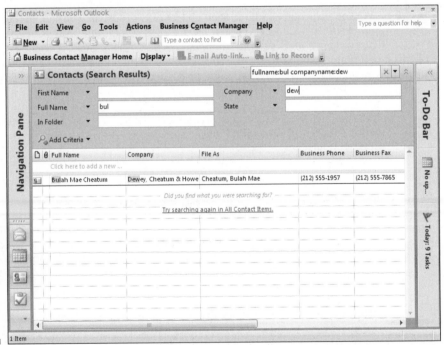

Figure 2-8:
You can
perform
more
detailed
searches.

Figure 2-9:
Change the
search
types by
clicking a
label to
reveal a list.

The best way to learn about the Instant Search feature is to try it out. Just
type some information into the box to see what you get, then click the X to
create a new search.

Getting Help in Outlook

Even though Outlook is as user-friendly a program as you could hope to find,
at times you may want to take advantage of the efficient Windows online Help
system when you're temporarily stumped (of course, you can turn to this
book for help, but sometimes online help is faster).

The Windows Outlook Help system appears as a separate pop-up window (as
shown in Figure 2-10) whenever you press F1. The Windows Help system
finds answers to any question you type in the text box at the top of the
screen. When you type a question in the text box and press Enter, a list of
possible answers appears in the box following the text box. Click the answer
that seems best related to your question, and a full explanation appears in a
new window. The Help system includes lots of blue underlined text, just like
you see in your Web browser, which you can click to make the Help system
show you more information about the underlined topic.

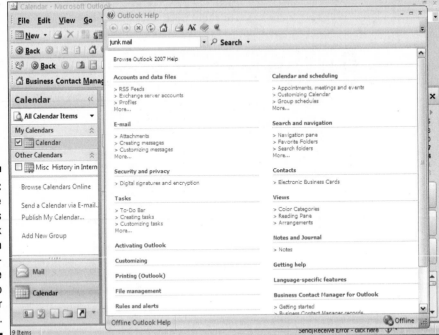

Figure 2-10:
The
Windows
Outlook
Help system
gives no-
nonsense
answers to
your
questions.

Chapter 3

On the Fast Track: Drag 'til You Drop

*T*yping — ugh! Who needs it? It's amazing to think that we still use a 19th century device — the typewriter keyboard — to control our computers in the 21st century. We appear to be stuck with the QWERTY keyboard (the standard we all know and, uh, *love*) for a while longer, but we can give our carpal tunnels a rest now and then: By using the mouse, trackball, or touch-pad, we can drag and drop rather than hunt and peck.

Drag

When I say *drag,* I'm not referring to Monty Python's men in women's cloth-ing. I mean the process of zipping items from one place to another with quick, easy mouse moves rather than slow, laborious menu choices. Throughout the rest of this book, I tell you how to do nearly everything in Outlook by the menu method only because it's the clearest way to explain how to do most things reliably. But if you want to work quickly in Outlook, drag and drop is the ticket to the simple and speedy completion of your tasks.

Before you can drag an item, you have to *select* it, which simply means to click the item once. Then the rest of the process is straightforward:

> ✔ *Dragging* means clicking your mouse on something and moving the mouse to another location while holding the mouse button down at the same time. The item you're dragging moves with the mouse pointer.

> ✔ *Dropping* means letting go of the mouse button. The mouse pointer detaches from the object you dragged and leaves it in its new location.

When you drag an item, you see an icon hanging from the tail of the mouse pointer as you move the pointer across the screen. The icon makes the pointer look like it's carrying baggage, and to some degree, that's true; dragging your mouse between Outlook modules "carries" information from one type of item to another.

When you drag and drop items between different Outlook modules, you can keep creating new types of items from the old information, depending on what you drag and where you drop it.

Everything you can do by using the drag-and-drop method can also be done through menu choices or keystroke shortcuts, but you lose the advantage of having the information from one item flow into the new item, so you have to retype information. I'm too lazy for that, so I just drag and drop.

Because I'm using this chapter to extol the benefits of drag and drop, I describe every action in terms of a drag-and-drop movement rather than through menu choices or keyboard shortcuts. Throughout the rest of the book, however, I describe how to do things in terms of menu choices. That's because the menus stay the same, whereas the Navigation Pane changes its appearance from time to time. So when you read other parts of the book, don't think I'm discouraging you from trying drag and drop; I'm just trying to offer you the clearest explanation I can. (Whew! I'm glad that's off my chest.)

Creating E-Mail Messages

Anything you drag to the Inbox becomes an outgoing e-mail message:

> ✔ If the item you drag to the Inbox contains an e-mail address (for example, a contact), Outlook automatically creates the message with that person's e-mail address filled in.

> ✔ If the item you drag to the Inbox contains a subject (for example, a task), Outlook automatically creates the message with that subject filled in.

From a name in your Address Book

Addressing messages is one of the most useful drag-and-drop techniques in Outlook. E-mail addresses can be cumbersome and difficult to remember, and if your spelling of an e-mail address is off by even one letter, your message won't go through. It's best to just keep the e-mail addresses of the people to whom you sent messages in your Contacts List and use those addresses to create new messages.

Create an e-mail message from your Contacts list this way:

1. **Click the Contact button in the Navigation Pane (or press Ctrl+3).**

   The Contacts list appears, as shown in Figure 3-1. You can use any view, but Address Cards view is easiest; you can click the first letter of the person's name to see that person's card. (For more about viewing your Contacts list, see Chapter 7.)

2. **Drag a name from your Contacts list to the Mail button in the Navigation Pane.**

   The Message form appears, with the address of the contact filled in.

3. **Type a subject for your message.**

   Keep it simple; a few words will do.

4. **Click in the text box and type your message.**

   You can also format text with bold type, italics, and other effects by clicking the appropriate buttons on the toolbar.

5. **Click Send.**

   The display returns to the Contacts list and your message is sent.

Figure 3-1:
Dragging a contact to the Mail button creates a new message addressed to that person.

From an appointment

After you enter the particulars about an appointment, you may want to send that information to someone to tell that person what the appointment is about, where it occurs, and when it occurs.

To send an e-mail message with information about an appointment:

1. **Click the Calendar button in the Navigation Pane (or press Ctrl+2).**

   The calendar appears, as shown in Figure 3-2.

2. **Drag the appointment you're interested in from the calendar to the Mail button.**

   The Message form appears. The subject of the message is already filled in.

3. **In the To text box, type the name of the person to whom you want to send a copy of the appointment.**

   Alternatively, you can click the To button and choose the person's name from the Address Book. If you use the Address Book, you have to click To again and then click OK.

4. **Click the Send button.**

   Your recipient gets an e-mail message with details about the meeting. You can add additional comments in the text box.

Figure 3-2:
Dragging an appointment to the Mail button creates a new message.

If you plan to invite other people in your organization to a meeting, and you want to check their schedules to plan the meeting, you can also use the Attendee Availability tab of the Appointment form. For this method to work, the people whom you plan to invite to the meeting must be sharing their schedules through Microsoft Exchange Server.

Creating Appointments from E-mail

The most popular way to announce an event is by e-mail; it's cheap, fast, and complete. Whether you are inviting people to a meeting, a party, a show, or a conference, you probably already know how convenient e-mail can be for organizing events where people get together.

When you receive an announcement about an event and you want to plug its details into your calendar, you can do that in Outlook by following these steps:

1. **Click the Mail button in the Navigation Pane (or press Ctrl+1).**

   A list of your current incoming e-mail messages appears.

2. **Select the message from which you want to make an appointment.**

3. **Drag the selected message to the Calendar button.**

   The New Appointment form opens with the text from the message you dragged in the note section of the New Appointment form. Figure 3-3 shows an appointment created in this way.

4. **If you want to include more information about the event, type that information in the appropriate box on the New Appointment form.**

   You probably want to fill in the Start Time and End Time boxes to reflect the actual time of your appointment.

5. **Click the Save and Close button.**

   You now have all the event information stored right in your calendar for future reference.

The great thing about creating an appointment from an e-mail message is that all the details included in your message end up right in your calendar. If you need driving directions, agenda details, or whatever information was included in the message, just double-click the appointment in your calendar to get the lowdown. And if you synchronize a Palm or other handheld computer to Outlook, all the information from your Outlook calendar ends up on your handheld. As a result, you'll have your appointment details handy wherever you go. For more tips on dealing with your Palm device, I humbly suggest you read *Palm For Dummies* (Wiley) written by (yes) yours truly.

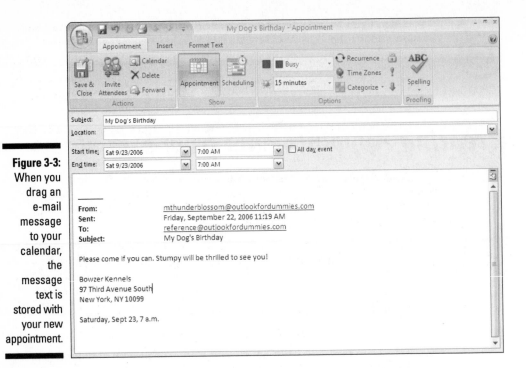

Figure 3-3: When you drag an e-mail message to your calendar, the message text is stored with your new appointment.

Creating Contact Records from E-Mail

You can drag an item from any other Outlook module to the Contacts button, but the only item that makes sense to drag there is an e-mail message. That is, you can drag an e-mail message to the Contacts button in order to create a contact record that includes the e-mail address. You not only save work by dragging a message to the Contacts button, but also eliminate the risk of mis-spelling the e-mail address.

To create a new contact record, follow these steps:

1. **Click the Mail button in the Navigation Pane (or press Ctrl+1).**

    A list of your current incoming e-mail messages appears.

2. **Select the message for which you want to make a contact record.**

3. **Drag the selected message to the Contacts button in the Navigation Pane.**

    The New Contact form opens, with the name and e-mail address of the person who sent the message filled in. Figure 3-4 shows a New Contact form created this way.

4. If you want to include more information, type it into the appropriate box on the New Contact form.

You can change existing information or add information — the company for whom the person works, the postal mail address, other phone numbers, personal details (say, whether to send a complimentary gift of freeze-dried ants for the person's pet aardvark), and so on.

If the body of the e-mail message contains information you want to use as contact information, select that information and drag it to the appropriate box of the New Contact form.

5. Click the Save and Close button.

You now have the e-mail address and any other information for the new contact stored for future reference.

Another quick way to capture an e-mail address from an incoming message is to right-click the name of the sender in the From line of the incoming message block. The From line is not a normal text box, so you may not think that right-clicking it would do anything, but it does: A shortcut menu appears. Click Add to Contacts to open the New Contact form and then follow the last two steps of the preceding list.

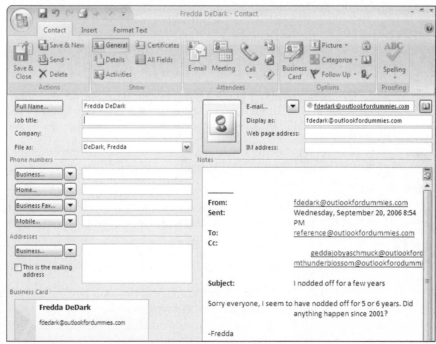

Figure 3-4: Somebody is about to create a contact record.

Drag-and-Drop Dead: Deleting Stuff

If in doubt, throw it out. You know the drill.

Here's how to delete an item using drag and drop:

1. **Click the Mail button in the Navigation Pane (or press Ctrl+1).**

   Your list of messages appears. You can click any button that has items you want to delete. (I'm just using e-mail as an example; you can delete any Outlook item by using the drag-and-drop feature.)

2. **If you don't see a Deleted Items folder in the Navigation Pane, choose Go ➪ Folder List (or press Ctrl+6) and find the Deleted Items folder there.**

   Sometimes the Folder List isn't displayed, but you can always bring it back.

3. **Drag an e-mail message to the Deleted Items folder in the Folder List.**

   Kiss it goodbye — it's gone.

If you change your mind after deleting something, just click the Deleted Items folder. The folder opens and a list of everything you've deleted is there. It's like being a hit man in the afterlife — you get another chance to see everyone you've disposed of. Except in this case, you can bring items back to life. Just drag them back to where they came from. (Even Don Corleone couldn't do that.)

Performing Right-Button Magic

So far I've talked about holding down your mouse button as if your mouse has only one button. But most up-to-date PC mice have two buttons; some have even more. Many people use only the left button and they get along just fine.

Just to confuse matters, you can change your mouse into a left-handed mouse by adjusting some settings in Windows. When you do that, the left and right buttons exchange functions. Shazam!

When you *right-drag* an item (drag it by holding down the right button instead of the left button), something different happens when you drop the item off: A menu asks what result you want. I don't always remember what's going to happen when I drag an item and drop it off, so I like to use the right-drag feature just to be sure.

For example, if you right-drag a contact to the Mail button, a menu with a half-dozen choices appears. The choices include

- ✔ Copy here as message with text
- ✔ Copy here as message with shortcut
- ✔ Copy here as message with attachment
- ✔ Move here as message with attachment

Part II
Taming the
E-Mail Beast

The 5th Wave   By Rich Tennant

Okay, enlarge the chicken bone by 900 percent and attach it to an e-mail to the museum saying, "Getting close...send more money."

In this part . . .

I've trained people who felt like their entire workday was taken up with e-mail. Experts say that the typical office worker now spends two hours each day on e-mail, but you can easily lose more time than that if you don't approach e-mail efficiently. In this part, I'll acquaint you with the tools that will help free your time from e-mail chores.

Chapter 4

The Essential Secrets of E-Mail

In This Chapter

▶ Sending, saving, opening, and replying to messages

▶ Previewing, forwarding, and deleting messages

▶ Saving messages as files

*W*hen I wrote the first edition of *Outlook For Dummies* some ten years ago, many readers had yet to celebrate the sending of their very first e-mail. After this much time, e-mail isn't something to celebrate anymore — not unless you celebrate washing the dishes or changing the cat box. (Woohoo!) E-mail has become every working person's biggest chore. I find that many of the people I train put a lot more effort into e-mail than is really necessary, especially if they have a tool as powerful as Outlook to speed things up.

Front Ends and Back Ends

You need two things to send and receive e-mail:

✔ A program that helps you create, save, and manage your messages

✔ A program that actually transports the messages to and from the other people with whom you exchange messages

Some technical people call these two parts the front end and the back end, respectively. Outlook is a *front end* for e-mail; it helps you create, format, store, and manage your messages, but it has little to do with actually getting your messages to your destination. That work is done by a *back-end* service (such as Microsoft Exchange Server in your office), by your *Internet service provider* (ISP), or by an online e-mail service (such as AOL or Hotmail).

If you feel that you're the last person on earth without Internet e-mail capability (and if you still don't have it, you might be right), you've got that capability now with Outlook. Computer manufacturers make it fiendishly simple to sign up for several online services through the Windows desktop. Remember, though, that your easiest choice isn't always your best choice. Literally hundreds of companies are out there ready to give you Internet access, so it pays to shop around. (I tell you more about connecting Outlook to an e-mail system in Chapter 12.)

Creating Messages

In many ways, electronic mail is better than regular paper mail (now sneeringly referred to as *snail mail*). E-mail is delivered much faster than paper mail — almost instantaneously. I find that speedy delivery is really handy for last-minute birthday greetings. E-mail is also incredibly cheap; in fact, it's free most of the time.

The quick-and-dirty way

Creating a new message is insanely easy. You can probably figure it out without my help, but here's a hint: Start Outlook, click the New button, enter an address in the To box, a subject in the Subject box, a message in the message box, and click Send. (Nailed that one, didn't you? Was that easy or what?)

The slow, complete way

You may prefer a more detailed approach to creating an e-mail message. If you have a yen for fancy e-mail — especially if you want to take advantage of every bell and whistle Outlook can add to your message — follow these steps:

1. **Click the Mail button in the Navigation Pane (or press Ctrl+1).**

   The e-mail Inbox appears.

2. **Click the New button at the top of the screen (or press Ctrl+N).**

   The New Message form appears (as shown in Figure 4-1).

3. **Click the To text box and type the e-mail address of the person to whom you're sending your message.**

   You can also click the To button itself, find the name of the person to whom you're sending the message in the Address Book, and then click OK. (Or you can use the AutoName feature, which I describe in the "What's in an AutoName?" sidebar in this chapter.)

4. **Click the Cc text box and type the e-mail addresses of the people to whom you want to send a copy of your message.**

   If you're sending messages to multiple people, separate their addresses; you can use either commas or semicolons.

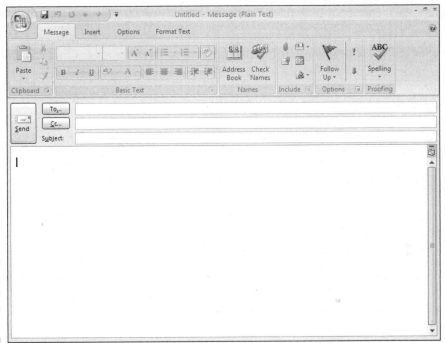

Figure 4-1:
The New
Message
form.

5. **Click the Check Names button at the top of the message screen (or press Ctrl+K).**

   If you haven't memorized the exact e-mail address of everyone you know (gasp!), the Check Names feature lets you enter a part of an address then looks up the exact address so you don't have to be bothered. Double-check what Check Names enters; sometimes it automatically enters the wrong address, which can yield embarrassing results.

6. **Type the subject of the message in the Subject box.**

   Your subject can be quite long, but keep it brief. A snappy, relevant subject line makes someone want to read your message; a long or weird subject line doesn't. (Well, you never know with a weird subject line — but don't send weird e-mail at the office unless everybody does.)

7. **Type the text of your message in the text box.**

   If you use Microsoft Word as your word processor, you're probably familiar with the formatting, graphics, tables, and all the tricks available in Word to make your e-mail more attractive. Those same tricks are available in Outlook by using the tools at the top of the message form.

I've listed a few message formatting tricks you can use in Chapter 20. You can also read Dan Gookin's *Word 2007 For Dummies* (Wiley) for more complete information about using Microsoft Word. If you're completely at home with Microsoft Word, you'll be happy to know that your word-processing skills are useful in Outlook, too. You can just type a message using all the formatting you'd use in any other document (including italics, bold, bullets) and then click Send. Simply type a message in Word by choosing File ⇨ Send To ⇨ Mail Recipient, type an address and subject, and then click Send.

Be careful how you format e-mail to send to people on the Internet. Not all e-mail systems can handle graphics or formatted text, such as bold-face or italics, so the masterpiece of correspondence art that you send to your client on the Internet may arrive as gibberish. If you don't know what the other person has on his or her computer, go light on the graphics. When you're sending e-mail to your colleagues in the same office, or if you're sure the person you're sending to also has Outlook, the formatting and graphics should look fine.

8. **Click Proofing Tools, then choose Spelling & Grammar (or press F7).**

    Outlook runs a spell check to make sure your message makes you look as smart as you actually are.

9. **Click the Send button.**

    Your mail is sent to the Outbox. If you use Outlook at an office where all the computers are connected on a network, your mail automatically goes from your Outbox to the Inbox of the person you're sending the message to. If you're using an online service such as MSN, press F9 to send the e-mail message along.

What's my e-mail address?

When you have an e-mail account, you want to tell other people your e-mail address so they can send stuff to you. E-mail addresses are a little like long-distance telephone numbers. If you live in Chicago, and you're calling someone in New York, you tell that person your number is (312) 555-9780; if the other person lives in Chicago, you leave off the (312) and just tell him or her to call you at 555-9780. If you work in the same office, you say you're at extension 9780; the other person knows the rest.

Likewise, your e-mail address comes in short, medium, and long versions for different people, depending on how much of the address they share with you. If you use the Microsoft Network and your account name is Jane_Doe, your e-mail address to the world at large is Jane_Doe@msn.com. The same is true if you're on an office e-mail system. If you work for International Widgets Corporation, you may be Jdoe@widgets. com. (Check with your company's computer guru about your corporate e-mail address.) Your coworkers can send you messages at Jdoe.

Setting priorities

Some messages are more important than others. The momentous report you're sending to your boss demands the kind of attention that wouldn't be appropriate for the wisecrack you send to your friend in the sales department. Setting the importance level to High tells the recipient that your message requires some serious attention.

Here's how you set the priority of a message:

1. **While composing your message, click the arrow to the right of the word Options in the Ribbon, as seen in Figure 4-2.**

   The Message Options dialog box appears, as shown in Figure 4-2. The Message Options dialog box enables you to define qualities about your message that are, well, *optional.* (Clever name, eh?)

2. **Click the arrow at the right end of the Importance box.**

   A menu of choices drops down.

Figure 4-2: Use the Message Options dialog box to set the priority of your message.

3. **Choose High, Normal, or Low.**

   Usually Importance is set to Normal, so you don't have to do anything. Putting a Low importance on your own messages seems silly, but you can also assign importance to messages received in your Inbox, to tell yourself which messages can be dealt with later, if at all.

4. **To close the Message Options dialog box, click Close (or press Esc).**

An even quicker way to set the priority of a message is to use the buttons in the Ribbon. The button with the red exclamation point marks your message as a high-importance message. The button with the arrow pointing downward marks your message as a low-importance message. You might wonder why anyone would mark a message low importance. After all, if it's so unimportant, why send the message in the first place? Apparently, some bosses like their employees to send in routine reports with a Low importance marking so the bosses know to read that stuff *after* all those exciting new e-mail messages they get to read every day.

Setting sensitivity

Sensitivity isn't just something Oprah talks about. You may want your message to be seen by only one person, or you may want to prevent your message from being changed by anyone after you send it. *Sensitivity* settings enable you to restrict what someone else can do to your message after you send it and who that someone else can be. Even Oprah.

What's in an AutoName?

One neat Outlook feature is that you can avoid memorizing long, confusing e-mail addresses of people to whom you send mail frequently. If the person to whom you're sending a message is entered in your Contacts List (see Chapter 7 for more information about contacts) and you've included an e-mail address in the Contact record, all you have to type in the To box of your e-mail form is the person's name or even just a part of the person's name. Outlook helps you fill in the rest of the person's name and figures out the e-mail address. You know you got it right when Outlook underlines the name with a solid black line after you press the Tab key or click outside the To box. If Outlook underlines the name with a wavy red line, that means Outlook thinks it knows the name you're entering but the name isn't spelled quite right — so you have to correct the spelling. If Outlook doesn't put any underline below the name, it's telling you it has no idea to whom you're sending the message — but it will still use the name you typed as the literal e-mail address. Making doubly sure that the name is correct is a good habit to cultivate.

To set the sensitivity of a message

1. **While composing your message, click the arrow to the right of the word Options in the Ribbon.**

   The Message Options dialog box appears.

2. **Click the scroll-down button (the triangle) at the right end of the Sensitivity box.**

   A menu scrolls down, showing the words *Normal, Personal, Private,* and *Confidential* (as shown in Figure 4-3). Most messages you send will have Normal sensitivity, so that's what Outlook uses if you don't say otherwise. The Personal and Confidential settings only notify the people getting the message that they may want to handle the message differently from a Normal message. (Some organizations even have special rules for dealing with Confidential messages.) Marking a message Private means no one can modify your message when forwarding or replying to it.

3. **Choose Normal, Personal, Private, or Confidential.**

4. **To close the Message Options dialog box, click Close.**

5. **When you finish composing your message, click Send (or press Alt+S).**

   Outlook sends your message off.

Figure 4-3:
Set the
sensitivity
of your
message
from the
Message
Options
dialog box.

Sensitivity means nothing, as a practical matter. Setting the sensitivity of a message to Private or Confidential doesn't make it any more private or confidential than any other message; it just notifies the recipient that the message contains particularly sensitive information. Many corporations are very careful about what kind of information can be sent by e-mail outside the company. If you use Outlook at work, check with your system administrators before presuming that the information you send by e-mail is secure.

Another feature you'll notice on the Message form is Permissions, which actually has the potential to prevent certain things from happening to your message, such as having someone forward your message to everyone you know. (How embarrassing.) However, both you and your recipient have to be set up on a compatible e-mail system with something called an *Information Rights Management program* to make that work. You also can't be sure it will work on systems such as Hotmail or Yahoo! You can find out more about Information Rights Management at www.microsoft.com.

Setting other message options

When you click the Options button and open the Options page the way I describe in the previous section, you may notice a number of strange-sounding options. The other options include Request Read Receipt (which notifies you when your recipient reads your message) and Expires After (which makes a message disappear if your recipient doesn't open it before a time you designate). Those are handy options, but if you want to use them, there's a catch: Both your e-mail system and your recipient's mail system must support those features, or they won't work at all. If you and your recipient are both on the same network using Microsoft Exchange Server, then everything should work just fine. If you're not using Outlook on an Exchange Network, then (frankly) it's a gamble. (See Chapter 14 for more about how to use the features of Outlook that work only on Exchange Server.)

Adding an Internet link to an e-mail message

All Microsoft Office programs automatically recognize the addresses of items on the Internet. If you type the name of a Web page, such as www.outlook fordummies.com, Outlook changes the text color to blue and underlines the address, making it look just like the hypertext you click to jump between different pages on the Web. That makes it easy to send someone information about an exciting Web site; just type or copy the address into your message. If the recipient is also an Outlook user, he or she can just click the text to make the Web browser pop up and open the page you mentioned in your message.

Reading and Replying to E-Mail Messages

Outlook has a couple of ways to tell you when you receive an e-mail message. The Status Bar in the bottom-left corner of the Outlook screen tells you how many e-mail messages you have overall and how many of those are unread; see Figure 4-4. The word *Inbox* in the Folder List changes to boldface type when you have unread e-mail, and when you look in the Inbox, you see titles of unread messages in bold as well. Also, when you log on to Windows XP, you'll see a little notice.

To open and read an e-mail message, follow these steps:

1. **Click the Mail button in the Navigation Pane (or press Ctrl+1).**

    The Inbox screen opens, showing your incoming mail.

2. **Double-click the title of the message you want to read.**

    The message opens, and you can see the text of the message (as in Figure 4-5). If the message is really long, press the down-arrow key or the PgDn key to scroll through the text.

Figure 4-4: Numbers next to your Inbox icon tell you how many unread messages are there.

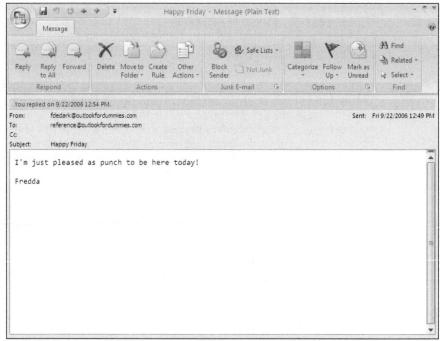

Figure 4-5:
Double-click
a message
to open it
and read the
contents.

3. **To close the Message screen, press Esc+Alt+F4.**

   The Message screen closes, and you see the list of messages in your Inbox.

Previewing message text

When you start getting lots of e-mail, some of it will be important, but some of it will be relatively unimportant — if not downright useless. When you first see the mail in your Inbox, it's nice to know which messages are important and which are not so you can focus on the important stuff. You can't count on the people who send you e-mail to say, "Don't read this; it's unimportant" (although a Low priority rating is a good clue). Outlook tries to help by enabling you to peek at the first few lines of a message so you know right off the bat whether it's worth reading.

To see previews of your unread messages:

1. **Click the Mail button in the Navigation Pane (or press Ctrl+1).**

   The Inbox screen opens, showing your incoming mail.

2. **Choose View ➪ AutoPreview.**

   The list of messages in your Inbox appears with the first few lines of each unread message displayed in blue. See Figure 4-6.

Figure 4-6:
You can see
a preview
of your
messages
after
choosing
Auto-
Preview.

Every module in Outlook has a collection of views you can use to make your information easier to use. The view called Messages with AutoPreview is the best way to look at your incoming e-mail. In Chapter 16, I show you some other views that can make your collection of e-mail messages more useful.

An even better way to zoom through your Inbox is to open the Reading Pane, an area of the Outlook screen that displays the contents of any message you select. To set up your Reading Pane, choose View ➪ Reading Pane, then choose either Right, Bottom, or Off. You can't go wrong with any of the three choices; if you don't like one, change to another. When you've turned on the Reading Pane, you can skim through your messages by pressing either your up-arrow or down-arrow keys.

Sending a reply

The thing I love about e-mail is that sending a reply is so easy. You don't even need to know the person's address when you're sending a reply; just click the Reply button and Outlook takes care of it for you.

Here's how you reply to a message:

1. **Click the Mail button in the Navigation Pane (or press Ctrl+1).**

   The Inbox screen opens, showing your incoming mail.

2. **Double-click the title of the message to which you want to reply.**

   The message you double-clicked opens, and you can see the contents of the message.

   If the message is already open, you can skip the first two steps and go directly to Step 3.

3. **Choose one of these options:**

   • **To reply to the people in the From line, click the Reply button.**

   • **To reply to the people in the Cc line *and* the From line, click the Reply to All button.**

   The Reply screen appears (as shown in Figure 4-7).

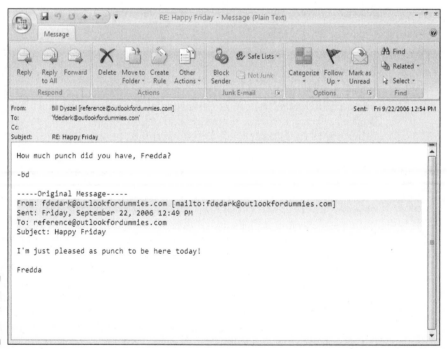

Figure 4-7:
The Reply
screen.

You may get (or send) e-mail that's addressed to a whole bunch of people all at one time. At least one person must be named in the To line; more than one person can be in the Cc line, which is for people to whom you're sending only a copy. Little difference exists between what happens to mail that's going to people in the To line and mail that's going to the people in the Cc line — all of them can reply to, forward, or ignore the message. You don't always need to reply to the people on the Cc line, or you may want to reply to only some of them. If you do that, you must click the Reply button (not Reply to All) and add them again to the Cc line.

4. **Type your reply in the Message box.**

   Don't be alarmed when you discover some text already in the text box — it's part of the message to which you're replying. Your blinking cursor is at the top of the screen, so anything you type precedes the other person's message. (This arrangement means the person who gets your message can review the original message as a memory-jogger when your reply comes back.)

5. **Click the Send button.**

   On your office network, clicking Send speeds the message to its intended recipient.

   If you're a standalone user who's sending mail using an online service, such as The Microsoft Network or CompuServe, you must also choose Tools ➪ Send/Receive ➪ Send/Receive All or press F9 to send your message out over the Internet. See Chapter 12 for more about sending e-mail from your home computer with Outlook.

6. **Press Esc to close the Message screen.**

   The Message form disappears and your Inbox reappears.

Using a Web link from your e-mail

When you open a message, sometimes you see blue, underlined text with the name of a Web page or other Internet resource, such as www.outlook fordummies.com. If you want to look at that page, all you have to do is double-click the text — if everything is installed correctly, your Web browser pops up and opens the Web page whose name you've clicked.

After you open the page, you can save the page to your Favorites folder so you can find it again easily.

Don't get caught by phishing

Sneaky people are always looking for new ways to trick you, especially on the Internet. In recent years, a common scam called *phishing* has cost people time, money, and grief after they responded to an e-mail by an impostor who claimed to represent a bank or other financial institution.

If you get an e-mail that purports to be from a bank or other business and asks you to click a link to log on to "verify" personal information, especially passwords, don't fall for it. They'll probably direct you to a Web site where you'll be asked to enter personal information that will then be used for fraud or identity theft. Contact the business directly, preferably by phone, to make sure the e-mail isn't a fake. One way to confirm that an e-mail is phony is to hover your mouse over a link in the message until the URL or Internet address pops up. If the address it links to isn't the same as the address of the institution that claims to be sending the message, it's a phishing scam. Just delete it.

That's Not My Department: Forwarding E-Mail

You may not always have the answer to every e-mail message you get. You may need to pass a message along to somebody else to answer, so pass it on.

To forward a message, follow these steps:

1. **Click the Mail button in the Navigation Pane (or press Ctrl+1).**

   The Inbox screen opens, showing your incoming mail.

2. **Click the title of the message you want to forward.**

   The message you selected appears in the Reading Pane; see Figure 4-8. You can forward the message as soon as you read it. If you've already opened the message, you can skip the first two steps.

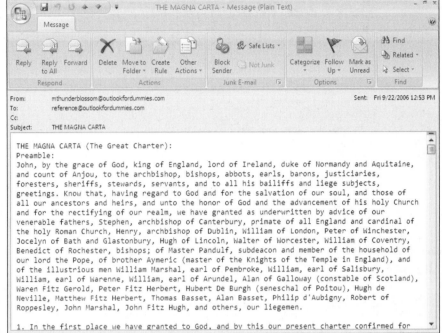

THE MAGNA CARTA - Message (Plain Text)

Message

Reply | Reply to All | Forward | Delete | Move to Folder | Create Rule | Other Actions | Block Sender | Safe Lists | Not Junk | Categorize | Follow Up | Mark as Unread | Find | Related | Select

Respond | Actions | Junk E-mail | Options | Find

From: mthunderblossom@outlookfordummies.com   Sent: Fri 9/22/2006 12:53 PM
To: reference@outlookfordummies.com
Cc:
Subject: THE MAGNA CARTA

THE MAGNA CARTA (The Great Charter):
Preamble:
John, by the grace of God, king of England, lord of Ireland, duke of Normandy and Aquitaine,
and count of Anjou, to the archbishop, bishops, abbots, earls, barons, justiciaries,
foresters, sheriffs, stewards, servants, and to all his bailiffs and liege subjects,
greetings. Know that, having regard to God and for the salvation of our soul, and those of
all our ancestors and heirs, and unto the honor of God and the advancement of his holy Church
and for the rectifying of our realm, we have granted as underwritten by advice of our
venerable fathers, Stephen, archbishop of Canterbury, primate of all England and cardinal of
the holy Roman Church, Henry, archbishop of Dublin, William of London, Peter of Winchester,
Jocelyn of Bath and Glastonbury, Hugh of Lincoln, Walter of Worcester, William of Coventry,
Benedict of Rochester, bishops; of Master Pandulf, subdeacon and member of the household of
our lord the Pope, of brother Aymeric (master of the Knights of the Temple in England), and
of the illustrious men William Marshal, earl of Pembroke, William, earl of Salisbury,
William, earl of Warenne, William, earl of Arundel, Alan of Galloway (constable of Scotland),
Waren Fitz Gerold, Peter Fitz Herbert, Hubert De Burgh (seneschal of Poitou), Hugh de
Neville, Matthew Fitz Herbert, Thomas Basset, Alan Basset, Philip d'Aubigny, Robert of
Roppesley, John Marshal, John Fitz Hugh, and others, our liegemen.

1. In the first place we have granted to God, and by this our present charter confirmed for

Figure 4-8:
The message you want to forward is opened.

3. Click the Forward button.

The Forward screen appears; see Figure 4-9. The subject of the original message is now the subject of the new message, except the letters *FW:* (for Forward) are inserted at the beginning.

4. Click the To text box and type the e-mail address of the person to whom you're forwarding the message.

If the person to whom you're forwarding is entered in your Contacts List, just type the person's name — Outlook figures out the e-mail address for you.

5. Click the Cc text box and type the e-mail addresses of the people to whom you want to forward a copy of your message.

Many people forward trivia (such as jokes of the day) to scads and scads of their friends by e-mail. Most recipients are included as Cc addresses.

Remember, business e-mail etiquette is different from home e-mail etiquette. Many employers have strict policies about appropriate use of their corporate e-mail systems. If you work for such a company, be aware of your company's policies.

Figure 4-9:
The
Forward
screen.

If you want to pester your friends by sending silly trivia from your home computer to their home computers (as I do), that's your own business.

6. **In the text box, type any comments you want to add to the message.**

   The text of the original message appears in the text box, preceded by the words Original Message and a couple of blank lines. You can preface the message that you're forwarding if you want to give that person a bit of explanation — for example, **This is the 99th message I've had from this person; somebody needs to get a life.**

7. **Click the Send button.**

   Your message is on its way.

Blind Copying for Privacy

When you send a message to a large group, everyone receiving the message can see the e-mail addresses in the To and Cc fields, which means that you've just given out e-mail addresses that some people might rather keep private. Everybody already gets way too many weird, unsolicited e-mails, and many people get peeved when you broadcast their address without permission.

Blind copies give you the best of both worlds. If you put all the e-mail addresses in the Bcc field, nobody's privacy is compromised. By using *BCCs* (an old abbreviation for Blind Carbon Copy, a quaint reminder to those who'll admit that they're old enough to remember carbon paper), you can keep secret addresses secret.

The Bcc field isn't always displayed when you create a message in Outlook. If you don't see a box labeled Bcc right below the Cc box, click the Options tab, then click the Show Bcc button.

Deleting Messages

You can zap an e-mail message without a second thought; you don't even have to read the thing. As soon as you see the Inbox list, you know who's sending the message and what it's about, so you don't have to waste time reading Burt's Bad Joke of the day. Just zap it.

If you accidentally delete a message you didn't want to lose, click the Deleted Items folder; you find all the messages you've deleted in the last few months. To recover a deleted message, just drag it from the Deleted Items list to either the Inbox icon or the Outbox icon.

Here's how you delete a message:

1. **Click the Mail button in the Navigation Pane (or press Ctrl+1).**

   The Inbox screen opens, showing your incoming mail.

2. **Click the title of the message you want to delete.**

   You don't have to read the message; you can just delete it from the list.

3. **Choose Edit ➪ Delete (or press Delete).**

Another quick way to delete a message is to click the Delete tool that appears at the top of a message you're reading. It's easy to recognize the Delete tool; it's marked with a huge, black X. You know it doesn't mean buried pirate treasure — it means make this message walk the plank.

When you delete messages, Outlook doesn't actually eliminate deleted items; it moves them to the Deleted Items folder. If you have unread items in your Deleted Items folder, Outlook annotates the Deleted Items icon with the number of unread items, the same way it annotates the Inbox with the number of unread items. You can get rid of the annotation by choosing Tools ➪ Empty Deleted Items Folder. Or you can just ignore the annotation. After you empty your Deleted Items folder, the messages that were in it disappear forever.

Saving Interrupted Messages

If you get interrupted while writing an e-mail message, all is not lost. You can just save the work you've done and return to it later. Just click the Save icon (or press Ctrl+S), and your message is saved to the Drafts folder, as shown in Figure 4-10 (unless you had reopened the message from the Outbox, in which case Outlook saves the unfinished message to the Outbox).

When a message is ready to be sent, its name appears in the Outbox in italics. If you've saved it to work on later, its name appears in normal text, not italics. If you're not finished with the message and plan to return to it later, save it (press Ctrl+S). If the message is ready for prime time, send it by pressing Alt+S.

Figure 4-10:
You can
save
incomplete
messages
and return
to finish
them later.

Saving a Message as a File

You may create or receive an e-mail message that's so wonderful (or terrible) that you just have to save it. You may need to print the message and show it to someone else, save it to a floppy disk, or export it to a desktop-publishing program.

To save a message as a file, follow these steps:

1. **Click the Office icon in the upper left of the message form, and then choose Save As (or press F12).**

   The File Menu appears.

2. **Choose Save As.**

   The Save As dialog box appears.

2. **Click the triangle at the end of the Save In box to choose the drive to which you want to save your file.**

   If you do all your work on drive C, Outlook chooses drive C first, so you don't have to do anything. To save to a floppy disk, choose the A drive.

   The triangle is called the *scroll-down* button.

3. **Click the name of the folder in which you want to save the file.**

   A list appears of all folders and files in the folder you select.

4. **Click the File Name text box and type the name you want to give the file**.

   Type any name you want, up to 256 characters.

5. **If you want to change the type of the file, click the triangle at the end of the Save as Type box and choose a file type.**

   The list offers text, Outlook Template, and two versions of the Outlook message format; see Figure 4-11. Use text. The Outlook Template format is for a message you want to use repeatedly in Outlook.

Figure 4-11:
The Save As
dialog box.

6. Click Save (or press Enter).

The message is saved to the file and folder you specified in Steps 2
through 4.

Postscript

Sending e-mail is simple. Keeping track of all the tens of millions of people to whom you want to send e-mail is a bigger task. Fortunately, Outlook does both things, so you can go to one program to get the names of the people you know, find what you know about them, and send them e-mail asking them to tell you more. Don't forget to stop when you know enough.

Chapter 5

E-Mail Tools You Can't Do Without

*O*utlook can do all sorts of tricks with the mail you send out, as well as with the messages you receive. You can flag messages with reminders, customize your messages with a signature, or add special formatting to the messages you send as replies.

As the automobile ads say, "Your mileage may vary." Outlook is just the pretty face on an elaborate arrangement of programs that make e-mail work. Outlook is like the dashboard of your car; you can use the dashboard to make the car do what you want it to do, but what your car *can* do depends more on what's under the hood than what's on the dashboard. In the same way, some Outlook features work only if the system that's backing it up supports those same features. In addition, some Outlook features work only if the person to whom you're mailing uses a system that supports the same features you're using.

Microsoft Exchange Server — a program that runs on many corporate networks — adds a number of features to Outlook, such as delaying delivery of messages or diverting messages to someone else. In this chapter, I don't discuss features you may not have, but if you want to know more about the features you may have on a corporate network with Microsoft Exchange Server, see Chapter 14. If you're not among the fortunate ones who have Exchange Server, don't worry — Outlook can do plenty all by itself.

Nagging by Flagging

Over time, *flags* have become my favorite Outlook feature. Back when I received only a few dozen e-mail messages a week, flags didn't matter that much. Now that I get thousands of messages each week, I need help remembering to get back to important messages that otherwise might get lost in the shuffle. If I can't respond to an important message right away, I like to flag that message as soon as I read the message. Then I'm sure to get back to it. You can also plant a flag in a message you send to others to remind them of a task they have to do if both you and the other person are on an Exchange network.

One-click flagging

Why flag a message? To help get your work done faster! So you need to know the fastest possible way to flag a message, right? Of course.

When you look at the list of messages in your Inbox, you see a little box at the right end of each subject line containing a little, gray outline of a flag, sort of a shadow flag. When you click that little shadow, it changes from gray to a bright red color to show you've flagged it. Now whenever you look at your list of messages, you know which messages need further attention. Those you've flagged also appear in the To-Do Bar on the right side of the Outlook screen so that you can see flagged messages even after they've slipped below the bottom of the screen. See Figure 5-1.

Figure 5-1:
The Inbox
screen with
your mail.

Once you've attended to your flagged message, click the flag again. That replaces the flag with a check mark to show you've taken care of that message.

Setting flags for different days

If you only click once on a message to add a flag, a copy of the message appears in your To-Do Bar along with the list of things you're scheduled to do today. You might not be ready to deal with a certain message today; you might prefer to put it off until tomorrow or next week. If you right-click the flag button on the message form (shown in Figure 5-1), you see a list of possible due dates for a flag, including Today, Tomorrow, This Week, Next Week, No Date, and Custom. (The 12th of Never remains unavailable. Sorry.) Once you've picked a due date, you can always change it by dragging the item from one due date to another. For example, you can drag an item from the Today group to the Next Week group (if both groups are visible). You can also double-click the item to reopen it and choose a different due date.

Changing the default flag date

For unusually busy people and compulsive procrastinators, you can change the default due dates of your flags by following these steps:

1. **Right-click any flag.**

   The flag shortcut menu appears.

2. **Choose Set Defaults.**

   Another shortcut menu appears, offering several choices of due date; see Figure 5-2.

3. **Pick the date that suits you.**

   The date you choose becomes the default flag due date.

If you have trouble committing to a date (you're so fickle), you can choose "No Date" and just wait until someone complains. I call that the Squeaky Wheel school of time management; put everything off until somebody yells about something, then just do that. It's a popular approach with people who work for the government.

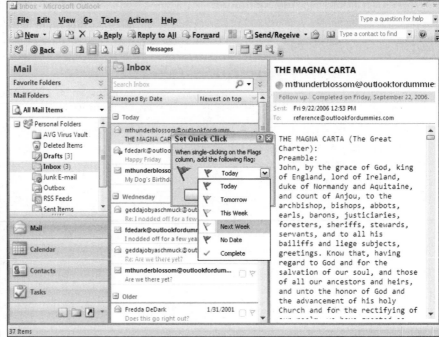

Figure 5-2:
Choose
from a
lovely
assortment
of default
flag
choices.

Adding a flag with a customized reminder

Of course, flags can do a lot more than stand there looking pretty for a week
or so. Outlook flags can pop up and remind you to do something at anytime
you choose. They can also pop up and pester someone *else* when you put a
flag on a message you send. (Who could resist that?) Adding a reminder to a
flag takes more than one click — but not much more. To attach a flag to your
e-mail messages (those you send and those you receive), follow these steps:

1. **Click the Mail button in the Navigation Pane (or press Ctrl+1).**

   The Inbox screen opens, showing your incoming mail.

2. **Right-click the flag on the message you want to flag.**

   The flag shortcut menu appears.

3. **Choose Add Reminder.**

   The Flag for Follow Up dialog box appears. At this point, if you click OK (or press Enter), your message is flagged and set to remind you at the end of the day today. That may be a wee bit too soon, so you can set more detailed options by using the remaining steps.

4. **Click the triangle at the right end of the Flag To text box and choose one of the menu items (or type your own choice).**

   One handy flag is Follow Up, which reminds you to confirm an appointment or other arrangement.

5. **Enter dates in the Start Date box, Due Date box, Reminder box, or all the boxes.**

   The date you type in the Reminder box is when a reminder will pop up to jog your memory. The other two dates help you keep track of how many tasks you're juggling at once. You can be pretty loose about how you enter dates in Outlook. You can type the date **3/5/08**; Outlook understands. You can type **first wednesday of march**; Outlook understands. You can type **a week from Wednesday**; Outlook understands that to mean "seven days after the Wednesday that comes after today." You don't even have to worry about capitalization. (Don't type **I hate mondays,** though — Outlook doesn't understand that. But I do.)

   If you'd rather just pick a date from a calendar, you can click the little down arrow at the right end of any of the boxes to reveal a calendar, and then just click the date you want.

6. **Click OK.**

When the date you entered in the Flag for Follow Up dialog box arrives, a reminder dialog box helps give you a gentle nudge.

Changing the date on a flag

Procrastination used to be an art; Outlook makes it a science. When someone nags you with flags, you can still put it off. Yes, dear, you *can* do it later.

To change the date on a flag, follow these steps:

1. **Click the Mail button in the Navigation Pane (or press Ctrl+1).**

   The Inbox screen opens, showing your incoming mail; see Figure 5-3.

Figure 5-3:
A mass of messages, waiting for flags.

2. **Click the message that has a flag you want to change.**

    The message appears highlighted to show that you've selected it.

3. **Choose Action ➪ Follow Up ➪ Add Reminder (or press Ctrl+Shift+G).**

    The Custom reminder dialog box appears; see Figure 5-4.

4. **Click the Reminder box and type the new date when you want the reminder flag to appear.**

    Type the date when you think you'll feel ready to be flagged again. Typing **999 years from now** will work — really!

5. **Click OK.**

Of course, you can always put something off if you really try. When a flag reminder pops up, hit the snooze button to put it off for a while, as you do with your alarm clock.

Figure 5-4:
The Custom
dialog box
for adding
reminders to
your e-mail.

Saving Copies of Your Messages

Nothing is handier than knowing what you've sent and when you sent it. You can save all your outgoing mail in Outlook so you can go back and look up the messages you've sent. Outlook starts saving sent items when you first install the program, but you can turn this feature on and off. So before you go changing your options, look in your Sent Messages folder to see whether it contains messages.

To save copies of your messages, follow these steps:

1. **Choose Tools ⇨ Options.**

   The Options dialog box appears.

2. **Click the E-mail Options button.**

   The E-mail Options dialog box appears, as shown in Figure 5-5.

Figure 5-5:
You can
decide
whether to
save copies
of the
messages
you send by
using the
E-mail
Options
dialog box.

3. **Click the Save Copies of Messages in Sent Items Folder check box.**

   If the box already contains a check mark, leave it alone. (That's the way Outlook is set up when you first install it.) If you click the box when it's already checked, you turn off your option for saving messages. Don't worry if you make a mistake; you can always change it back. Just make sure a check appears in the box if you want to save messages.

4. **Click OK.**

Outlook saves two months' worth of saved messages and sends older messages to an archive file to save disk space on your computer.

Automatically Adding Your Name to a Reply

When you reply to a message, it helps to include parts of the original message you're replying to so the person reading your message knows exactly what you're responding to. The trick is, how will the reader know which comments are his or hers and which are yours?

Outlook enables you to preface your comments with your name or any text you choose. If you want to be understood, it's best to use your name. (If you want to confuse the issue, you could always use a phrase such as "Simon says.")

To tag your replies with your name, follow these steps:

1. **Choose Tools ➪ Options.**

   The Options dialog box appears.

2. **Click the E-mail Options button.**

   The E-mail Options dialog box appears, as shown in Figure 5-6.

Figure 5-6:
Preface your replies with your name by checking the box at the bottom of the E-mail Options dialog box.

3. **Click the Mark My Comments With check box to put a check there.**

   If the check box is already checked, don't click it; doing so would remove the check.

4. **In the Mark My Comments With text box, type the text you want to accompany your annotations.**

   Your best bet is to enter your name here. Whatever you enter will be used as the prefix to all text you type when you reply to messages.

5. **Click OK.**

You can select and delete the text of the original message when you create a reply, but including at least a part of the message you're replying to makes your response easier to understand. You also have the option of selecting and deleting the parts of the original text that aren't relevant to your reply.

Setting Your Options

You can control the appearance of the messages you forward, as well as your replies. If all your e-mail stays in your office among other Microsoft Office users, you can make your text look pretty incredible in messages you send to one another by adding graphics, wild-looking fonts, or special effects, such as blinking text. If you're sending mail to poor ol' Internet users or to people on an online service, such as CompuServe (see Chapter 12 for more about sending e-mail to online services and the Internet), pay attention to how messages look to those people.

To set your options, follow these steps:

1. **Choose Tools ⇨ Options.**

   The Options dialog box appears.

2. **Click the E-mail Options button.**

   The E-mail Options dialog box appears (looking a lot like Figure 5-7).

3. **Click the triangle at the right end of the When Replying to a Message box.**

   A menu of options drops down. When Outlook is first installed, Include and Indent Original Message Text is the default option. The diagram to the right of the scroll-down menu illustrates how the message will be laid out when you choose each option.

4. **Choose the style you prefer to use for replies.**

   The little diagram to the right of the menu changes when you make a choice to show you what your choice will look like. If you don't like the choice you've made, try another and see how it looks in the diagram.

5. **Click the triangle at the right end of the When Forwarding a Message box.**

   The When Forwarding a Message box has one choice fewer than the When Replying to a Message box does, but the two menus work the same way. Also, they both have that little diagram of the page layout off to the right.

Figure 5-7:
Change the
appearance
of your
outgoing
messages
by selecting
what you
need in the
E-mail
options
dialog box.

6. **Choose the style you prefer to use for forwarding messages.**

   Just pick one; you can always change it.

7. **Click OK.**

You can do all sorts of fancy, exciting, and even useful tricks with e-mail by taking advantage of Outlook's options. If the advanced options seem confusing, you can easily ignore them. Just click Reply and type your answer.

Sending Attachments

If you've already created a document that you want to send, you don't have to type the document all over again in a message; just send the document as an attachment to an e-mail message. You can attach any kind of file — word-processing documents, spreadsheets, and presentations from programs, such as PowerPoint. You can even send pictures or music. Any kind of file can be sent as an attachment.

The easiest way to send a file from a Microsoft Office program (such as Microsoft Word) is to open that file in Word, click the Office icon in the upper-left of the screen, and then choose Send To. If you'd rather not do that, you can send a file attachment straight from Outlook by following these steps:

1. **Click the Mail button in the Navigation Pane (or press Ctrl+Shift+I).**

   The Inbox screen opens, showing your incoming mail.

2. **Choose File ⇨ New ⇨ Mail Message (or press Ctrl+N).**

   The New Message form appears.

3. **Click the Attach File button in the Message Form Ribbon.**

   The Insert File dialog box appears; see Figure 5-8. It looks like the dialog box you use for opening files in most Windows programs, and it works like opening a file, too. Just click the name of the file you want to send and press Enter.

Figure 5-8:
The Insert
File dialog
box.

4. In the list of files, click the name of the file you want to send.

An icon appears in your text, representing the file you attached to your message.

5. Click OK.

Your Message form now contains an icon that has the same name as the file you selected — which means the file is attached. When you send this e-mail message, a copy of the file you selected goes to your recipient.

6. Type your message (if you have a message to send).

You may not have a message; perhaps you want to send only the attachment. If what you want to say is in the attachment, that's fine, but remember that the contents of an attachment don't show up on the recipient's screen until he or she double-clicks to open the attachment.

7. Click the To button in your Message form.

The Select Names dialog box appears.

8. Select a name from your Address Book.

If the name of the person to whom you want to send your message isn't in the list, you can click the Cancel button and return to the Message form. Then just type the person's e-mail address in the To text box.

9. Click the To button in the Select Names dialog box.

The name of the selected person appears in the Message Recipients box of the Select Names dialog box.

10. Click OK.

The name of the selected person is now in the To box of the message.

11. Click the Subject text box and type a subject for your message.

A subject is optional, but if you want somebody to read what you send, including a subject helps.

12. Click the Send button.

Your message and its attachment are sent.

Another approach is to find the file on your computer by choosing Start ⇨ Documents, right-clicking that file, and choosing Send To from the shortcut menu. That allows you to send nearly anything to anybody.

Creating Signatures for Your Messages

Many people like to add a signature to the end of every message they send. A *signature* is usually a small portion of text that identifies you to everyone reading your message and tells something you want everyone to know. Many people include their name, the name of their business, their motto, a little sales slogan, or some squib of personal information.

You can tell Outlook to add a signature automatically to all your outgoing messages, but first you must create a signature file. Here's how to create your signature file:

1. **Choose Tools ⇨ Options.**

   The Options dialog box appears.

2. **Click the Mail Format tab.**

   The Mail Format dialog box appears.

3. **Click the Signature button.**

   The Signatures and Stationery dialog box appears, as shown in Figure 5-9.

Figure 5-9: The Signatures and Stationery dialog box.

4. Click the New button.

The New Signature dialog box appears.

5. Type a name for your new signature.

The name you type appears in the New Signature box. You can name a signature anything you want.

6. Click OK.

The New Signature dialog box closes.

7. Type the text of the signature you want to create and add any formatting you want.

The text you type appears in the Signature text box. To change the font, size, color, or other text characteristics, use the buttons just above the text box. If you're more comfortable creating highly formatted text in Microsoft Word, you can create your signature in Word, then select and copy it to the Signature box.

Many people receive e-mail on cell phones and other kinds of devices that don't know what to do with fancy formatting, so you may be best off with a fairly plain signature. Also, try to be brief. You don't want your signature to be longer than the message to which it's attached.

8. Click OK.

The Signature Picker dialog box appears.

9. Click OK.

The Mail Format dialog box appears.

10. Click OK.

The Options dialog box appears.

11. Click OK.

Your new signature will now appear on every message you send. If you create more than one signature, you can switch to a different default signature by following Steps 1 and 2 and then choosing the signature you want from the scroll-down menu next to the words Use This Signature by Default.

If you use more than one e-mail address, you can choose them a couple ways:

✔ **Set up Outlook to use different signatures on different e-mail addresses.** For example, assume one address is for business and another is for personal messages. You can create a businesslike signature for the first and a more casual signature for the latter. To designate which signature goes with which address, click Select the Signatures to Use with the Following Account, and then pick the signatures you want to use.

> ✔ **Choose signatures one at a time.** When you finish writing the body of an e-mail message, click the Insert tab at the top of the message form, then click the Signature button to see the list of signatures you've created. Clicking the name of the signature that you want to use makes that signature appear in your message.

One of my favorite timesavers is to create a signature that contains a message that I send out frequently. For example, when I'm working on a book like this, I often contact many different people asking for information about products that improve or work with Outlook. Instead of typing the same message over and over, I turn that message into a signature, then insert that "signature" each time I send the message. It's sneaky, because that's not what signatures were designed to do, but it saves a lot of typing.

Chapter 6

Conquering Your Mountain of Messages

- -

In This Chapter

▶ Setting up a new mail folder

▶ Filing messages in folders

▶ Using and customizing stationery

▶ Looking at your messages

▶ Using the Rules Wizard

▶ Dealing with junk e-mail

- -

*Y*ou spend too much time on e-mail. I know you do. Everybody does. Some experts estimate that the average business employee spends up to two hours each day on e-mail, and it's getting worse every year. Pretty soon, you'll spend more time on e-mail than you spend working. (Some people already do.) Then you'll spend more time on e-mail than you spend awake. After that . . . I don't want to think about it. I'd rather get Outlook to cut down the time I spend wrestling with e-mail.

Outlook has some handy tools for coping with the flood of electronic flotsam and jetsam that finds its way into your Inbox. You can create separate folders for filing your mail, and you can use Outlook's view feature to help you slice and dice your incoming messages into manageable groups.

Even better than the View feature is the Rules Wizard, which automatically responds to incoming messages according to your wishes. You can move all messages from certain senders to the folder of your choice — for instance, consigning everything from Spam-O-Rama.com to oblivion — send automatic replies to messages about certain subjects, or delete messages containing words that offend you.

Speaking of spam, an even more effective way to deal with offensive or aggressively useless messages is to use the new junk e-mail filters built into Outlook. You turn the filters on only once — after you do, you'll have a lot less junk mail cluttering up your Inbox.

Organizing Folders

You're probably familiar with organizing items into folders. Windows organizes all of your other documents into folders, so why should Outlook be any different? Well, Outlook *is* a little different than Windows regarding folders. But the idea is the same: create a folder and drag stuff to it.

Creating a new mail folder

The simplest way to manage incoming mail is just to file it. Before you file a message, you need to create at least one folder in which to file your messages. You have to create a folder only once; it's there for good after you create it. You can create as many folders as you want; you may have dozens or just one or two.

I have folders for filing mail from specific clients, for example. All the e-mail I've received in connection with this book is in a folder called *Outlook For Dummies*. (Clever title, eh?) Another folder called *Personal* contains messages that aren't business-related.

To create a folder for new mail, follow these steps:

1. **Click the Mail button in the Navigation Pane (or press Ctrl+1).**

   The list of messages in your Inbox appears.

2. **Choose Go ➪ Folder List.**

   The Folder List appears on the left side of the screen.

3. **Right-click the word Inbox in the Folder List.**

   A shortcut menu appears.

4. **Choose New Folder from the shortcut menu.**

   The Create New Folder dialog box appears (as in Figure 6-1).

Figure 6-1:
The Create
New Folder
dialog box.

5. **In the Name text box, type a name for your new folder, such as**
   Personal.

   You can name the subfolder anything you like. You can also create many
   folders for saving and sorting your incoming e-mail. Leaving all your mail
   in your Inbox gets confusing. On the other hand, if you create too many
   folders, you may be just as confused as if you had only one.

6. **Click OK.**

   Your new folder appears in the Folder List.

You now have a new folder named Personal (or whatever name you entered)
for filing messages you want to save for future reference. I like to use three or
four mail folders for different types of mail to make finding what I'm looking
for easier.

Moving messages to another folder

Filing your messages is as easy as dragging them from the folder they're in to the folder where you want them. Just click the Inbox to look at your messages when they arrive, and then drag each message to the folder where you want your messages to stay.

To move messages to another folder, follow these steps:

1. **Click the Mail button in the Navigation Pane (or press Ctrl+Shift+I).**

   Your list of incoming mail messages appears.

2. **Click the title of the message you want to move.**

   The message is highlighted.

3. **Click the Move to Folder button.**

   The Move Items dialog box appears.

4. **Click the name of the folder to which you want to move your message, and then click OK.**

   Your message is moved to the folder you chose. If you created a folder named *Personal* (or anything else) in the preceding section of this chapter, you can drag the message there.

The Outlook toolbar has a button called Move to Folder that you can click to move a selected message to the folder of your choice. The best thing about the button is that it remembers the last ten folders to which you moved messages. That feature makes it easy to move messages to folders that may be tricky to find in the Folder List.

Organizing Your E-Mail with Search Folders

The Search Folders feature in Outlook is designed to help you organize the messages in your Inbox. Search Folders provide a single place where you can always look to find a certain kind of message. A Search Folder doesn't actually move your messages; it's really a kind of imaginary location for your messages so you only have to look at one type of message at a time.

When you first start Outlook, you find these Search Folders already installed:

✔ **For Follow-Up:** This folder shows only the messages you've flagged. When you remove the flag from a message, you'll no longer see it in this Search Folder, but you can still find it in your Inbox.

✔ **Large Messages:** This Search Folder organizes your messages in order of how much storage space they require. Normally, you're probably not too concerned with the size of the messages you receive — but don't be surprised if the system administrators where you work ask you not to store too much mail in your Inbox. If you have lots of messages with attachments (or messages in which friends include their photographs), you may find your Inbox filling up quickly.

You can use the Large Messages Search Folder to figure out which messages are taking up the most space — and eliminate the largest ones. The messages you'll see in this folder are categorized by size, starting with Large and moving up to Huge and Enormous.

✔ **Unread Mail:** This folder shows you only the messages you haven't read yet. When you read a message in this folder, it disappears from the folder, but you'll still be able to find it in your Inbox.

Using a Search Folder

You don't need to do anything special to use a Search Folder; just click the name of the search you want to look at, and those messages appear in the Reading Pane. When you're ready to go back to your Inbox, just click the Mail button in the Navigation Pane to see your whole collection of messages again.

Setting up a new Search Folder

You need not limit yourself to the Search Folders that Outlook provides. You can create your own custom folders as well. For example, if you receive regular messages about sales in a certain region, you can set up a Search Folder that automatically shows you all the messages you've received containing that information.

To set up a new Search Folder, follow these steps:

1. **Choose File ➪ New ➪ Search Folder (or press Ctrl+Shift+P).**

   The New Search Folder dialog box appears.

2. **Select the type of Search Folder you'd like to create from the list in the New Search Folder dialog box.**

   About a dozen different kinds of folders are available. You can either use a predefined folder or create your own type of Search Folder (by choosing Create Custom Search Folder).

3. **If a button appears at the bottom of the New Search Folder dialog box, click the button and fill in the requested information.**

    When you click one of the folder types to select it, the bottom of the New Search Folder dialog box changes, offering you a choice suitable to the type of folder you're creating.

4. **Click OK.**

    The New Search Folder dialog box closes.

Deleting a Search Folder

After your Search Folder has served its purpose, there's no reason for you to keep it. Remember, the contents of the Search Folder are really just imaginary; deleting this folder does not delete the messages it contains. Just click the Search Folder you want to delete and then click the Delete button (the button with the big black X) in the toolbar to make your Search Folder disappear.

Using (Electronic) Stationery

It has been only a few centuries now since preprinted stationery came into fashion for paper mail, so I suppose it's not too early for the same idea to catch on for electronic mail.

Stationery is designed to convey a visual impression about your message. With the right choice of stationery, you can make your message look uniquely important, businesslike, or just plain fun.

Unlike paper stationery, an unlimited selection (and supply!) of stationery is available for your e-mail messages — and you don't have to spend any money on printing and paper. Just pick the design you want from a menu, and there you are! Correspondence Art!

To use stationery, follow these steps:

1. **Choose Actions ⇨ New Mail Message Using ⇨ More Stationery.**

    The Select a Stationery dialog box appears, containing a list of stationery types you can choose (as shown in Figure 6-2). Each time you click the name of a type of stationery, you see what that stationery looks like in the Preview window.

Figure 6-2:
The Select a
Stationery
dialog box.

If the New Mail Message Using command on the Actions menu isn't black and doesn't work when you click it, turn the feature on. Choose Tools ⇨ Options, click the Mail Format tab, and choose HTML from the scroll-down menu at the top of the Mail Format page.

2. **Click the name of the stationery you want to use.**

   The name of the stationery you click is highlighted to show you've selected it.

3. **Click OK.**

   The stationery you choose appears. For this example (see Figure 6-3), I chose the Citrus Punch Stationery.

4. **Fill in the information in the form.**

   You can customize stationery to fit any need. Just click any box where you can put information and type your desired text. You can replace any existing text on a piece of stationery; just select the text you want to replace by dragging the mouse pointer over the text, and then type the text you want.

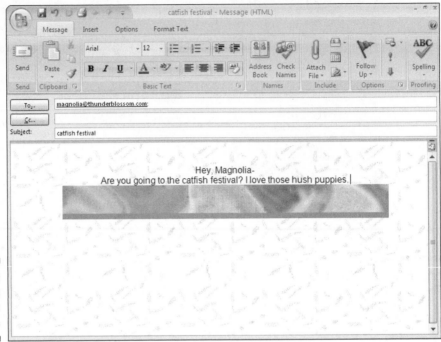

Figure 6-3:
The Citrus Punch stationery.

5. **Click the To button.**

   The Select Names dialog box appears (as shown in Figure 6-4).

6. **Select the name of the person to whom you want to send the message.**

   The name you click is highlighted to show you've selected it.

7. **Click the To button.**

   Yes, I know, you clicked the To button before. This time it's for entering the person's name into your e-mail message.

8. **Click OK.**

   The Select Names dialog box disappears and the stationery reappears.

9. **Click Send.**

   If your computer is on a network at your office, your message is on its way. If you're using Outlook at home, you have to send your message by choosing Tools ⇨ Send/Receive. You can also press F9.

Figure 6-4:
The Select
Names
dialog box.

Not everyone uses Outlook to read his or her e-mail, which means the beauty
of your stationery may be lost on some people to whom you send messages.
Don't be offended if your stationery design is lost in shipment (or arrives as
an attachment), as long as the text of your message arrives.

Using the Reading Pane

If you want to skim through a whole bunch of messages quickly, the Reading
Pane can help. The Reading Pane is normally open when you first install
Outlook. If it got closed somehow, choose View ⇨ Reading Pane ⇨ Right to
open it.

When you do, the Inbox screen divides into two sections:

✔ The left shows your list of messages.

✔ The right shows the contents of the message you've selected; see
Figure 6-5.

To move from one message to the next, just press the ↓ key. You can also view any message in your Inbox by clicking the message title. If you prefer to see the text of your messages on the bottom of the screen, you can also choose View ➪ Reading Pane ➪ Bottom, but you can't see as much of your message. I generally prefer setting the Reading Pane to appear on the right, although sometimes the To-Do Bar cramps the Reading Pane. You can make more room for the Reading Pane by clicking the two little arrows to the left of the words To-Do Bar, which squeezes the bar into a skinny little ribbon on the right edge of the screen. You can click the double arrows above the words To-Do Bar to reopen it.

The Reading Pane displays quite a lot more text than AutoPreview mode, in addition to graphics and formatting. If your friends send messages using Outlook stationery, for example, you can appreciate their graphic genius much better by viewing their messages in the Reading Pane.

Figure 6-5:
The Reading Pane displays the list of messages along with the contents of one message.

Playing by the Rules

Rules are probably my favorite feature in Outlook. The rules feature lets you make Outlook act on certain kinds of e-mail messages automatically. For example, I get tons of e-mail messages, and I can easily waste the whole day sorting through them. I have much more entertaining ways to waste my time, such as pasting sticky notes to my forehead and having imaginary conversations with Donald Trump. ("Oh, yeah? Well, you're fired too, ya jerk!") That's why I set up rules in Outlook to automatically sort my incoming mail into different folders; it lets me spend a little less time wading through all those messages and more time on my overactive fantasy life.

The question of how many different rules you can create with the Rules Wizard may be one of those vast cosmic mysteries, but I'm sure you can create more rules than you and I will ever need.

Creating a rule the quick-and-dirty way

You usually discover the need to create a rule right after getting a message that ticks you off. Your first impulse may be to kick your computer, but don't do that; you might hurt yourself, especially if the computer is on top of the desk. Besides, you can create an Outlook Rule while you're still reading the message (that you'd rather not be reading at all). Just click the Create Rule button at the top of the message form and check the appropriate boxes in the Create Rule dialog box. You never have to read another message from that so-and-so again. Unless that so-and-so is your boss, then you may have to make another kind of rule.

Creating a rule the regular way

The Rules Wizard is called a *wizard* because of the way the program leads you step by step to create each rule. The process is pretty simple. To create a simple rule to move an incoming message from a certain person to a certain folder, follow these steps:

1. **Click the Inbox icon in the Navigation Pane (or press Ctrl+Shift+I).**

   The list of messages in your Inbox appears.

2. **Choose Tools ➪ Rules and Alerts.**

   The Rules and Alerts dialog box appears (see Figure 6-6).

Figure 6-6:
The Rules
Wizard's
dialog box
enables you
to make the
rules.

3. Click the New Rule button.

A dialog box for creating new rules appears. The dialog box contains a list of the types of rules you can create.

4. Choose the type of rule you want to create.

The Rules Wizard offers several common types of rules you may want to create:

- Move messages from someone to a folder

- Move messages with specific words in the subject to a folder

- Move messages sent to a distribution list to a folder (as shown in Figure 6-7)

The collection of suggested rules is divided into useful categories such as Stay Organized and Stay Up-To-Date. I'm disappointed that the list doesn't include *Stay Sane, Stay Employed,* or even *Stay Home but Still Get Paid.* I'm sure those will be available in a future version of Outlook. For this example, I suggest choosing Move Messages from Someone to a Folder. After doing so, you see, in the Rule Description box at the bottom of the dialog box, the words Apply This Rule After the Message Arrives from People or Distribution List . . . Move It to the Specified Folder. (That's a mouthful, but Outlook understands.)

Figure 6-7:
Choose the
type of rule
you want to
create.

5. **Click the first piece of underlined text in the Rule Description box, which says People or Distribution List.**

   The Rules Address dialog box appears.

6. **Double-click the name of each person whose messages you want to move to a new folder.**

   The name of each person you choose appears in the right column of the Rules Address dialog box.

7. **Click OK when you've chosen all the people whose messages you want to move.**

   The Rules Address dialog box closes and the names you've selected replace the words People or Distribution List.

8. **Click the next piece of underlined text in the Rule Description box.**

   Another dialog box opens, offering you a choice of folders to which you can move the message (as shown in Figure 6-8).

Figure 6-8:
Choose the
folder to
which your
messages
will go.

9. **Double-click the name of the folder to which you want to move messages.**

   The dialog box closes, and the name of the folder you choose appears in the sentence in the Rule Description box.

10. **Click Finish.**

    The first Rules Wizard dialog box appears, providing a list of all your rules. Each rule has a check box next to it. You can turn rules on and off by clicking the check boxes. If a check mark appears next to a rule, it's turned on; otherwise the rule is turned off.

11. **Click OK to close the Rules Wizard.**

Rules can do much more than just sort incoming messages. You can create rules that automatically reply to certain messages, flag messages with a particular word in the subject, delete messages about specific topics . . . the sky's the limit.

Running a rule

Normally, rules go into action when messages arrive in your Inbox. When you create a rule to move messages from a certain person to a certain folder, the messages that arrive after you create the rule get moved, but the messages sitting in your Inbox keep sitting there. If you want to apply a rule to the messages already sitting in your Inbox, use the Run Now button at the top of the Rules and Alerts dialog box. When the Run Rules Now dialog box appears, check the rule you want to run and then click the Run Now button at the bottom of the dialog box.

Filtering Junk E-Mail

If you feel overwhelmed by junk e-mail, you're not alone; more junk e-mail messages are now sent over the Internet than legitimate ones. It's now safe to assume that if you get e-mail, you get junk e-mail, also known as *spam*. Outlook includes a filtering system that looks over all your incoming mail and automatically moves anything that looks like junk e-mail to a special folder. You can delete everything that gets moved to your Junk E-Mail folder now and again — after checking to make sure Outlook didn't mistakenly move real e-mail to your Junk E-Mail folder.

No machine is perfect, and no program that runs on a machine is perfect. I don't entirely know how Outlook figures out which messages are junk and which are real. I find that some junk e-mail still gets through, but Outlook catches more than half the junk messages I get. Once or twice I've seen it dump items from real people into the Junk E-Mail folder. (Outlook once sent a message from my father to the Junk E-Mail folder; I've been checking the Junk E-Mail folder regularly ever since.)

Fine-tuning the filter's sensitivity

You don't need to do anything to turn on Junk E-Mail filtering in Outlook. The program already guards against junk e-mail the first time you start it up; however, the protection level is set at Low.

Whether you feel that Outlook moves too many incoming messages — or too few — to the Junk E-Mail folder, you can adjust Outlook's sensitivity to suit your taste by changing the Junk E-Mail settings.

To adjust Outlook's Junk E-Mail Settings, follow these steps:

1. **Choose Actions ➪ Junk E-Mail ➪ Junk E-Mail Options.**

   The Junk E-Mail Options dialog box appears (as in Figure 6-9) with the Options tab on top.

Figure 6-9:
Set your
Junk E-Mail
protection
as high or
low as
you like.

2. **Click the option you prefer.**

The circle next to the option you click darkens to show what you've selected. The options that Outlook offers you include

- **No protection:** At this setting, every sleazy message goes right to your Inbox, unchallenged. If that's your cup of tea, fine. Most people want a little more filtering.

- **Low:** The junkiest of the junk gets moved, but a lot of nasty stuff still gets through.

- **High:** This setting is aggressive enough that you can expect to see a certain amount of legitimate e-mail end up in the Junk E-Mail folder. If you choose this setting, be sure to check your Junk E-Mail folder from time to time to be sure that important messages don't get trashed by mistake.

- **Safe Lists only:** This setting moves all messages out of your Inbox except for the ones from people or companies that you've designated in your Safe Senders lists.

Also, the check boxes at the bottom of the Options tab offer you a range of other choices:

- **Permanently Delete Suspected Junk E-Mail:** I think that might be a bit too aggressive, but it's your choice. I haven't seen a perfect Junk E-Mail filter yet, so it's probably better to push junk messages over to the Junk E-Mail folder and empty the folder occasionally. On the other hand, you may work in a company that limits the amount of e-mail you're allowed to store, and the messages in your Junk E-Mail folder count against your limit. So zapping junk e-mail may be the best option.

- **Disable Links in Phishing Messages:** *Phishing* isn't just incorrectly spelled; it's a way of doing something very wrong to lots of unsuspecting e-mail recipients. That's the term used for an e-mail message that tries to impersonate a bank or financial institution in an effort to steal your personal information. It's the first step in an identity theft operation. This kind of crime is on the rise, so Outlook now tries to detect false e-mails and disable the Web links they contain. Even so, you should never give personal financial information or passwords to anyone in response to an e-mail message. Go straight to your financial institution by phone or log on to their Web site directly (not by clicking the links in an e-mail). You could be the victim of all kinds of bad stuff if you're not careful.

- **Warn About Suspicious Domains:** Some places have a bad reputation, both on the Web and off. If you receive an e-mail from a suspicious location, Outlook will warn you so that you don't get yourself into trouble. Mother told you there's be webs like this. She also told you to eat your vegetables. Did you? I didn't think so.

3. Click OK.

The Junk E-Mail Options dialog box closes.

There you are! With any luck, you'll no longer need to wade through messages about get-rich-quick schemes or pills that enlarge body parts you don't even have.

Filtering your e-mail with sender and recipient lists

Outlook's Junk E-Mail handling feature includes an option that you can choose if you want to set up your own *safe lists* for handling where your e-mail comes from or goes to. You can make a list of people whose messages should *always* be moved to the Junk E-Mail folder (or people whose messages should *never* be moved there). Check out the other tabs of the Junk E-Mail Options dialog box for descriptions of the types of senders you can enter:

✔ **Safe Senders:** When a message arrives with an e-mail address or domain on this list in the From line of the message, Outlook makes sure not to treat the message as Junk E-Mail — no matter what else the message says.

✔ **Safe Recipients:** If you receive messages from an online mailing list, the messages often appear to come from many different people, but they're always addressed to the list. (For example, if you belong to any of the groups on yahoogroups.com, you'll see this.) In this case, you'd put the name of the list in your Safe Recipients list.

✔ **Blocked Senders:** This is the opposite of the two preceding choices; messages from the addresses on this list are always treated as Junk E-Mail.

Adding an individual to your Blocked Senders List is pretty simple: When you receive a message from someone you don't want to hear from anymore, select the message and choose Actions ➪ Junk E-Mail ➪ Add Sender to Blocked Senders List. This same method works for adding people to the Safe Senders and Safe Recipients Lists. Just select the message, choose Actions ➪ Junk E-Mail, and then choose the list to which you want the sender added.

Of course, if you want to be more precise, you can go directly to the appropriate tab in the Junk E-Mail Options dialog box and type in the addresses you want to filter.

Some other Junk E-Mail options that could save you time include these:

✔ **Contacts List:** A check box at the bottom of the Safe Senders tab is labeled Also Trust E-Mail from My Contacts. If that box is checked, messages from anyone in your Contacts List automatically get treated as safe messages.

✔ **Your Recipients:** If you check the box labeled Automatically Add People I E-Mail to the Safe Senders List, Outlook will automatically accept messages from the people to whom you've sent messages.

✔ **Import and Export:** If you have a particularly long list of people to add to your Safe Senders List or your Blocked Senders List, you can create a list in Notepad and then import that list to Outlook. Companies with lengthy client lists might make this feature available to all.

Filtering domains

Outlook gives you one rather powerful option among your junk e-mail choices that you need to be careful about. That option involves filtering domains. If you do business with people at a certain company, you can enter that entire company in your Safe Senders List by selecting the message and then choosing Actions ➪ Junk E-Mail ➪ Add Senders Domain (@example.com) to Safe Senders List.

However, if you accidentally add the domain of a friend who sends you e-mail via America Online to your Safe Senders List, you partly defeat the purpose of your Junk E-Mail filters (because so much junk e-mail comes from aol.com — or at least pretends to come from aol.com). So use the domain-filtering feature with care.

Archiving for Posterity

It doesn't take long to accumulate more messages than you can deal with. Some people just delete messages as they read them. Others hold on to old messages for reference purposes. I hold onto all the messages I've ever sent or received in Outlook because I never know when I'll need to check back to see what someone said to me (or, for that matter, what I said).

Also, some companies are required by law to retain all messages for a certain period of time. This is a serious issue if you work in a highly-regulated industry such as banking, finance, or health care. Failure to save messages for the right amount of time can land you or your company in deep doo-doo, so it pays to be aware of your company's retention policy. On the other hand, many large companies automatically back up all messages and save the backups in a "secure, undisclosed location," which lets individual employees off the hook when it comes to document retention.

The problem with storing lots of messages is that Outlook slows down when you store too many of them. A huge collection of messages is not only cumbersome to manage, system administrators at a large company may not let you store more than a certain amount of e-mail because it clogs up the system.

Archiving is a feature built right into Outlook to help you store messages and other Outlook items that you don't need to look at right now, but that you still might want to refer to in the future. If you use Outlook on an Exchange network at work, Archiving makes it easy for you to get along with your system administrators by slimming down the number of messages you're storing in the e-mail system.

Even if you don't want to use the Archiving feature right now, you may want to understand how it works. Outlook sometimes archives items automatically — which may look to you as if your Outlook items are disappearing. In this section, I show you how to find the items that Outlook has archived for safekeeping.

If the AutoArchive feature seems scary and complicated to you, try not to worry. I agree that Microsoft hasn't done a good job of making the Archive feature understandable. When you get the hang of it, however, AutoArchiving could become valuable to you.

Although e-mail messages are what people archive most often, all Outlook items can be sent to the archive — appointments, tasks, everything. People don't usually archive contacts and notes, but you can even archive those if you want.

Setting up AutoArchive

You don't have to do anything to make Outlook archive your items; the program is set up to archive items automatically. If you want to see how Outlook is set up to archive your old items, or change the way Outlook does the job, follow these steps:

1. **Choose Tools ➪ Options.**

   The Options dialog box appears.

2. **Click the Other tab.**

   The Other options page appears.

3. **Click the AutoArchive button.**

   The AutoArchive dialog box appears (shown in Figure 6-10).

Don't go barging through the AutoArchive dialog box changing things willy-nilly — at least not until you look to see what's already set up. Four important tidbits that the AutoArchive dialog box normally tells you are as follows:

✔ How often Outlook archives items

✔ How old items have to be for Outlook to send them to the archive

✔ The name and location of the archive file

✔ Whether the AutoArchive feature is turned on

When you first install Outlook, the program automatically archives items every 14 days, sending items over six months old to the archive file listed in the AutoArchive dialog box. For most people, those settings are just fine. Some people prefer to turn off the AutoArchive feature and run the Archive process manually, as I describe in the next section. You can turn off the AutoArchive process by clicking the check box labeled Run AutoArchive Every 14 Days at the top of the AutoArchive dialog box.

Activating the archive process manually

You can archive messages any time you want by choosing File ⇨ Archive
from the Outlook menu and following the prompts. The advantage of running
the Archive process manually is that you get slightly better control of the
process; you can give Outlook a cutoff date for archiving items, say the first
of the year. You can also tell Outlook which folders to archive and where to
send the archived items. You can even archive different Outlook folders to
different archive files. The disadvantage to all this control is that it's possible
to make an innocent mistake and send archived items to a place you can't
find again easily. Try not to change the name or location of the files to which
your archived items are sent, because it's surprisingly easy to lose track of
what went where, and Outlook doesn't provide much help with keeping track
of archived files.

Finding and viewing archived items

Sometimes AutoArchive seems like magic. Older items are mysteriously filed away without any action on your part. Isn't that easy? Sure — until you suddenly need to *find* one of those items that moved magically to your archive. Then you have to figure out where it went and how to get at it again.

I usually like to talk up the good points of Outlook, but honestly, this is one place where the Outlook developers fell down on the job. Although it's easy to move items into your Archive, it's pretty confusing to get them back. What's the point of archiving items if you can't find them again?

Anyway, when you want to take another look at the items you've archived, open the Archive folder, which Outlook also refers to as a *data file*.

To open a data file containing your archive items, follow these steps:

1. **Choose File ➪ Open ➪ Outlook Data File.**

   The Open Outlook Data File dialog box appears.

2. **Type the name of the file you want to open in the File Name box.**

   The name you enter appears in the File Name box.

3. **Click OK.**

   The name of the data file you opened appears in the Folder Banner in large letters. Your Folder List also appears, showing two sets of folders: Normal and Archive.

Simple enough, right? Yes, but there's a virtual fly in the virtual ointment. You probably don't know the name of the archive file you want to open, and it doesn't usually show up in the list in the Create or Open Outlook Data File dialog box.

To find out the name of the archive file to open, choose File ➪ Archive and look in the box labeled Archive File. Be careful not to change anything about the information; otherwise Outlook may start sending your archived items someplace else. The information in the Archive File box is usually complex gobbledygook with colons and slashes and all sorts of stuff that normal people can't remember.

My favorite trick for capturing a long name in a dialog box is to copy the information. Here's what it looks like in fast-forward: Click the name once, press Tab, press Shift+Tab, press Ctrl+C, and then click Cancel. After you copy the file name, you can follow the steps given earlier in this section — pasting the name you want into the File Name box by pressing Ctrl+V, and rejoicing that you don't have to remember that long, crazy file name.

Closing the Archive file

You can keep your Archive file open in the Outlook Folder List as long as you want, but most people prefer to close it after they find what they need. Outlook runs a little faster when you close any unnecessary data files.

To close a data file, follow these steps:

1. **With the Folder List open, right-click the name of your Archive folder.**

   A shortcut menu appears.

2. **Choose Close Folder from the shortcut menu.**

   Your archive folder disappears from the Folder List.

The way folders are named in Outlook is odd. You may find Personal Folders appearing several times in your Folder List. To make Outlook run as quickly as possible, close as many of them as you can. Your main set of folders — the set you use every day — won't close, so you don't have to worry about closing the folders you use every day.

Arranging Your Messages

Nobody gets a *little* bit of e-mail anymore. If you get one message, you get a ton of 'em. Fortunately, Outlook offers you a whole bunch of different ways to arrange that mess of messages so you have a fighting chance to figure out what's important and what can wait.

When Outlook is set up to display the Reading Pane on the right side of the screen, you'll see two buttons at the top of the list of messages. The leftmost button has a label that says something like Arranged By: Date. The Arranged By button describes the system Outlook is using to organize your messages. To the right of the Arranged By button sits another button with a label that offers some detail about the arrangement Outlook is currently using. (For example, if your messages are currently arranged by date, the button on the right will say either Newest on Top or Oldest on Top.)

To change the way Outlook is arranging your messages, simply click the Arranged By button to reveal a shortcut menu of all the arrangements you can use. These are the arrangements Outlook offers:

✓ **Date:** The most common way to organize messages is by date. When you first set up Outlook, this is how your messages will be arranged. Click the button on the right to alternate between newest messages on top and oldest messages on top.

✔ **Conversation:** This arrangement groups messages of the same topic together. If you've been exchanging a series of messages with someone about a specific project or idea, you can choose the Conversation arrangement to follow the thread of the conversation.

✔ **From:** As you might guess, this arrangement organizes your message collection according to the person from whom the message was sent. Choosing the From arrangement is a little bit faster than setting up a Search Folder, but sometimes a Search Folder is still the best way to track messages from *specific* important people.

✔ **To:** Most messages you receive are addressed to you, but not always. Sometimes you receive messages addressed to a list of people, so your name doesn't appear on the To line of the message. This arrangement separates your messages according to whether your name is on the To line of each message.

✔ **Folder:** When you're viewing messages in a Search folder, the messages you're viewing may actually be located in a variety of different folders. If you want to know exactly which folder contains each message, use the Folder arrangement. When you're viewing your Inbox, the Folder arrangement is not available; it's only for Search Folders.

✔ **Size:** Everyone knows that size doesn't matter; it's the sentiment that counts. Well, okay, not always. Size is important to certain system administrators — and it isn't *always* a personal problem. Some e-mail messages include photographs, music, and all sorts of heavyweight files that can really clog up your company's e-mail servers. So when your system administrator asks you to thin out your Inbox, make some use of this feature: Identify and delete the messages that are the most over-weight.

✔ **Subject:** This arrangement is similar to the Conversation arrangement, except it doesn't follow the thread of a conversation, it just lumps together messages that have the same subject.

✔ **Type:** Not every item that arrives in your Inbox is a simple message; you may also receive Meeting Invitations, Task Requests, and all sorts of other items. When you want to separate the messages from the Meeting Requests, switch to the Type arrangement so the most interesting messages rise to the top of the list.

✔ **Attachment:** When you go to your Inbox, you may not be looking for a message, you may be hunting for an attachment. Arranging your messages by attachment enables you to examine the likely suspects first.

✔ **E-mail accounts:** You can set up Outlook to collect e-mail from several different e-mail addresses. Sometimes you want to know which message came from which of those addresses, or just to look at the messages sent to one of those addresses. If you want to see only the messages sent to a single address, choose the E-Mail Accounts arrangement and then click the minus sign (–) next to the names of accounts you don't want to see. With this arrangement, Outlook shows you only the messages from the accounts that interest you.

✔ **Importance:** First things first — you know the saying. When you need to see the messages marked with high importance first, this is the arrangement you want to use.

✔ **Categories:** You can assign categories to any message you send, and sometimes other people can assign categories to the messages they send you. To see which message falls into which category, use the Categories arrangement.

✔ **Availability:** If you get an e-mail from someone cute and want to know if they're married, this setting won't help. The Availability setting is for people who use a laptop on a corporate network with Microsoft Exchange. Exchange can be set up so that when your connection speed is slow, such as on a dial-up connection (remember those?), it only sends *headers* of each e-mail message — just the subject, date, and sender name — but not the main body of the message. Until you actually click the message to read it, the rest of the message stays back on the main computer in the home office. Those kinds of messages are *unavailable*. The messages you can access in their entirety are considered *available*. Some of them are kind of cute, too.

The Arrange By button appears at the top of your Message List only when the Reading Pane is set to appear on the right side of the screen. You can turn the Reading Pane on by choosing View ➪ Reading Pane ➪ Right. If you want to arrange your messages when the Reading Pane is off, choose View ➪ Arrange By to see the list of arrangements and then pick the one you want.

Part III
Managing Contacts, Dates, Tasks, and More

The 5th Wave   By Rich Tennant

"Hold on, Barbara. Let me launch Outlook and
see if I can find a newsgroup on this."

In this part . . .

The vast majority of the people I've trained started out using less than ten percent of Outlook's power to organize tasks, appointments and contacts. Since you already have Outlook right on your desk, it makes sense to harness the power it offers to cut through your workload and get more done. In this part, I show you faster ways to manage the world outside your desktop.

Chapter 7

Your Little Black Book: Creating Contact Lists

You've heard people say "It's not what you know, it's who you know." Well, how do you keep track of what you know about who you know? You either need a terrific memory or a convenient tool for keeping track of all those whatshisnames and whoziwhatzits out there.

Years ago I had a habit of keeping track of all the people I needed to know by memory. Then something happened that changed that habit. What was it? I forget. But take my word for it; I don't go around memorizing names and numbers anymore. I put them all into Outlook and make my computer do the memorizing. Now, instead of wasting hours memorizing, I can spend quality time with my dear friends whatshisname and whoziwhatzit.

All kidding aside, I work as a consultant and speaker and writer for computer magazines. The information I need to keep about consulting clients (hours, locations, and whatnot) differs from the information I need for dealing with people in the publishing business (editors, deadlines, topics, and so on). I'm also active as a musician and filmmaker, and my contacts in those businesses are two entirely different kettles of fish. But when someone calls on the phone, or when I want to do a mailing to a group from one world or another, I need to be able to look up the person right away, regardless of which category the person fits in.

Outlook is flexible enough to let you keep your entire collection of name and address information in a single place — but you can also sort, view, find, and print it differently, depending on what kind of work you're doing. You can also keep lists of family and friends stored in Outlook right alongside your business contacts, and still distinguish them from one another quickly when the need arises.

Storing Names, Numbers, and Other Stuff

Storing lots of names, addresses, and phone numbers is no big trick, but finding them again can take magic unless you have a tool like Outlook. Other programs can store names and related numbers, but Outlook, by far, is the most popular program for doing work that uses names, addresses, and phone numbers.

If you've ever used a little pocket address book, you pretty much know how to use the Outlook Contacts feature. Simply enter the name, address, phone number, and a few juicy tidbits, and there you are!

The quick-and-dirty way to enter contacts

Entering a new name in your Contacts List is utterly simple. With the Contacts List open, click the New button on the toolbar to open the New Contact entry form, fill in the blanks on the form, and then click Save ⇨ Close. That's really all there is to it. If you don't enter every detail about a contact right away, it's okay — you can always add more information later.

The slow, complete way to enter contacts

If you want, you can enter scads of details about every person you enter in your Contacts List and choose from literally dozens of options, but if all you do is enter the essentials and move on, that's fine. If you're more detail-minded, here's the way to enter every jot and tittle for each contact record:

1. **Click the Contacts button in the Navigation Pane (or press Ctrl+3).**

   The Contacts List appears; see Figure 7-1.

2. **Click the New button.**

   The New Contact form appears.

   To be really quick, press Ctrl+Shift+C to see the New Contact form shown in Figure 7-2.

Figure 7-1:
The
Contacts
List.

Figure 7-2:
The New
Contact
form.

3. Click the Full Name button.

The Check Full Name dialog box appears (as shown in Figure 7-3):

- Click the triangle (called the *scroll-down button*) on the right edge of the Title text box and choose a title (such as Mr., Ms., or Dr.) from the list that drops down, or type one — such as *Reverend, Guru,* or *Swami.*

- Click in the First text box and type the contact's first name.

- Click in the Middle text box and type the contact's middle initial (if any). If there's no middle initial, you can leave this box blank.

- Click in the Last text box and type the contact's last name.

- Click in the Suffix drop-down list and choose a suffix, such as Jr., III, or type one in the box, such as *Ph.D., D.D.S.,* or *B.P.O.E.*

- Click OK. The Check Full Name dialog box closes, and you're back in the New Contact form, where the name you entered is now shown in both the Full Name and File As text boxes.

Figure 7-3:
The Check
Full Name
dialog box.

4. **Click in the appropriate box and enter the information requested on the New Contact form.**

   If the information isn't available — for example, if the contact has no job title — leave the box blank. A triangle after the box indicates a drop-down list with choices. If your choice isn't listed, type it in the box.

   - If you've entered a name in the Full Name box, the File As box will already contain that name.

   - If you want this person filed under something other than his or her name, click in the File As box and type in your preferred designation.

     For example, you may want to file your dentist's name under the term *Dentist* rather than by name. If you put Dentist in the File As box, the name turns up under Dentist in the alphabetical listing rather than under the name itself. Both the Full Name and the File As designation exist in your Contacts List. That way (for example), you can search for your dentist either by name or by the word *Dentist.*

5. **Click the triangle in the Address section to choose the type of address you want to enter.**

   You can choose to enter a Business address, Home address, or Other type of address.

6. **Click the button in the Address section to open the Check Address dialog box, then enter the following information in the appropriate boxes:**

   - Street

   - City

   - State/Province

   - ZIP/Postal Code

   - Country

   See Figure 7-4 for a look at a completed Check Address dialog box.

7. **Click OK.**

   The Check Address dialog box closes.

8. **Click the check box on the New Contact form next to This Is the Mailing Address if the address you just entered is the one you'll use for sending mail to the contact.**

9. **Click in the text box to the right of the Business Phone box and type in the contact's business phone number.**

Figure 7-4:
The Check
Address
dialog box.

10. Click in the text box to the right of the Home Phone box and type in the contact's home phone number.

For numbers other than Business and Home phones, click the triangle to the right of the phone-number type block, choose the kind of number you're entering, and then enter the number.

The New Contact form has four phone-number blocks. You can use any of them for any of the 19 phone-number types available in the drop-down list. You can also add custom fields so you can include more than four phone numbers for a single contact. For the person who has everything, you can create custom fields for that person's Ski Phone, Submarine Phone, Gym Phone — as many as you want.

You can choose any of 19 phone number types to enter, depending on what types of phone numbers your contacts have; see Figure 7-5.

11. Click in the E-mail text box and enter your contact's e-mail address.

If your contact has more than one e-mail address, click the triangle at the left edge of the E-mail box (shown in Figure 7-6), select E-mail 2, click in the text box, and then enter the second address.

Figure 7-5:
You can always reach your contact at one of these phone numbers.

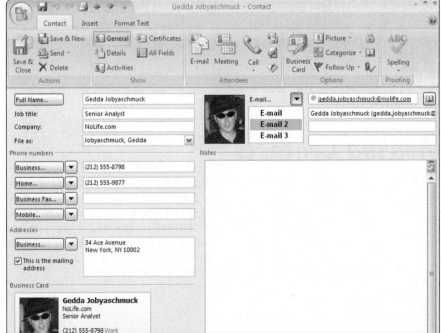

Figure 7-6:
You can enter more than one e-mail address for each person in your Contacts List.

12. Click in the Web Page text box and type the page's address if you want to link to that page directly from the Address Card.

URL is a fancy name for the address of a page on the World Wide Web. When you see ads on TV that refer to `www.discovery.com` or `www.dummies.com`, what you're seeing is a *Uniform Resource Locator* (the even fancier term that URL stands for — essentially an Internet address).

You can view a Web page by entering the URL for the page in the Address box of your Web browser. If a person or company in your Outlook Contacts List has a Web page, you can enter the URL for that page in the Web Page box. To view the Web page for a contact, open the contact record and choose Actions ➪ Explore Web Page (or press Ctrl+Shift+X); your Web browser opens and loads the contact's Web page.

13. Click in the large text box at the bottom of the form and type in anything you want.

You can enter directions, details about meetings, the Declaration of Independence — anything you want (preferably something that can help you in your dealings with the contact).

Format the text in the big text box (see Figure 7-7) by clicking the Write tab and using the buttons on the Formatting Ribbon, if you want. The tools on the formatting Ribbon are just like the ones that all other word-processing programs use: font, point size, bold, italic, justification, and color. Select the text you want to format. You can change the formatting of a single letter or the whole text box. You can't format the text in the smaller data text boxes in the other parts of the Contact form — only that in the big text box at the bottom of the form.

14. When you're done, click Save and Close.

After you enter anything you want or need (or may need) to know about people you deal with at work, you're ready to start dealing.

Viewing Contacts

After you enter your contact information, Outlook lets you see the information arranged in many different and useful ways, called *views*. Viewing your contact information and sorting the views are quick ways to get the big picture of the data you've entered. Outlook comes with anywhere from 5 to 12 predefined views in each module. You can easily alter any predefined view. Then you can name and save your altered view and use it just as you would the predefined views that come with Outlook.

Figure 7-7:
Have fun with formatting in the Contact text box.

To change the view of your Contacts List, follow these steps:

1. **Click the Contacts button in the Navigation Pane (or press Ctrl+3).**

   The Contacts List appears in the main part of the Outlook screen; a list of views appears in the top part of the Navigation Pane.

2. **Pick the view you want from the Current View menu on the Navigation Pane.**

   The view you picked appears. If you chose the Business Cards view, you'd get something like what's shown in Figure 7-8. You can also choose Address Cards, Detailed Address Cards, Phone List, By Category, By Company, By Location, or whatever other views are listed. To use one of the other views, repeat the preceding steps and choose the view you want.

   You can shift between views as you can switch television stations, so don't worry about changing back and forth. Figure 7-9 shows the Current View menu and its list of views for contacts, with the Detailed Address Cards view selected.

Figure 7-8:
The
Business
Cards view.

Figure 7-9:
Your
contacts in
the Detailed
Address
Cards view.

Sorting a view

Some views are organized as simple lists, such as the Phone List view of the Contacts module. Figure 7-10 shows the Phone List: a column of names on the left, followed by a column of company names, and so on.

If you're unable to find a certain contact in a view that is arranged in columns, all you have to do to sort that column is click once on the title of the column. For example, suppose you want to see the names of the people who work for IBM who are entered in your Contacts List. One easy way to see all their names simultaneously is to run a sort on the Company column, like this:

1. **Click the Contacts button in the Navigation Pane (or press Ctrl+3).**

   The Contacts List appears in the main part of the Outlook screen and a list of views appears in the top part of the Navigation Pane.

2. **Choose the Phone List view.**

   Your list of contacts appears in the Phone List view.

3. **Click the heading at the top of the Company column.**

   Your contacts appear in alphabetical order according to the name in the Company column. If you click the heading a second time, your contacts appear in reverse alphabetical order.

Figure 7-10:
The Phone List view.

After you sort your list, it's easier to find someone's name by scrolling down to that part of the alphabet. If you sort by company, all the contacts line up in order of company name, so you can scroll down to the section of your list where all the people from a certain company are listed.

Rearranging views

You can rearrange views simply by dragging the column title and dropping the title where you want it. For example, to move the Business Phone column in the Phone List view, follow these steps:

1. **Choose the Phone List view from the list in the Navigation Pane.**

   The Phone List view of your contacts appears.

2. **Click the Business Phone heading and drag it on top of the column to its left.**

   You see a pair of red arrows pointing to the border between the two columns to the left of the Business Phone column. The red arrows tell you where Outlook will drop the column when you release the mouse button (as shown in Figure 7-11).

Figure 7-11:
You can rearrange the columns by dragging the column heading to the location you desire.

3. **Release the mouse button.**

   The Business Phone column is now to the left of the File As column (instead of to the right). If it makes more sense to you to have File As to the right of Business Phone, you can set up your view in Outlook to put it there.

You can use the same process to move any column in any Outlook view. Because the screen is not as wide as the list, you may need to move columns around at times to see what you really want to see. For example, the Phone List in Figure 7-11 shows 6 columns, but the list in that view really has 12 columns. You must use the scroll bar at the bottom of the list to scroll to the right to see the last column, Categories. If you want to see the Categories column at the same time as the Full Name column, you have to move the Categories column to the left.

Using grouped views

Sometimes sorting just isn't enough. Contacts Lists can get pretty long after awhile; you can easily collect a few thousand contacts in a few years. Sorting a list that long means that if you're looking for stuff starting with the letter *M*, for example, the item you want to find will be about three feet below the bottom of your monitor screen, no matter what you do.

Groups are the answer, and I don't mean Outlook Anonymous. Outlook already offers you several predefined lists that use grouping.

You can view several types of lists in Outlook: A sorted list is like a deck of playing cards laid out in numerical order, starting with the deuces, then the threes, then the fours, and so on up through the picture cards. A grouped view is like seeing the cards arranged with all the hearts in one row, then all the spades, then the diamonds, and then the clubs. Outlook also has several other view types that don't apply to contacts, such as Timeline and Day/Week/Month.

Gathering items of similar types into groups is handy for tasks such as finding all the people on your list who work for a certain company when you want to send congratulations on a new piece of business. Because grouping by company is so frequently useful, the By Company view (shown in Figure 7-12) is set up as a predefined view in Outlook.

To use the By Company view, follow these steps:

1. **Click the Contacts button in the Navigation Pane.**

   The Contacts module opens with its current view displayed.

Figure 7-12:
The By
Company
view.

2. **Choose the By Company view from the list in the Navigation Pane.**

   Each gray bar labeled Company: *name of company* has a little box at the left with a plus or minus sign on it. Click a plus sign to see additional names under the company's heading; a minus sign indicates that no more entries are available.

3. **Click the plus icon to see entries for the company listed on the gray bar.**

If the predefined group views don't meet your needs, you can group items according to just about anything you want, assuming that you've entered the data.

To see the By Category view, follow these steps:

1. **Click the Contacts button in the Navigation Pane.**

   The Contacts view appears.

2. **Choose the By Category view from the list in the Navigation Pane.**

   Each gray bar has an icon on the left side with a plus or a minus sign, followed by Category: *name of category*. A minus sign indicates that no entries are hidden under that category heading; a plus sign means more entries are available (see Figure 7-13).

Figure 7-13:
In the By Category view, if a plus sign appears to the left, click it to see more entries.

3. **Click a plus sign to see more entries for the category listed on the gray bar.**

Grouping is a good way to manage all Outlook items, especially contacts. After you get a handle on using groups, you'll save a lot of time when you're trying to find things.

Flagging Your Friends

Sometimes you need a reminder to do something involving another person — but tying a string around your finger looks silly and doesn't help much anyway. Outlook offers a better way. For example, if you promise to call someone next week, the best way to help yourself remember is to flag that person's name in the Contacts List. A reminder will pop up in your calendar to prompt you to make the call.

Adding a flag to a contact

Contacts aren't the only items you can flag. You can add reminders to tasks, e-mail messages, and appointments to achieve the same effect.

To attach a flag to a contact, follow these steps:

1. **With the Contacts screen open, right-click the contact you want to flag.**

   A shortcut menu appears (as shown in Figure 7-14).

2. **Choose Follow Up.**

   The Follow Up menu appears.

3. **Choose the date you plan to follow up with the contact you chose.**

   Your choices include Today, Tomorrow, This Week, and Next Week. Sadly, When-Heck-Freezes-Over is not included.

4. **Click OK.**

Flagging a contact for a specific day makes that contact's name appear on your Outlook calendar on the day you chose. If you prefer, you can add a reminder to your flag by choosing Add Reminder. That makes a reminder window pop up and play a sound at the time you choose, just in case you have big reasons to avoid talking to that person. A reminder is Outlook's way of telling you to get it over with.

Using Contact Information

Call me crazy, but I bet you actually plan to use all that contact information you enter. I'm sure you'll indulge me while I show you a few ways to dig up and exploit the valuable nuggets you've stashed in your Contacts list.

Finding contacts in the Contacts module

The whole reason for entering names in a Contacts List is so you can find them again. Otherwise what's the point of all this rigmarole?

Finding names in the Outlook Contacts module is child's play. The easiest way is to look in the Address Cards view under the last name.

To find a contact by last name, follow these steps:

1. **Click the Contacts button in the Navigation Pane.**

   Your list of contacts appears.

2. **Choose the Address Cards view from the list in the Navigation Pane.**

   The Address Cards view appears (as shown in Figure 7-15).

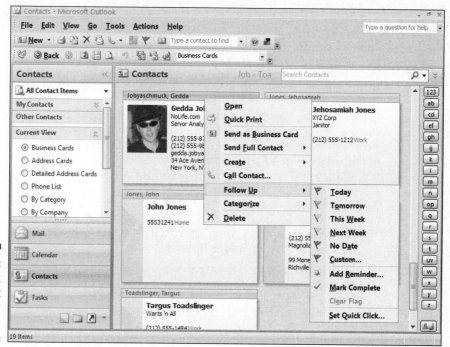

Figure 7-14:
Right-click
any contact
to add
a flag.

Figure 7-15:
The
Address
Cards view.

The Address Cards view has a set of lettered tabs along the right edge. You can click a tab to go to that lettered section, but you can use an easier way: Simply type the first letter of the name you're looking for. For example, if you're looking for Magnolia Thunderblossom (and you've had Outlook make her File As name *Thunderblossom, Magnolia*), then type the letter **T**. You see the names that start with T.

Of course, you may need to base a search for a contact name on something like the company the contact works for. Or you may want to find all the people on your list who live in a certain state. Or people who put you in a certain state of mind (now, *there's* a useful tidbit to include in their contact records). In such a case, the Find Items tool is your portal to your contact.

To use the Find Items tool to search for a contact, follow these steps:

1. **With the Contacts screen open, type the text you want to find in the search box in the Folder Banner.**

   The search box is to the right of the word Contacts. The list of contacts shrinks to those containing the information you typed (as shown in Figure 7-16).

Figure 7-16:
Choose what kind of item you're looking for with the Find tool.

2. **Double-click the name of the contact in the list at the bottom of the screen to see the Contact record.**

   If you get no contacts that match your search, check to see whether you correctly spelled the search text you entered.

It's hard to be as stupidly literal as computers — close doesn't count with them. If you see *Grge Wshngtn,* you know to look for *George Washington;* but a computer doesn't. George would have to have his vowels removed before a computer would see those two names the same way.

On the other hand, if you have only a scrap of the name you're looking for, Outlook can find that scrap wherever it is. A search for *Geo* would turn up George Washington, as well as any other Georges in your Contacts List, including Boy George and George of the Jungle (provided they're all such close, personal friends of yours that they're featured in your Contacts List).

Searching for details about contacts

It doesn't take long to amass a large collection of names in your Outlook Contacts List. That's good — the more people you know, the more good things you can do for other people (or *bad* things you can do *to* other people if you're someone like Tony Soprano). However, a long list of names is no good if you can't find a specific person in that list. Or dig up someone you added a few years back from XYZ company, but whose name you forgot. Outlook has a pretty powerful search tool that helps you find the people you want in a hurry.

To do a "power search" for a name in your Contacts List, follow along:

1. **Click the arrow to the right of the search tool in the Contacts Folder Banner to the right of the word Clear.**

   A shaded box drops down, containing several boxes labeled Business Address, Home Address, Company, and Full Name; see Figure 7-17.

2. **Type the information you want to find in the box whose label corresponds to that type of information.**

   For example, type a company name in the box labeled Company. The list of contacts shrinks to those containing the information you typed.

Figure 7-17:
Searching
for contact
details.

3. **To narrow the list further, type information into a second box.**

   For example, if you're seeking someone named Jones at XYZ Company, you already found everyone at XYZ by typing that in the Company box. Now type **Jones** in the Name box to find all the Joneses at XYZ.

   You can change the types of information you're searching for by clicking the label next to each box to see how many types of information you can search on. It's a big number, more than you're likely to need.

Finding a contact from any Outlook module

A box on the toolbar with the words Type a Contact to Find can help you dig up a contact record in a jiffy from any Outlook module.

1. **Click the Type a Contact to Find box.**

2. **Type the contact name.**

3. **Press Enter to make Outlook open the record for that contact.**

   If you just type in a fragment of a name, Outlook lists names that contain that fragment and enables you to choose which contact you had in mind. For example, if you type *Wash,* you get George Washington, Sam Washburn, and anyone else in your list whose name includes *Wash.* Double-click the name of the contact record you want to see.

The Type a Contact to Find box has a scroll-down button (triangle) at the right side.

If you click the button, you see a list of the last dozen people you looked up, which is handy when you look for the same people repeatedly. When the list appears, just click the name of the contact you want to see.

Using the Activities page

When you open a contact record, you see an icon labeled Activities. That's the place to look for a summary of every Outlook item you've associated with that person (see Figure 7-18). When you click the Activities icon, Outlook opens a page that displays all items linked with your contact. If you're sure you want to find something specific, such as an e-mail message, click the scroll-down button (triangle) next to the word Show and choose the type of item you want. That way Outlook looks only at the kind of items you've specified.

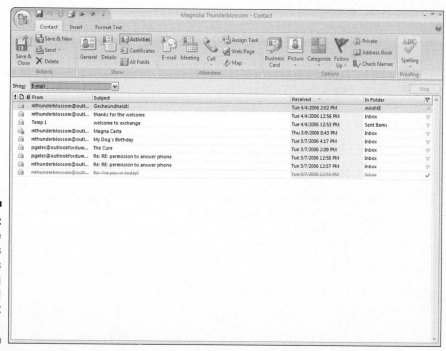

Figure 7-18:
The Activities page finds everything associated with that contact.

Sending a business card

Outlook also has the capability to forward an electronic "business card" to any other person who uses Outlook (or any other program that understands how to use digital business cards). It's a handy way to e-mail any contact record in your list to anybody else.

The most obvious thing you may want to send this way is your own contact information. All you need to do is create a contact record for yourself that contains all the information you want to send someone. Then follow these steps:

1. **Click the Contacts button in the Navigation Pane.**

   Your list of contacts appears.

2. **Double-click the contact record containing the information you want to send.**

   The contact record you double-clicked opens.

3. **Click the Send button.**

   A menu offers three choices: Send as Business Card (both Internet Format and Outlook Format), In Internet Format, and In Outlook Format.

4. **Choose the format you prefer.**

   If you're not sure, choose Send as Business Card. That sends both kinds of card, as seen in Figure 7-19.

5. **Type the address of the person to whom you want to send the message in the To text box.**

   You can also click the To button and pick a name from the Address Book.

6. **Click the Send button (or press Alt+S).**

   Your message and the attached vCard are sent to your recipient.

When you receive a business card in an e-mail message, you can add the card to your Contacts List by double-clicking the icon in the message that represents the business card. Doing so opens a new contact record; simply click Save and Close to add the new name — along with all the info on the business card — to your Contacts List.

Figure 7-19:
Sending a
business
card.

Distribution Lists

You can create a Distribution List in your Contacts module that includes the name of more than one person for those times when you send a message to several people simultaneously. You can also assign categories to your Distribution Lists (just as you can with individual contacts), and you can send a Distribution List to other people as an attachment to an e-mail message so they can use the same list you do if they're also using Outlook.

Creating a Distribution List

Creating a Distribution List is a simple matter of making up a name for your list and choosing from the collection of names you've stored on your system. A Distribution List doesn't keep track of phone numbers and mailing addresses, just e-mail addresses.

To create a Distribution List in your Contacts module, follow these steps:

1. **Choose File ⇨ New ⇨ Distribution List (or press Ctrl+Shift+L).**

   The Distribution List dialog box appears.

2. **Type the name you want to assign to your Distribution List.**

   The name you type appears in the Name text box.

3. **Click the Select Members button.**

   The Select Members dialog box appears, displaying a list of available names on the left side and a blank box on the right side; see Figure 7-20.

4. **Double-click the name of each person you want to add to your Distribution List.**

   Each name you double-click appears in the Add to Distribution List column on the right side of the dialog box.

5. **When you're done picking names, click OK.**

   The Select Members dialog box closes.

Figure 7-20:
Picking members for your Distribution List.

6. Click Save and Close (or press Alt+S).

The Distribution List dialog box closes and your Distribution List appears in boldface in your list of contacts.

When you're creating a Distribution List, you may also want to include the e-mail addresses of people who aren't included in your Contacts list or any of your other Outlook Address Books. To do so, click Add New (instead of Select Members) in Step 3. Enter the name and e-mail address of the person you want to add in the Add New Members dialog box, click OK, and follow the rest of the steps exactly the same way.

Editing a Distribution List

People come and people go in Distribution Lists, just as they do everywhere else. It's a good thing you can edit the lists. Just click the Contacts icon in the Navigation Pane and double-click the name of one of your Distribution Lists (the entries that show a little two-headed icon to the right of their names). When you open a Distribution List entry, you see the same screen you saw when you first created the list. Here you have some useful options:

✔ To remove a member of the list, click that name and click the Remove button.

✔ To select a new member from the names already in your Contacts List or Global Address List, click Select Members and follow the same routine you used when you created the list.

✔ To add a person whose e-mail address isn't listed in any of your Address Books, click the Add New button, fill in the person's name and e-mail address, and click OK.

Using a Distribution List

Distribution Lists show up as items in your Contacts List along with people's names — so (as you'd guess) you can use a Distribution List to address an e-mail message just as you would with any contact. You can drag the card for a Distribution List to your Inbox to create a new e-mail message to that list. You can also type the name of the Distribution List in the To line of an e-mail message and click the Check Names button in the toolbar. When Outlook adds an underline to the name in the To box, you know your message will go to the people on your Distribution List.

Adding pictures to contacts

You can include a picture with the contact information you collect, and not just for decoration. Now that many cell phones and other mobile devices synchronize with the Outlook Contacts List, you can make someone's picture appear on your cell phone screen every time they call or send you a text message. Those pictures will also appear when you pick the Business Cards view of your Outlook contacts. If you're the type who forgets names but never forgets a face, you can collect both names and faces.

Add a picture to a contact record:

1. **With the Contacts screen open, double-click a contact to which you want to add a picture.**

   The contact record you chose opens.

2. **Double-click the picture icon at the top center of the contact record.**

   The Add Picture dialog box opens; see Figure 7-21.

Figure 7-21:
The Add
Contact
Picture
dialog box.

3. Double-click the picture you want to add.

The picture you chose appears in the contact record.

4. Click Save and Close.

Another smiling face now adorns your world, as shown in Figure 7-22. Isn't it wonderful? If you're likely to be sending out your own business card, it's probably worthwhile to add a nice-looking picture to help make a good impression.

Also, if you have one of those fun picture-editing programs, you can add mustaches and blacked-out teeth to the people you find unappealing just for a laugh. But if your boss is likely to see his picture on your screen with some (ahem!) unflattering adjustments, you might think twice before "improving" his contact photo.

Figure 7-22:
A picture is worth a thousand words — sometimes.

Chapter 8

The Calendar: How to Unleash Its Power

Do working people work all day? No. Most working people spend the day going to meetings. When all the meetings are over, they stay late at the office to do the work that was supposed to happen during all those meetings. As if an endless parade of meetings wasn't bad enough, there's the meeting to schedule the next meeting. Which comes right after the meeting to schedule the meeting to schedule the meeting. It's enough to send anyone to Over Meeters Anonymous. The Outlook calendar can't stop the relentless tedium of meetings, but it can speed up the scheduling process and help you budget your time for more meetings!

No doubt you've been looking at calendars your whole life, so the Outlook calendar will be pretty simple for you to understand — it looks like a calendar: plain old rows of dates, Monday through Friday plus weekends, and so on. You don't have to learn to think like a computer to understand your schedule.

If you want to see more information about something in your calendar, most of the time all you have to do is click the calendar with your mouse. If that doesn't give you enough information, click twice. If that doesn't give you everything you're looking for, read on; I fill you in on the fine points. (I suspect the Outlook calendar will be so easy that you won't need much special training to find it useful.)

The Date Navigator: Really Getting Around

The Date Navigator is actually the name of this feature, but don't confuse it with Casanova's chauffeur. The Date Navigator (shown at the upper-right of Figure 8-1) is a trick you can use in Outlook to change the part of the calendar you're seeing or the time period you want to look at.

Believe it or not, that unassuming calendar scrap is probably the quickest way to change how you look at the calendar and make your way around in it. All you have to do is click the date you want to see, and it opens in all its glory. It couldn't be simpler.

To use the Date Navigator, follow these steps:

1. **Click the Calendar button in the Navigation Pane (or press Ctrl+2).**

   The calendar appears.

Figure 8-1:
The Outlook
Date
Navigator.

2. **Choose View ⇨ To-Do Bar.**

   The To-Do Bar appears on the right side of the Outlook screen. The top part of the bar contains the Date Navigator; the bottom part shows an abbreviated list of your upcoming tasks and appointments. (To find out more about the To-Do Bar, see Chapter 9.)

3. **Click the word Day, Week, or Month in the Navigation Pane.**

   One of these words appears highlighted to indicate what you've selected. The Date Navigator appears as a small calendar in the upper-right corner of the screen, just below the words To-Do Bar.

   • To see details of a single date, click that day in the Date Navigator. You see the appointments and events scheduled for the day you clicked.

   • To advance the Date Navigator one month at a time, click one of the triangles on either side of the name of the month, just below the words To-Do Bar.

   • As time goes by (so to speak), you'll gravitate to the Calendar view that suits you best. I like the Week view because it includes both calendar and task information in a screen that's pretty easy to read. You can leave Outlook running most of the time to keep the information you need handy.

Time travel isn't just science fiction. You can zip around the Outlook calendar faster than you can say "Star Trek." Talk about futuristic; the Outlook calendar can schedule appointments for you well into the year 4500! Think about it: Between now and then there are more than 130,000 Saturday nights! That's the good news. There are also more than 130,000 Monday mornings. Of course, in our lifetimes, you and I have to deal with only about 5,000 Saturday nights at most, so we have to make good use of them. Better start planning.

So when you need to find an open date fast, follow these steps:

1. **Choose Go ⇨ Go To Date (or press Ctrl+G).**

   A dialog box appears (as in Figure 8-2) with a date highlighted.

2. **To go to another date, type the date you want as you normally would, such as** January 15, 2005, **or** 1/15/05.

   A really neat way to change dates is to type something like **45 days ago** or **93 days from now**. Try it. Outlook understands simple English when it comes to dates. Don't get fancy, though — Outlook doesn't understand **Fourscore and seven years ago**. (But who does?)

Figure 8-2:
The Go
To Date
dialog box.

If you want to go to today's date, just click the Today button at the top of the screen or choose Go ➪ Today. No matter which date you land on, you can plunge right in and start scheduling. You can double-click the time and date of when you want an appointment to occur and then enter the particulars, or you can double-check details of an appointment on that date by double-clicking the date and making changes to the appointment if necessary. You can also do something silly like find out what day of the week your birthday falls on 1,000 years from now. (Mine's on Saturday. Don't forget.)

Meetings Galore: Scheduling Appointments

Many people live and die by their datebooks. The paper type of datebook still exists. (How quaint.) I'll admit, I find them the easiest kind of datebook to put stuff in, although after it's in, the stuff can be a pain to find. Electronic gizmos like PDAs, cell phones, and iPods can also serve as datebooks, but they're so tiny it's hard to put appointments into them. Fortunately, many digital gadgets synchronize to Outlook, so you can have the best of both worlds!

Outlook makes it surprisingly easy to add appointments — and even easier to find items you've entered. It also warns you when you've scheduled two dates simultaneously. (Very embarrassing!)

The quick-and-dirty way to enter an appointment

Some appointments don't need much explanation. If you're having lunch with Mom on Friday, there's no reason to make a big production out of entering the appointment. When you're looking at a view of your calendar that shows the hours of the day in a column, such as the Workweek view, just click the starting time of your appointment, type a description, such as **Lunch with Mom**, and press Enter. Your appointment is now part of your official schedule, faster than you can say "Waiter!"

The complete way to enter an appointment

Appointments you set up at work often require you to include a little more information than you'd need for your lunch date with Mom. You might want to add details about the location of a meeting and some notes about the meeting agenda; you might also want to assign a category to a meeting so you can show the boss how much time you spend with your clients. When you want to give an appointment the full-Monty treatment, use the complete method.

To schedule an appointment the complete way:

1. **Choose File ➪ New from the menu bar.**

   The New Item menu appears (as in Figure 8-3).

   You may notice Ctrl+N next to the word Appointment. If you press Ctrl+N in any section of Outlook, a dialog box appears so you can create a new item in that section. Press Ctrl+Shift+A from any section of Outlook to create an appointment. The catch is that you won't see the appointment on the calendar until you switch to the Calendar view.

2. **Choose Appointment.**

   The Appointment form opens (as shown in Figure 8-4).

Figure 8-3:
Creating
a new
appointment.

Figure 8-4:
The
Appoint-
ment form.

3. Click in the Subject box and type something there to help you remember what the appointment's about.

For example, type **Dentist appointment** or **Deposit Lottery Winnings** or whatever. This text shows up on your calendar.

4. Click in the Location box and enter the location.

Notice the little triangle (scroll-bar button) at the right side of the box. If you click the triangle, you see a list of the last few locations where you scheduled appointments so you can use the same places repeatedly without having to retype them. Another advantage to having this recallable list of locations is that it makes entering locations easy — you can (for example) sort your list of appointments by location to see whether any conference rooms are free.

5. Double-click the name you want to link to your appointment.

The Select Contacts dialog box closes and the name you chose appears in the Contacts text box.

6. Click Save ➪ Close.

The appointment you created appears in your calendar (as shown in Figure 8-5). You may have to change your Calendar view by clicking the Date Navigator on the date the appointment occurs so you can see your new appointment.

Figure 8-5: When you finish creating an appointment, you'll find it in your calendar.

If you want to see reminders for all your important appointments, you must keep Outlook running so the reminders pop up. You can keep Outlook running in the background if you start up a second program, such as Microsoft Word. When the reminder time arrives, you see a dialog box, similar to the one in Figure 8-6.

Not this time: Changing dates

You can be as fickle as you want with Outlook. In fact, to change the time of a scheduled item, all you do is drag the appointment from where it is to where you want it to be (as shown in Figure 8-7). Or back again . . . maybe . . . if you feel like it. . . .

To change an appointment, follow these steps:

1. **Click the appointment in the Calendar view.**

   A dark border appears around the edge of the appointment.

2. **Drag the appointment to the time or date you want it to be.**

   If you're in the One-Day view, drag an appointment to a different date on the small calendar in the upper right just under the words To-Do Bar, also known as the Date Navigator.

Figure 8-6:
A dialog box pops up to remind you of your appointment.

Figure 8-7:
If your appointment is a drag, drop it in a new time slot.

If you want to create a copy of an appointment for another time, hold down the Ctrl key while you use the mouse to drag the appointment to another time or date. For example, if you're scheduling a Summer Intern Orientation from 9:00 a.m. to 11:00 a.m. and again from 1:00 p.m. to 3:00 p.m., you can create the 9:00 a.m. appointment and then copy it to 1:00 p.m. by holding Ctrl and dragging the appointment. Then you have two appointments with the same subject, location, and date, but different hours.

If you copy an appointment to a different date by dragging the appointment to a date on the Date Navigator, you retain the hour of the appointment but change the date.

You can change an appointment to a date you can't see on the calendar:

1. **Double-click the appointment.**

   The Appointment dialog box opens.

2. **Click in the leftmost Start time block and then click the scroll-down button to the right of the date.**

   A pull-down calendar (shown in Figure 8-8) appears.

3. **Pick the month by clicking one of the triangles beside the month's name.**

   Clicking the left triangle moves you one month earlier; clicking the right triangle moves you one month later.

4. **Click the day of the month you want.**

5. **Click in the rightmost Start Time text box and enter the appointment's new time, if needed.**

6. **Make any other changes you need in the appointment by clicking the information you want to change and typing the revised information over it.**

7. **Click Save and Close.**

Imagine your dentist calls to tell you that you *won't* need a root canal after all, but you'll still need a routine checkup. To change the length of an appointment, follow these steps:

1. **Click the appointment.**

2. **Move the mouse pointer over the "handles" at the top or bottom of the appointment.**

   When the pointer is in the right place, it turns into a two-headed arrow you can use to drag the lines of the appointment box.

Figure 8-8:
The pull-
down
calendar in
the Appoint-
ment form.

3. **Drag the bottom line down to make the appointment time longer; drag the bottom line up to make the appointment shorter.**

   You can change an appointment's length by dragging only in multiples of 30 minutes (as shown in Figure 8-9).

You also can shorten an appointment to fewer than 30 minutes:

1. **Double-click the appointment and click the End Time box.**

2. **Type the ending time.**

3. **Click Save and Close.**

You can enter times in Outlook without adding colons and often without using a.m. or p.m. Outlook translates **443** as 4:43 p.m. If you plan lots of appointments at 4:43 a.m., just type **443A**. (Just don't call *me* at that hour, okay?)

Figure 8-9:
Drag the
handles
to change
an appoint-
ment's
length.

Not ever: Breaking dates

Well, sometimes things just don't work out. Sorry about that. Even if it's hard for you to forget, with the click of a mouse, Outlook deletes dates that you otherwise fondly remember. Okay, *two* clicks of a mouse. *C'est la vie, c'est l'amour, c'est la guerre.* (Look for my next book, *Tawdry French Clichés For Dummies.*)

To delete an appointment (after you've called to break it, of course):

1. **Right-click the appointment (that is, click with the right mouse button).**

2. **Click Delete.**

   As far as Outlook is concerned, your appointment is canceled.

By pressing the Ctrl+D combination, you can delete an appointment in just one, brusque keystroke. How cold.

We've got to keep seeing each other: Recurring dates

Some appointments are like a meal at a Chinese restaurant: As soon as you're done with one, you're ready for another. With Outlook, you can easily create an appointment that comes back like last night's spicy Szechwan noodles.

To create a *recurring* (that is, regularly scheduled) appointment, follow these steps:

1. **Click the Calendar button in the Navigation Pane (or press Ctrl+2).**

   The calendar appears.

2. **Choose Actions ⇨ New Recurring Appointment (as shown in Figure 8-10).**

   The Appointment Recurrence dialog box appears (as shown in Figure 8-11). If you simply click OK to accept the preset choices in the Appointment Recurrence dialog box, your appointment will repeat at the same time each week forever. However, you might not be prepared to schedule meetings from now until Doomsday. Doomsday is not a Federal holiday, by the way; you'll still have to work (unless you take a Personal Doomsday). So you might want to fill in the rest of the Appointment Recurrence dialog box just to be sure.

Figure 8-10:
Create
recurring
appoint-
ments from
the Actions
menu.

Figure 8-11:
The
Appointment
Recurrence
dialog box.

3. **Click the Start text box and enter the starting time.**

   Outlook assumes that your appointment is 30 minutes long unless you tell it otherwise by entering an ending time as well. Click the End box and enter an ending time if you feel the need.

4. **In the Recurrence Pattern box, click the Daily, Weekly, Monthly, or Yearly option button to select how often the appointment recurs.**

5. **In the next part of the Recurrence Pattern box, choose how often the appointment occurs.**

6. **In the Range of Recurrence box, enter the first occurrence in the Start box.**

7. **Choose when the appointments will stop.**

   You can select No End Date, End After (a certain number of occurrences), or End By (a certain date).

8. **Click OK.**

   The Appointment Recurrence dialog box closes and the Appointment form appears; refer to Figure 8-4.

9. **Click the Subject box and enter the subject.**

10. **Click the Location box and enter the location.**

11. **Click Save and Close.**

Your appointment appears in your Outlook calendar with a symbol in the lower-right corner to show that it's a recurring appointment; see Figure 8-12. The symbol looks like two little arrows chasing each others' tails, a little bit like people who go to too many recurring meetings. Coincidence? I don't think so.

Even a recurring appointment gets changed once in awhile. Edit a recurring appointment this way:

1. **Double-click the appointment you want to edit.**

   The Open Recurring Item dialog box appears.

2. **Choose whether you want to change just the occurrence you clicked or the whole series.**

3. **Click OK.**

   The Recurring Appointment dialog box appears (as shown in Figure 8-13).

4. **Edit the details of the appointment.**

   To change the pattern, click the Recurrence button, change the recurrence, and click OK.

5. **Click Save and Close.**

Figure 8-12:
Repeating
appoint-
ments
display the
recurrence
symbol
in the lower-
right corner.

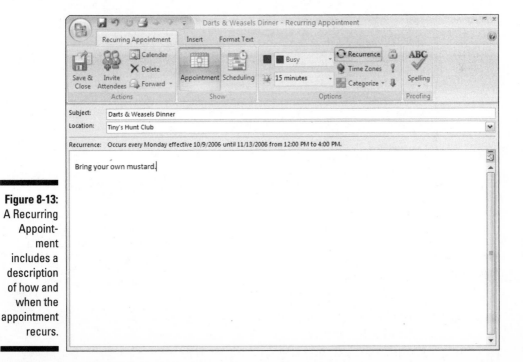

Figure 8-13:
A Recurring
Appoint-
ment
includes a
description
of how and
when the
appointment
recurs.

> I find it helpful to enter regular appointments, such as classes or regular recreational events, even if I'm sure I won't forget them. Entering all my activities into Outlook prevents me from scheduling conflicting appointments.

Getting a Good View of Your Calendar

Outlook enables you to slice and dice the information in every section nearly any way you can imagine, using different views. You could easily fill a cookbook with different views you can create, but I'm going to stick to the standard ways of looking at a calendar that most people are used to. If you want to cook up a calendar arrangement that nobody's ever thought of before, Outlook will probably let you. If you accidentally create a Calendar view you don't like — "Only Mondays? Yikes. What was I thinking?" — that's okay; you can delete it.

The basic Calendar views are Daily view (shown in Figure 8-14), Weekly view (shown in Figure 8-15), and Monthly view (shown in Figure 8-16). Other views (such as Active Appointments) are helpful when you're trying to figure out when you did something or when you will do something.

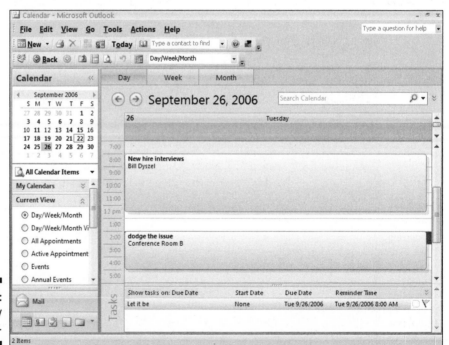

Figure 8-14:
The Daily view.

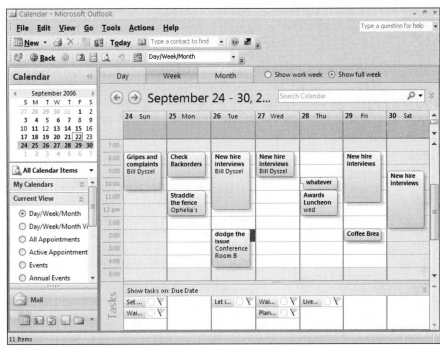

Figure 8-15:
The Weekly view.

Figure 8-16:
The Monthly view.

You can make Outlook display a list of the Outlook Calendar views in the upper part of the Navigation Pane by choosing View ⇨ Navigation Pane ⇨ Show Views in Navigation Pane. When you've done that, you can change Calendar views by clicking the name of the view you want to see. If the view you select doesn't suit you, don't worry — just click a different view. In Active Appointments view (shown in Figure 8-17), you can see details of your upcoming appointments in a list that's easy to read. You can also sort the view on any column, such as Location, Subject, or Start date, by clicking the column's title.

The Active Appointments view is only one of a half-dozen preprogrammed views that come with Outlook. Pull down the menu and try each of the other choices: You've seen the Daily/Weekly/Monthly views, which enable you to look at your schedule in the familiar calendar layouts. Events view shows you items that last more than a day. Annual Events view shows the list of items that last more than a day and return at the same time each year. Recurring view is the view of appointments you've set up to repeat themselves. By Category view groups your appointments according to the category you assigned them to.

Figure 8-17:
The Active Appoint-ments view.

Printing Your Appointments

Plain old paper is still everybody's favorite medium for reading. No matter how slick your computer organizer is, you may still need old-fashioned ink on paper to make it really useful. To be brutally honest, Outlook's calendar printing feature stinks. It hasn't changed one iota since the program was introduced some ten years ago. If you can't figure out how to print your calendar the way you want, it's probably not your fault.

You use the same basic steps to print from any module in Outlook. Here's how to print your appointments:

1. **Click a date within the range of dates you want to print.**

    If you want to print a single day, click just one day. If you want to print a range of dates, click the first date and then hold the Shift key and click the last date in the range. The whole range is highlighted to show which dates you've selected.

2. **Choose File ⇨ Print (or press Ctrl+P).**

    The Print dialog box appears (as shown in Figure 8-18).

Figure 8-18:
The Print
dialog box.

Scheduling your main events

You can enter more than just appointments in your calendar. You can also add events by clicking the All Day Event check box in the Appointment form, or you can begin by choosing Actions ⇨ New All Day Event and follow the same steps you use to create an appointment. (Refer to the section "Meetings Galore: Scheduling Appointments," earlier in this chapter.)

Events correspond to occurrences that land on your calendar (such as business trips or conferences) that last longer than an appointment — and you can still enter routine appointments that may take place at the event. For example, you can create an event called "2005 Auto Show" and then add appointments to see General Motors at 9:00 a.m., Chrysler at noon, and Ford at 3:00 p.m.

3. **In the Print Style group, make a choice from the Style box.**

   Daily, Weekly, Monthly, Trifold, and Calendar Details are the basic choices. You can also define your own print styles in Outlook, so you may eventually have quite a collection of choices showing up in this box.

4. **In the Print Range box, set the range of dates you want to print.**

   Because you began by clicking a date in that range, it should already be correct. If it's not correct, you can change the range in the Print dialog box to the print range you want.

5. **Click OK.**

   Your dates are sent to the printer.

Clicking the Print icon on the toolbar is another handy way to start the print process. The icon looks like a tiny printer.

Adding Holidays to Your Outlook Calendar

What days are most important to working people? The days when they don't have to work! Outlook can automatically add calendar entries for every major holiday so you don't forget to take the day off (as if you'd forget!). In fact, Outlook can automatically add holidays from over 70 different countries and several major religions. So if you have a yen (so to speak) to celebrate Japanese Greenery Day, an urge to observe Estonian Independence Day, or suddenly want to send a gift for Ataturk's birthday, your Outlook calendar can remind you to observe those monumental events.

To add holidays to your calendar, choose Tools ⇨ Options and click the Calendar Options button, then click the button marked Add Holidays. You then see a list of nations and religions whose holidays you can add to your calendar; just click the ones you want to add. Think about it; if you made a promise that you'd only eat chocolate on holidays, you can now make just about every day of the year a holiday by adding enough international celebrations to your calendar. It's just a thought (yum).

Chapter 9

Task Mastery: Discovering All the Bells and Whistles

. . . .

In This Chapter

▶ Entering a new task

▶ Changing, copying, and deleting tasks

▶ Creating recurring and regenerating tasks

▶ Completing tasks — what a concept!

▶ Using views to control your tasks

. . . .

*Y*ou can store and manage more information about your daily tasks in Outlook than you may have wanted to know, but you'll certainly find that Outlook makes it easy to remember and monitor your daily work. Organizing your tasks doesn't have to be a task in itself.

Some people say that work expands to fill the available time — and chances are that your boss is one of those people. (Who else would keep expanding your work to fill your available time?) One way of saving time is to keep a list of the tasks filling your time. That way, you can avoid getting too many more tasks to do.

I used to scrawl a to-do list on paper and hope I'd find the list in time to do everything I had written down. Now Outlook pops up and reminds me of the things I'm trying to forget to do just before I forget to do them. It also keeps track of when I'm supposed to have done my daily tasks and when I actually did them. That way, I can use all the work I was supposed to do yesterday as an excuse not to do the drudgery I'm supposed to do today. Sort of. (Outlook still won't *do* the stuff for me — it just tells me how far I'm falling behind. Be forewarned.)

The To-Do Bar

Outlook 2007 has a new feature called the To-Do Bar that pulls together all the things you need to do and displays them in a single part of the Outlook screen (see Figure 9-1). The goal of the To-Do Bar is to let you know what you need to do at a glance rather than making you check your calendar, then check your e-mail Inbox, and then check your Task List. The items you'll see most often in the To-Do Bar include

✔ Tasks you've entered

✔ Your next few appointments

✔ E-mail messages you've flagged for action

At first the To-Do Bar can seem a little confusing because things turn up there that you may not have put there directly. For example, if you receive an e-mail message on a Monday and apply the flag labeled This Week, it'll turn up for action two Fridays later, when you might have forgotten about it. That's what the To-Do Bar is for — to prevent you from forgetting.

Figure 9-1: The To-Do Bar — more than you'll ever want to do.

Adding a new item to the To-Do Bar

I don't mean to add work to your busy schedule; you already have plenty of that. But adding an item to the To-Do Bar in Outlook isn't such a big to-do. Even though you can store gobs of information about your tasks in Outlook, you have both a quick way and a really quick way to enter a new task.

There's a little box in the To Do Bar on the right side of the screen that says Type a New Task. Do what the box says. (If you can't see the box, go on to the following section to discover the regular, slightly slower way to enter the task.)

To enter a task by using the quick-and-dirty method, follow these steps:

1. **Click the text that says Type a New Task.**

   The words disappear and you see the insertion point (a blinking line).

2. **Type the name of your task.**

   Your task appears in the To-Do Bar Task List, as shown in Figure 9-2.

Figure 9-2: Entering your task into the To-Do Bar.

3. Press the Enter key.

Your new task moves down to the To-Do Bar Task List with your other tasks.

Isn't that easy? If only the tasks themselves were that easy to do. Maybe in the next version of Outlook, the tasks will get easier, too (in my dreams).

Of course, all you have is the name of the task — no due dates, reminders, or any of the cool stuff. If you want that information, you have to enter the task the regular way through the Tasks module.

Customizing or minimizing the To-Do Bar

Although the To-Do Bar is handy, it takes up quite a bit of space on the screen, which is a nuisance when you're reading e-mail or checking your calendar. You can clear the To-Do Bar out of the way by clicking the double arrow to the left of the words To-Do Bar. That shrinks it into a tiny ribbon along the right side of the screen (see Figure 9-3).

Click the ribbon along the right side of the screen to get a quick glance at the To-Do Bar; clicking anywhere else on the screen makes the To-Do Bar shrink up again.

Figure 9-3:
The To-Do Bar shrinks down to a ribbon on the right side of the screen when you minimize it.

Customizing the To-Do Bar

Three types of information can appear in the To-Do Bar:

- ✔ The Date Navigator, which is a small calendar
- ✔ A few of your next appointments
- ✔ A list of tasks

If you want to adjust how much of each of those items to display, or to turn one of them off, choose View ⇨ To-Do Bar ⇨ Options and enter your preference. If you don't like the first choice you make, go back and make another. You can always change your To-Do Bar options.

Closing the To-Do Bar

Clicking the X to the right of the words To-Do Bar closes the bar completely, and it disappears without a trace. You can reopen the To-Do Bar by choosing View ⇨ To-Do Bar ⇨ Normal.

Entering New Tasks in the Tasks Module

The regular way to enter a task is through the Task form, which looks like more work, but it's really not. As long as you enter a name for the task, you've done all you really must do. If you want to go hog-wild and enter all sorts of due dates or have Outlook remind you to actually *complete* the tasks you've entered (heaven forbid!), you just need to put information in a few more boxes.

To add a task to your Task List, follow these steps:

1. **Click the Tasks button in the Navigation Pane (or press Ctrl+4).**

   Your Task List appears.

2. **Choose File ⇨ New⇨ Task (or press Ctrl+N).**

   The Task form appears (see Figure 9-4).

3. **Type the name of the task in the Subject box.**

   Use a subject that will help you remember what the task is. The main reason to create a task is to help you remember to do the task.

You can finish at this point by jumping to Step 14 (choose Save and Close or press Alt+S) if you want to add only the name of the task to your list. If you want to note a due date, start date, reminders, and so on, you have more to do. All the rest of the steps are optional; you can skip the ones that don't interest you.

Figure 9-4:
Enter your
new task in
the Task
form.

4. **(Optional) To assign a due date to the task, click the Due Date box.**

5. **(Optional) Enter the due date in the Due Date box.**

You can enter a date in Outlook in several ways. You can type **7/4/07**, **the first Friday of July**, or **Three weeks from Friday**. You can also click the scroll-down button (triangle) at the right end of the Due Date text box and choose the date you want from the drop-down calendar.

6. **(Optional) To assign a start date to the task, click the Start Date box and enter the start date.**

If you haven't started the task, you can skip this step. You can use the same tricks to enter the start date that you use to enter the due date.

When you're entering information in a dialog box such as the Task form, you can press the Tab key to move from one text box to the next. You can use the mouse to click each text box before you type, but pressing the Tab key is a bit faster.

7. **(Optional) Click the Status box to choose the status of the task.**

If you haven't begun, leave Status set to Not Started. You can also choose In Progress, Completed, Waiting on Someone Else, or Deferred.

8. **(Optional) Click the triangle at the right end of the Priority box to choose the priority.**

If you don't change anything, the priority stays Normal. You can also choose High or Low.

9. **(Optional) Click the Reminder check box if you want to be reminded before the task is due.**

   If you'd rather forget the task, forget the reminder. But then, why enter the task at all?

10. **(Optional) Click the date box next to the Reminder check box and enter the date when you want to be reminded.**

    If you entered a due date, Outlook has already entered that date in the Reminder box. You can enter any date you want (see Figure 9-5). If you choose a date in the past, Outlook lets you know that it won't be setting a reminder. If you open the scroll-down menu by clicking the triangle on the right of the date box, a calendar appears. You can click the date you desire in the calendar.

There's no reason that the reminder date you enter has to be the same as the due date of the task. You might consider setting a reminder some time before the task is due. That way you avoid that last minute angst over things that you forgot until the last minute. Unless you enjoy last-minute anxiety, then don't use reminders at all.

Figure 9-5:
A calendar drops down to show the date your task is due.

11. **(Optional) Enter the time you want to activate the reminder in the Time box.**

    The easiest way to set a time is to type the numbers for the time. You don't need colons or anything special. If you want to finish by 2:35 p.m., just type 235. Outlook assumes you're not a vampire — it schedules your tasks and appointments during daylight hours unless you say otherwise. (If you *are* a vampire, then type 235a and Outlook translates that to 2:35 a.m. If you simply *must* use correct punctuation, Outlook can handle that, too.)

12. **(Optional) In the text box, enter miscellaneous notes and information about this task.**

    If you need to keep directions to the appointment, a list of supplies, or whatever, it all fits here.

    The Select Contacts dialog box appears.

13. **(Optional) Double-click the name you want to link to your task.**

    The Select Contacts dialog box closes and the name you chose appears in the Contacts text box.

14. **Click the Save & Close button to finish.**

    Your new task is now included in your Task List, waiting to be done by some fortunate person. Unfortunately, that person is probably you.

Adding an Internet link to a task

If you type the name of a Web page, such as www.outlookfordummies.com, in the text box at the bottom of the Task form, Outlook changes the text color to blue and underlines the address, making it look just like the hyperlink you click to jump between different pages on the World Wide Web. That makes it easy to save information about an exciting Web site; just type or copy the address into your task. To view the page you entered, just click the text to make your Web browser pop up and open the page.

Editing Your Tasks

No sooner do you enter a new task than it seems that you need to change it. Sometimes I enter a task the quick-and-dirty way and change some of the particulars later — add a due date, a reminder, an added step, or whatever. Fortunately, editing tasks is easy.

The quick-and-dirty way to change a task

For lazy people like me, Outlook offers a quick-and-dirty way to change a task, just as it has a quick-and-dirty way to enter a task. You're limited in the number of details you can change, but the process is fast.

If you can see the name of a task, and if you want to change something about the task you can see, follow the steps I describe in this section. If you can't see the task or the part you want to change, use the regular method, which I describe in the next section of this chapter.

To change a task the quick-and-dirty way, follow these steps:

1. **Double-click the thing you want to change.**

   You see a blinking line at the end of the text, a triangle at the right end of the box, or a menu with a list of choices.

2. **Select the old information.**

   The old text is highlighted to show it's selected (as shown in Figure 9-6).

Figure 9-6:
A task highlighted in the Task List.

3. **Type the new information.**

   The new information replaces the old. If you click the Status box, a menu drops down and you can choose from the list.

4. **Press the Enter key.**

Isn't that easy? If all you want to change is the name, status, or due date, the quick-and-dirty way will get you there.

The regular way to change a task

If you don't want to be quick and dirty, or if the information you want to change about a task isn't on the list you're looking at, you have to take a slightly longer route. The regular way is a little more work, but not much.

To make changes to a task the clean-and-long way (also known as the regular way), follow these steps:

1. **Click the Tasks button in the Navigation Pane (or press Ctrl+4).**

   The Tasks module opens.

2. **Click the words Simple List in the Current View section of the Navigation Pane.**

   You can choose a different current view if you know that the view includes the task you want to change. The Simple List view is the most basic view of your tasks; it's sure to include the task you're looking for.

3. **Double-click the name of the task you want to change.**

   The Task form (shown in Figure 9-7) appears. Now you can change anything you can see in the box. Just click the information you want to change, type the new information, and click Save and Close (or press Alt+S).

4. **Change the name of the task.**

   The name is your choice. Remember to call the task something that helps you remember the task. There's nothing worse than a computer reminding you to do something that you can't understand.

5. **To change the due date, click the Due Date box.**

6. **Enter the new due date in the Due Date box.**

   Plenty of date styles work here — **7/4/04**, **the first Friday in July**, **Six weeks from now**, whatever. Unfortunately, **the 12th of Never** isn't an option. Sorry.

7. **Click the Start Date box and enter the new start date.**

   If you haven't started the task, you can skip this step. You don't absolutely need a start date; it's just for your own use.

Figure 9-7:
The Task
form.

8. **Click the scroll-down button (triangle) at the right end of the Status box to see a menu that enables you to change the status of the task.**

If you're using Outlook at work and you're hooked up to a network, the Status box entry is one way of keeping your boss informed of your progress. You'll need to check with your boss or system administrator if this is the case.

If you're using Outlook at home, chances are that nobody else will care, but you may feel better if you know how well you're doing. You can't add your own choices to the Status box. (I'd like to add, "Waiting, hoping the task will go away." No such luck.) Figure 9-8 shows the Task box with the Status line highlighted.

9. **Click the scroll-down button (triangle) at the right end of the Priority box to change the priority.**

Switch the priority to High or Low, if the situation changes (see Figure 9-9).

10. **Click the Reminder check box if you want to turn the reminder on or off.**

Reminders are easy and harmless, so why not? If you didn't ask for one the first time, do it now.

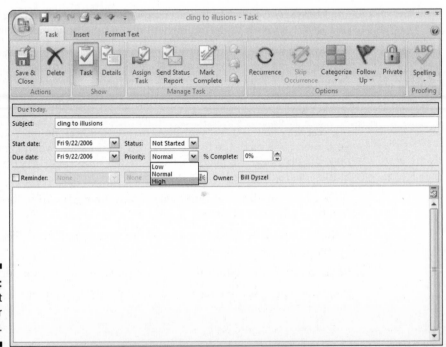

Figure 9-8:
This task
hasn't been
started yet.

Figure 9-9:
Let's hear it
for a lower
priority.

11. **Click the date box next to the Reminder check box to enter or change the date when you want to be reminded.**

    You can enter any date you want. Your entry doesn't have to be the due date; it can be much earlier, reminding you to get started. You can even set a reminder after the task is due, which isn't very useful. You should make sure that the reminder is before the due date. (The default date for a reminder is the date the task is due.)

12. **Change the time you want to activate the reminder in the time box.**

    When entering times, keep it simple. The entry **230** does the trick when you want to enter 2:30 p.m. If you make appointments at 2:30 a.m. (I'd rather not know what kind of appointments you make at that hour), you can type **230a**.

13. **Click the text box to add or change miscellaneous notes and information about this task.**

    You can add detailed information here that doesn't really belong anywhere else in the Task form (as shown in Figure 9-10). You see these details only when you open the Task form again; they don't normally show up in your Task List.

14. **Click the Save and Close button to finish.**

    There! You've changed your task.

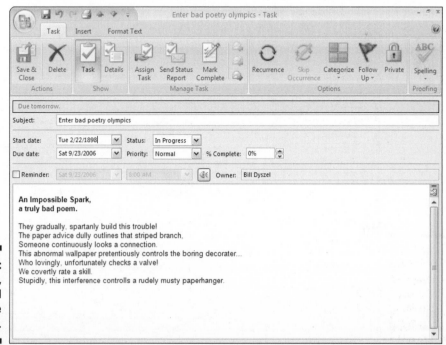

Figure 9-10:
Details, details. Add 'em in the text box.

Copying a task

By now, you're probably saying, "I had so much fun setting up a task for myself, I'd like to set up another one." If it's the same task on a different day, the easiest approach is to copy the task.

To copy a task, follow these steps:

1. **Select the task you want to copy.**

   The selected task is highlighted in blue (see Figure 9-11).

2. **Choose Edit ➪ Copy (or press Ctrl+C).**

3. **Choose Edit ➪ Paste (or press Ctrl+V).**

   A new, identical copy of your task appears just following the old one. The problem is that it's exactly the same task. You don't need Siamese-twin tasks, so you probably want to change the date of the new task. Double-click the new task and change the date.

For creating tasks that recur every day, copying the task is pretty laborious. That's why you can set up a task as a recurring task the way I describe in the section "Managing Recurring Tasks," later in this chapter.

Figure 9-11: Your selected task is highlighted.

Deleting a task

The really gratifying part about tasks is getting rid of them, preferably by completing the tasks you entered. You may also delete a task you changed your mind about. Of course, nothing is stopping you from deleting tasks you just don't want to bother with; this version of Outlook can't really tell whether you've actually completed your tasks. (Rumor has it that the next version of Outlook will know whether you've finished your tasks and report to Santa. So don't be naughty!)

To delete a task, follow these steps:

1. **Select the task.**

2. **Choose Edit ⇨ Delete.**

   Alternatively, you can press Ctrl+D or click the Delete button in the toolbar. Poof! Your task is gone.

Managing Recurring Tasks

Lots of tasks crop up on a regular basis. You know how it goes — same stuff, new day. To save you the effort of entering a task, such as a monthly sales report or a quarterly tax payment, over and over again, just set it up as a recurring task. Outlook can then remind you whenever it's that time again.

To create a recurring task, follow these steps:

1. **Open the task by double-clicking it.**

   The Task form appears (see Figure 9-12).

2. **Click the Recurrence button in the Task Form toolbar (or press Ctrl+G).**

   The Task Recurrence dialog box appears (see Figure 9-13).

3. **Choose the Daily, Weekly, Monthly, or Yearly option to specify how often the appointment occurs.**

   Each choice you make — Daily, Weekly, or Monthly — changes the types of exact choices available for when the task recurs. For example, a daily recurring task can be set to recur every day or every five days or whatever. A monthly recurring task can be set to recur on a certain day of the month, such as the 15th of each month, or on the second Friday of every month.

Figure 9-12:
Getting a
handle on
recurring
tasks.

Figure 9-13:
How often
should this
task be
done?

4. **In the next box to the right, specify how often the appointment occurs, such as every third day or the first Monday of each month.**

   If you choose to create a monthly task, for example, you can click the scroll-down buttons (triangles) to choose First, then Monday to schedule a task on the first Monday of each month.

5. **In the Range of Recurrence box, enter the first occurrence in the Start box.**

6. **Choose when you want the appointments to stop (no end date, after a certain number of occurrences, or at a certain date).**

7. **Click OK.**

   A banner appears at the top of the Task form describing the recurrence pattern of the task.

8. **Click Save and Close.**

Your task appears in the list of tasks once, but it has a different type of icon than nonrecurring tasks so you can tell at a glance that it's a recurring task.

Creating a regenerating task

A *regenerating task* is like a recurring task except it recurs only when a certain amount of time passes after the last time you completed the task. Suppose that you mow the lawn every two weeks. If it rains for a week and one mowing happens a week late, you still want to wait two weeks for the next one. If you schedule your mowings in Outlook, you use the Regenerating Task feature to enter your lawn-mowing schedule.

To create a regenerating task:

1. **Open the task by double-clicking it.**

   The Task form appears.

2. **Click the Recurrence button in the toolbar in the Task form (or press Ctrl+G).**

   The Task Recurrence dialog box appears.

3. **Click Regenerate New Task (shown in Figure 9-14).**

4. **Enter the number of weeks between regenerating each task.**

5. **Click OK.**

   A banner appears in the Task form describing the regeneration pattern you've set for the task.

6. **Click Save and Close.**

Figure 9-14:
You can
regenerate
a task in
the Task
Recurrence
dialog box.

Your task appears in the list of tasks once, but it has a different type of icon than nonrecurring tasks have so you can tell at a glance that it's a regenerating task.

Skipping a recurring task once

When you need to skip a single occurrence of a recurring task, you don't have to change the recurrence pattern of the task forever; just skip the occurrence you want to skip and leave the rest alone.

To skip a recurring task, follow these steps:

1. **Click the Tasks button in the Navigation Pane (or press Ctrl+4).**

   Your list of tasks appears.

2. **Click the words Simple List in the Current View section of the Navigation Pane.**

   It doesn't matter which view you use, as long as you can see the name of the task you want to skip. I suggest the Simple List because it's . . . well, simple.

3. **Double-click the name of the task you want to change.**

   The Task form appears.

4. **Choose Actions ⇨ Skip Occurrence.**

   The due date changes to the date of the next scheduled occurrence.

5. **Click Save and Close.**

   Your task remains in the list with the new scheduled occurrence date showing.

Marking Tasks Complete

Marking off those completed tasks is even more fun than entering them, and it's much easier. If you can see the task you want to mark complete in either the To-Do Bar or your Task List, just right-click the item and choose Mark Complete. Nothing could be simpler.

To mark a task complete, follow these steps:

1. **Click the Tasks button in the Navigation Pane (or press Ctrl+4).**

   The Tasks module opens.

2. **Click the words Simple List in the Current View section of the Navigation Pane.**

   Actually, you can choose any view you want, as long as the task you're looking for shows up there. If the task that you want to mark complete isn't in the view you chose, try the Simple List, which contains every task you've entered.

3. **Click the box next to the name of the task that you want to mark complete.**

   The box in the second column from the left is the one you want to check (see Figure 9-15).

   When you check the box, the name of the task changes color and gets a line through it. You're finished.

You can view a list of the tasks you've marked complete by clicking the words Completed Tasks in the Current View menu on the left side of the screen. All the jobs you've polished off show up there in a nice, neat list. Ah! How satisfying!

Outlook has more than one place for marking tasks complete. You can look at the Task List I just described, as well as certain views of your calendar, and also the list of tasks in Outlook Today.

Figure 9-15:
A check
marks
the task
complete.

Marking several tasks complete

Perhaps you don't race to your computer every time you complete a task. Marking off your completed tasks in groups is faster than marking them one by one. Outlook enables you to do that by making a multiple selection.

To mark several tasks complete, follow these steps:

1. **Click the Tasks button in the Navigation Pane (or press Ctrl+4).**

   The Tasks module opens.

2. **Click the words Simple List in the Current View section of the Navigation Pane.**

   Again, I'm just suggesting Simple List view because it's most likely to show you all your tasks. You can pick any view that enables you to see the tasks that you want to mark.

3. **Click the first task that you want to mark.**

4. **Hold down the Ctrl key and click each of the other tasks that you want to mark.**

   All the tasks you clicked are highlighted, showing that you've selected them.

5. **Right-click one of the tasks you highlighted.**

    A menu appears (as shown in Figure 9-16).

6. **Choose Mark Complete.**

    The tasks you selected are marked complete.

There are two good reasons for recording your tasks and marking them complete. One is to remember everything you have to do; the second is to tell other people everything you've done, like your boss at raise time, for instance. It pays to toot your own horn, and keeping a completed Task List helps you remember what to toot your horn about.

Picking a color for completed or overdue tasks

When you complete a task or when it becomes overdue, Outlook changes the color of the text for the completed tasks to gray and the overdue tasks to red, which makes it easy for you to tell at a glance which tasks are done and which tasks remain to be done. If you don't like Outlook's color choices, you can pick different colors.

Figure 9-16: A shortcut menu in the Task List.

Here's how to change the color of completed and overdue tasks:

1. **Choose Tools ⇨ Options.**

   The Options dialog box appears.

2. **Click the Task Options button.**

   The Task Options page appears (as shown in Figure 9-17).

3. **Click the box labeled Overdue Task Color.**

   A list of colors drops down.

4. **Choose a color for overdue tasks.**

5. **Click the box labeled Completed Task Color.**

   A list of colors drops down.

6. **Choose a color for completed tasks.**

7. **Click OK.**

Your completed and overdue tasks will appear on your list in the colors you chose.

Figure 9-17:
The Task
Options
page.

Viewing Your Tasks

Outlook comes with several ways to view your Task List and enables you to invent and save as many custom views as you like. The views that come with Outlook take you a long way when you know how to use them.

To change your view of your tasks, click the name of one of the following views from the Current View List in the Navigation Pane:

- **Simple List** view presents just the facts — the names you gave each task and the due date you assigned (if you assigned one). The Simple List view makes it easy to add new tasks and mark old ones complete. However, you won't see any extra information. If you want details. . . .

- **Detailed List** view is a little more chock-full of the fiddly bits than the Simple List view. It's really the same information, plus the status of the tasks, the percentage of each task complete, and whatever categories you may have assigned to your tasks.

- **Active List** view shows you only the tasks you haven't finished yet. After you mark a task complete — zap! Completed tasks vanish from the Active List view, which helps keep you focused on the tasks remaining to be done.

- **Next Seven Days** view is even more focused than the Active List view. The Next Seven Days view shows only uncompleted tasks scheduled to be done within the next seven days (as shown in Figure 9-18). It's just right for those people who like to live in the moment, or at least within the week.

- **Overdue Tasks** view means you've been naughty. These are tasks that really *did* need to be "done yesterday" (when it *was* yesterday) but are still hanging around today.

- **By Category** view breaks up your tasks according to the category you've assigned each task. You can open and close categories to focus on the type of tasks you're looking for. For example, you may assign a category of Sales to the sales-related tasks in your list. When you want to focus on sales, use the By Category view and click the Sales category.

- **Assignment** view lists your tasks in order of the name of the person upon whom you dumped, er, I mean *to whom you delegated*, each task.

- **By Person Responsible** view contains the same information as the Assignment view, but the list is grouped to let you see the assignments of only one person at a time.

- **Completed Tasks** view shows (you guessed it) tasks you've marked complete. You don't need to deal with completed tasks anymore, but looking at the list gives you a warm, fuzzy feeling, doesn't it?

Figure 9-18:
The Next
Seven Days
view helps
you focus
your work
for the
week.

- **Task Timeline** view draws a picture of when each task is scheduled to start and end (as shown in Figure 9-19). Seeing a picture of your tasks gives you a better idea of how to fit work into your schedule sensibly.

- **To-Do List** view includes all the tasks you've entered as well as any flagged e-mails that show up in the To-Do Bar. The other Task List views only show the items you've added directly to the Task List.

Tasks in the Calendar

The Task List and the To-Do Bar help you track what you need to do. After that, you need to figure out when you have time to do all that stuff. That's why Outlook offers a display of upcoming tasks in the Weekly view of your calendar (see Figure 9-20). In a strip along the bottom of the screen, there are icons representing tasks whose due dates fall on each of the days displayed. If you find that you've stacked up too many to-dos than can be done on a single day, just drag the task to a day when it can be done. You can even drag a task up to a particular hour in the calendar and reserve specific time to get that thing done.

Figure 9-19:
The Task
Timeline
helps you
balance
your
workload.

Figure 9-20:
You can
manage
both time
and tasks in
the Weekly
view of the
calendar.

Chapter 10

For the Record: Outlook Notes and Journal Entries

*T*he simple, dopey features of a program are often my favorites — the features I end up using all the time such as Outlook Notes and the Outlook Journal. Outlook Notes are my favorite underappreciated feature. There's really nothing earth shattering about them, and certainly nothing difficult. This feature is just there when you need it — ready to record whatever strange, random thoughts are passing through your head while you're doing your work. (As you can tell from my writing, strange, random thoughts are a common occurrence for me. That's why I love using Notes.)

The Journal is Outlook's most underappreciated feature, a place for recording who did what and when they did it. The feature gets so little use that it no longer rates a button in the Navigation Bar the way it did when Outlook was a new product. But just because the Journal is easy to overlook doesn't mean it can't do a lot for you.

Writing a Note

How did we ever live without those little yellow stick-on notes? They're everywhere! The funny thing about stick-on notes is that they came from an inventor's failure. A scientist was trying to invent a new formula for glue, and he came up with a kind of glue that didn't stick very well. Like the computer scientists who came later, he said, "That's not a bug; that's a feature!" Then he figured out how to make a fortune selling little notes that didn't stick too well. It's only natural that an invention like this would be adapted for computers.

A note is the only type of item you can create in Outlook that doesn't use a normal dialog box with menus and toolbars. Notes are easier to use — but somewhat trickier to explain — than other Outlook items; I can only describe the objects you're supposed to click and drag. No name appears on the Note icon, and no name exists for the part of the note you drag when you want to resize it (although you can see what one looks like in Figure 10-1).

Figure 10-1:
Your note begins as a nearly blank box.

Tricky notes

Each time you start a program, the Windows taskbar at the bottom of the screen adds an icon. That way, you know how many programs you're running. If you click an icon for a program in the taskbar, you switch to that program. If you start Word and Excel, for example, you see two icons in the taskbar. You can have two or more documents open in Word or Excel, but you see only one icon for each program.

When you choose File ⇨ New to create a new item in Outlook, a second icon remains available in the taskbar for the item you're creating (in Windows XP, the extra icon is stacked above the Outlook icon). The icon remains until you

close and save the item. It's like having two or more programs open in Windows simultaneously. The advantage of this arrangement is that you can leave something like a note open for a long time and keep switching to it to add comments. The disadvantage is that if you don't look at the taskbar to see how many notes you have open, you may be creating a clutter of notes when you may prefer just one.

Another advantage is that you can have two notes open at the same time, or a note and an e-mail message, and drag text from one to the other.

Here's the basic scoop on how to take virtual notes while doing your work:

1. **Choose Go ⇨ Notes (or press Ctrl+5).**

   The Notes List appears.

   You don't actually have to go to the Notes module to create a new note; you can go right to Step 2. I suggest going to the Notes module first only so you can see your note appear in the list of notes when you finish. Otherwise your note seems to disappear into thin air (even though it doesn't). Outlook automatically files your note in the Notes module unless you make a special effort to send it somewhere else.

2. **Click New (or press Ctrl+ N).**

   The blank Note box appears.

3. **Type what you want to say in your note (as shown in Figure 10-2) and click the Note icon in the upper-left corner of the note.**

Figure 10-2:
You can
write a note
to remind
yourself of
something.

4. Click Close (or press Esc).

An even quicker way to create a note is to press Ctrl+Shift+N in any Outlook module. You don't see your note listed with all the other notes until you switch to the Notes module, but you can capture that thought before you drift back to online shopping.

Finding a Note

Unlike paper stick-on notes, Outlook notes stay where you put them so you can always find them — or at least your computer can find them. As a matter of fact, you can find any item you create in Outlook just by using the Search tool. (I wish I had a Search tool to help me round up all my lost galoshes and umbrellas.)

Here's how to find a misplaced note:

1. Choose Go ⇨ Notes (or press Ctrl+5).

Your list of notes appears (see Figure 10-3). The Search box appears at the top of the screen.

Figure 10-3:
The Look
For box.

2. **In the Search box, type the word or phrase you're looking for.**

   Don't worry about capitalization. Outlook doesn't worry about it.

3. **If the note you're looking for turns up, double-click the Note icon to read what the note says.**

Reading a Note

When you write a note, no doubt you plan to read it sometime. Reading notes is even easier than writing them. To read a note, follow these steps:

1. **Choose Go ⇨ Notes (or press Ctrl+5).**

   Your list of notes appears.

2. **Double-click the title of the note you want to open.**

   The note appears onscreen (as shown in Figure 10-4). You can close the note when you're done by pressing Esc.

Funny how notes look the same when you're reading them as they do when you're writing them.

Figure 10-4:
Ah ha! The
missing note
is found.

Deleting a Note

What if you change your mind about what you wrote in a note? Fortunately, notes don't have to stick around forever. You can write one this morning and throw it out this afternoon. What could be easier?

Taking your pick: Multiple selections

When you're sorting your notes or assigning them to categories, one way to work a little faster is to select several notes simultaneously. If you want to select a group of notes that you can see one right after another in a list, click the first one and then hold down the Shift key while clicking the last one. That action selects not only the notes you clicked, but also all the notes in-between.

If you're selecting several items that aren't arranged next to one another, hold down the Ctrl key while clicking each item. The notes you click are highlighted and the others stay plain. Then you can open, move, delete, or categorize the entire group of notes you selected in a single stroke. To view several notes, right-click any notes you've selected and choose Open.

Here's how to delete a note:

1. **Choose Go ⇨ Notes (or press Ctrl+5).**

   Your list of notes appears.

2. **Click the title of the note you want to delete.**

3. **Choose Edit ⇨ Delete (or simply press Delete).**

   You can also click the Delete button in the Outlook toolbar.

Changing a Note's Size

You may be an old hand at moving and resizing boxes in Windows. Notes follow all the rules that other Windows boxes follow, so you'll be okay. If you're new to Windows and dialog boxes, don't worry — notes are as easy to resize as they are to write and read.

To change the size of a note, follow these steps:

1. **Choose Go ⇨ Notes (or press Ctrl+5).**

   Your list of notes appears.

2. **Double-click the title of the note you want to open.**

   The note pops up.

3. **Move your mouse pointer to the bottom-right corner of the note until the mouse pointer changes into a two-headed arrow pointed on a diagonal.**

   Use this arrow to drag the edges of the note to resize it. Don't be alarmed. Resizing boxes is much easier to do than to read about. After you resize one box, you'll have no trouble resizing another.

4. **Drag with your mouse until the note is the size you want it to be.**

   As you drag the mouse pointer around, the size of your note changes (as shown in Figure 10-5). Don't worry if the size doesn't come out right the first time; you can change the note size again by dragging with the mouse again.

Color-Coding Notes

Color may seem to be a trifling issue, but it can help you keep track of your notes. You can assign a color to a level of importance, for example, or to a specific task, so you can quickly see the note you want among the many notes in your list. Later in the chapter, I explain how you can sort your list of notes according to color categories. Sorting is useful, so spending your entire day changing the colors of your notes isn't just aesthetic; it's also productive.

Here's how to change your note's color:

1. **Open the note and click the Note icon in the top-left corner of the note.**

   I wish there was a better way to describe this icon than "the little thingy up on the left" (how's that for a high-tech term?) — but that's what it is. The icon is easy to see; it's the only little thingy in the top-left corner of your note. Anyway, when you click it, the Note menu appears.

2. **Choose Categorize.**

   A menu of color categories appears; see Figure 10-6. The list includes Green, Blue, Orange, Purple, Red, and Yellow. For a wider range of choices, choose All Categories.

3. **Pick a color.**

You can also change the colors of your notes when viewing a list of notes; just right-click the icon for a note and choose a color from the menu that appears.

Figure 10-5: Make your note larger if you need more room to expound.

Figure 10-6:
The Color
menu.

Viewing Your Notes

Notes are handy enough to stash tidbits of information any way you want, but what makes notes really useful is what happens when you need to get the stuff back. You can open your notes one by one and see what's in them, but Outlook's Notes module offers even handier capabilities for arranging, sorting, and viewing your notes in a way that makes sense for you.

Icons view

Some folks like Icons view — just a bunch of notes scattered all over, as they are on my desk. Because I can already see a mess of notes any time I look at my desk, I prefer organized lists for viewing my notes on my computer, but you may like the more free-form Icons view. To use Icons view, click the word Icons in the Current View section of the Navigation Pane (shown in Figure 10-7). When you do, the screen fills with a bunch of icons and incredibly long titles for each icon.

Outlook uses the entire text of your message as the title of the icon, so the screen gets cluttered fast. If you prefer creative clutter, this view is for you. If not, keep reading.

Figure 10-7:
The Icons
view — a
clutter of
notes.

Notes List view

The Notes List view is as basic as basic gets. Just the facts, ma'am. The Notes List view shows the subject and creation date of each note, as well as the first few lines of text. To see the Notes List view, click the words Notes List in the Current View section of the Navigation Pane to make a listing of your notes appear; see Figure 10-8.

I usually recommend Notes List view for opening, forwarding, reading, and otherwise dealing with notes because it's the most straightforward. Anything you can do to a note in Notes List view, you can do in the other Notes views. The difference is that the other views don't always let you see the note you want to do things to.

Last Seven Days view

The notes you dealt with in the last few days are most likely to be the notes you'll need today. So, Outlook includes a special view of the notes you modified in the last seven days. You're more likely to quickly find what you're looking for in the Last Seven Days view. To see your notes for the last seven days, click the words Last Seven Days in the Current View section of the Navigation Pane. Figure 10-9 shows what you get.

Figure 10-8:
Your Notes
List view.

Figure 10-9:
Your notes
for the past
week, in all
their glory.

If you haven't modified any notes in the past seven days, Last Seven Days view will be empty. If having an empty view bothers you, create a note. That'll tide you over for a week.

By Category view

Color coordination means more than making sure your socks match. Every item you create in Outlook can be assigned to a category and displayed as a color. That means that you can create an organization system that shows what's important about your notes at a glance. You use the same category list for all items, and you can create your own categories. With categories, you have another useful way to organize your views of Outlook items. To see your notes arranged by category, click the words By Category in the Current View section of the Navigation Pane (as shown in Figure 10-10).

By Category view is a *grouped view,* meaning that the notes are collected in bunches, according to the categories you've assigned. You can just look at the category of notes you're interested in to organize the information you've collected.

Figure 10-10:
Your notes
in By
Category
view.

The Reading Pane

Once you've accumulated a collection of squibs and jots in your Notes collection, you'll want a quick way to browse your collection easily. If you choose View ➪ Reading Pane ➪ Right, you'll see a list of your notes on the left and the contents of each note you select on the right (see Figure 10-11). That way you can scan your collection of notes quickly by clicking a note with your mouse or by pressing the up and down arrow keys on your keyboard to move from note to note.

Printing Your Notes

You can organize and view your notes in so many clever ways that you'll also want to print what you can see, or at least the list of what you can see.

Printing a list of your notes

To print a list of your notes, follow these steps:

1. **Choose Go ➪ Notes (or press Ctrl+5).**

   The Notes list appears.

2. **Choose File ➪ Print (or press Ctrl+P).**

   The Print dialog box appears (as shown in Figure 10-11).

3. **In the Print Style box, choose Table Style.**

   If you choose Memo Style, you print the contents of a note rather than a list of notes.

4. **Click OK.**

If you want to print only a portion of your list of notes, click the first note you want listed and then hold down the Shift key while clicking the last note you want in your printout. You can also hold down the Ctrl key while clicking the notes you want one-by-one. When the Print dialog box appears, choose Only Selected Rows in the Print Range section.

Figure 10-11:
The Print
dialog box.

Printing the contents of a note

Computer screens are pretty, but there's still nothing like ink on paper. Of course, you can print a note. Remember, though, that the pretty colors you've given your notes don't show when you print them, even if you have a color printer. Colors just provide a way of organizing your notes.

To print the note, follow these steps:

1. **Choose Go ⇨ Notes (or press Ctrl+5).**

   The Notes list appears.

2. **Click the title of the note you want to print.**

3. **Choose File ⇨ Print (or press Ctrl+P).**

   The Print dialog box appears.

4. **In the Print Style box, choose Memo Style (see Figure 10-12).**

   Choosing Memo Style prints the full contents of the note.

Figure 10-12:
The Print
dialog
box with
Memo style
selected.

5. **Click OK.**

   Outlook prints the full contents of your note.

If you want to print some, but not all, of your notes, click the first note you want listed and then hold down the Shift key while clicking the last note you want to appear in your printout.

Changing Your Default Options for New Notes

Plain old notes are fine; you really don't need to change anything. But if you want to make some changes, the Options dialog box in the Tools menu gives you lots of . . . well, options. All adjustments you make in the Options dialog box change the size, color, and other qualities of your note when you first create the note. You can also change these qualities after you create the note.

Changing size and color

To change the color and size of your notes:

1. **Choose Tools ⇨ Options.**

   The Options dialog box appears.

2. **Click the Note Options button.**

   The Notes Options dialog box is where you change the options for the Notes module of Outlook.

3. **Click the Color box.**

   A list of colors drops down (as shown in Figure 10-13). Choosing one changes the color of all your notes when you create them. I hope you like pastels, because Blue, Green, Pink, Yellow, and White are your only options at the moment. Perhaps Burgundy and Off-Mauve notes will be in next season for more color-conscious computer users.

Figure 10-13:
Changing colors in Notes Options.

4. **Choose a color.**

5. **Click the Size box.**

   The list reads Small, Medium, or Large. Choosing one of these options sets the size of your notes when you create them.

6. **Click OK.**

   Your notes appear in the size and color to which you changed them.

Turning the date and time display on or off

At the bottom of each note, Outlook displays the date and time when you most recently changed the contents of the note. You may notice that you change a lot of notes on Mondays around 9:45 a.m. You may not want to notice that fact, so you can turn this handy little feature off.

To turn off the date and time display, follow these steps:

1. **Choose Tools ⇨ Options.**

   The Options dialog box appears.

2. **Click the Other tab.**

   I don't know why Microsoft called this the Other tab. (Perhaps the programmers all kept arguing, "Don't put that option on MY tab! Put it on some OTHER tab!") Anyway, that's where you have to look. When you click the Other tab, the Other Options page appears.

3. **Click the Advanced Options button.**

   The Advanced Options dialog box appears (see Figure 10-14).

4. **Click the words When Viewing Notes, Show Time and Date.**

   A check mark appears in the check box if you click once, and then it disappears if you click a second time. If you want to turn off the time and date display, make sure that the box doesn't contain a check mark.

5. **Click OK.**

   The time and date will no longer show up on command, unless you follow the same steps you used in turning them off to turn them on again.

Figure 10-14:
Time for
some
advanced
options.

Forwarding a Note

Forwarding a note really means sending an e-mail message with a note included as an attachment. It's helpful if the person to whom you're forwarding the note uses Outlook, too.

To forward a note:

1. **Choose Go ➪ Notes (or press Ctrl+5).**

   The Notes list appears.

2. **Click the title of the note you want to forward.**

3. **Choose Actions ➪ Forward (or press Ctrl+F).**

   The New Message form appears (shown in Figure 10-15).

4. **Click the To text box and type the e-mail address of the person to whom you're sending your note.**

   You can also click the To button to open the e-mail Address Book. Then all you need do is look up the name of the person to whom you want to forward your note, click To, and then click OK.

Figure 10-15:
The New
Message
form with
a Note
attached.

5. **Type the subject of the note in the Subject box.**

   The subject of your note will already be in the Subject box of the New Message form. You can leave it alone or type something else.

6. **If you want, type the text of a message in the text box.**

   You don't really have to include a message. Your note may say all you want to say, but you can also add regular e-mail message text.

7. **Click the Send button.**

   Your message is off to its intended recipient(s).

If your Outlook note includes the address of a page on the World Wide Web (such as `www.dummies.com`), you can simply click the address to launch your Web browser — just as you can in all the other Outlook modules.

Keeping a Journal for Tidy Recordkeeping

Sometimes, when you want to find a document or a record of a conversation, you don't remember what you called the document or where you stored it, but you do remember *when* you created or received the item. In this case, you can go to the Journal and check the date when you remember dealing with the item and find what you need to know.

To get good use from the Journal, though, you have to use it (details, details . . .). You can set Outlook to make journal entries for nearly everything you do, or you can shut the Journal off entirely and make no entries to it. If you put nothing in the Journal, you get nothing out.

Don't Just Do Something — Stand There!

What's the easiest way to make entries in the Journal? Do nothing. After it's turned on, the Journal automatically records any document you create, edit, or print in any Microsoft Office application. The Journal also automatically tracks e-mail messages, meeting requests and responses, and task requests and responses. A few programs other than the Microsoft Office applications also have the capability to make entries in the Journal, but that feature is most often used with Office programs.

There's a catch: You have to tell Outlook that you *want* automatic Journal recording turned on. (All right, so you *do* have to do something besides just standing there.) Fortunately, if you haven't activated the Journal's automatic recording feature, Outlook asks you whether you want to turn the feature on every time you click the Journal icon.

To turn on the Journal's automatic recording feature, follow these steps:

1. **Choose Tools ⇨ Options.**

    The Options dialog box appears.

2. **Click the Journal Options button.**

    The Journal Options dialog box appears (as shown in Figure 10-16), offering check boxes for all the types of activities you can record automatically — and the names of all the people for whom you can automatically record transactions such as e-mail.

3. **Click the check box for items and files you want to automatically record and for contacts about whom you want information recorded.**

    The list of people in the For These Contacts box is the same as the list of people in your Contacts List. You can manually create Journal entries for people who are not in your Contacts List; see the following section, "Recording an Outlook item in the Journal manually."

Figure 10-16:
The Journal
Options
dialog box.

When you add names to your Contacts List in the Contacts module, those names aren't set for automatic recording in the Journal. If you want the Journal to keep track of them, then you have two ways to tell it so:

- Check the name(s) in the Journal Options dialog box.
- Open the Contact record, click the Journal tab, and check Automatically Record Journal Entries for These Contacts.

4. Click OK.

The Journal promptly begins automatically recording the items and files you selected for the contacts you named.

Recording an Outlook item in the Journal manually

If you don't want to clutter your Journal by recording everything automatically, you can enter selected items manually — just drag them to the Journal icon. For example, you may not want to record every transaction with a prospective client until you're certain you're doing business with that client. You can drag relevant e-mail messages to the Journal and retain a record of serious inquiries. When you actually start doing business with a new client, you can set up automatic recording.

To manually record items in the Journal:

1. **Choose Go ⇨ Folder List (or press Ctrl+6).**

   The Folder List, which includes a small icon for the Journal, appears in the top half of the Navigation Pane.

2. **Drag the item you want to record (such as an e-mail message) to the Journal icon in the Folder List.**

   The Journal Entry form appears (see Figure 10-17). At the bottom of the form is an icon representing the item you're recording, along with the item's name.

3. **Fill in the information you want to record.**

   You don't have to record anything. The text box at the bottom of the screen gives you space for making a note to yourself, if you want to use it.

4. **Click Save and Close.**

   The item you recorded is entered in the Journal. You can see your new entry when you view your Journal, as I describe in the section "Viewing the Journal," later in this chapter.

Viewing Journal Entries for a Contact

My friend Vinnie in Brooklyn says, "You gotta know who you dealt wit and when you dealt wit 'em." You can use the Contacts List — together with the Journal — to keep track of whom you dealt with and when. Just look in the person's Contact record to see when you made Journal entries:

1. **Click the Contacts icon in the Navigation Pane.**

   The Contacts List appears.

2. **Double-click the name of the contact you want to view.**

   The Contact record opens.

3. **Click the Activities button in the Contact form.**

   A list of every Journal entry you've made for that person appears (as in Figure 10-18), including the automatic entries Outlook made if you chose that option.

Figure 10-17:
A Journal
entry with a
shortcut to
an e-mail
message
attached in
the text box.

Figure 10-18:
Journal
entries for a
contact.

Finding a Journal Entry

When you don't remember exactly when you did something or dealt with somebody, you can look it up by searching for words in the Journal item.

To find a Journal entry when you don't know the *when,* follow these steps:

1. **Choose Go ⇨ Journal (or press Ctrl+8).**

   The list of Journal items appears.

2. **Click the words Search Journal at the top of the Journal screen.**

   A blinking bar appears, replacing the words Search Journal (as shown in Figure 10-19).

3. **Type a word or phrase that you can find in your Journal.**

   If you're looking for information about an upcoming meeting on the current Toad Inventory, type toad.

4. **Press Enter.**

   A list of matching items appears in your Journal List.

Figure 10-19:
The Search
Journal box.

5. **Double-click the icon to the left of your item in the Journal list.**

The Journal item you clicked appears. An icon in the text box at the bottom is a shortcut to any other Outlook item or document that the Journal entry represents. If you want to see the calendar item that has details about the Toad Inventory meeting, double-click the icon at the bottom of the Journal entry. The calendar item pops up.

Printing Your Journal

I can't explain why, but I just don't get a complete picture from information on a screen. I still like to print out my work on paper to really see what I've done. Printing your Journal (or segments of it) enables you to see a printed list of recent or upcoming activities. Stick it on the wall where you can look at it often.

To print your Journal, follow these steps:

1. **With the Journal open, select the entries you want to print.**

If you select nothing, you print the entire list. Also, if you use one of the views I describe later in this chapter (or even create your own view by grouping, sorting, or filtering), what you see is what you print.

2. **Choose File ⇨ Print (or press Ctrl+P).**

The Print dialog box appears (as shown in Figure 10-20).

3. **Choose Table or Memo style.**

Table style prints only a list of your Journal entries, not the contents of each entry. Memo style prints the contents of your Journal entries, with each item appearing as a separate memo.

4. **Choose All Rows or Only Selected Rows.**

If you want to print only certain rows, select the rows you want to print, choose File ⇨ Print, and then click the Only Selected Rows button to limit what you print to those rows.

5. **Click OK.**

The list of Journal entries you selected prints.

The printed list won't go up on the wall for you, however, unless you put it there.

Figure 10-20:
The Print
dialog box.

Viewing the Journal

As with other Outlook modules, the Journal comes with multiple views that show your entries in different ways, depending on what you want to see — whether that's a record of phone calls or a list organized by the names of the people you've dealt with. The Current View menu enables you to change quickly from one view to the next.

The Entry List

The Entry List is the whole tomato — all your Journal entries, regardless of whom, what, or when. To call up the Entry List, click the words Entry List in the Current View section of the Navigation Pane (shown in Figure 10-21).

You can click the heading at the top of any column to sort the list according to the information in that column. If you want to arrange your list of Journal entries by the type of entry, for example, click the header that says Entry Type. Your list is sorted alphabetically by type of entry, with conversations before e-mail, e-mail before faxes, and so on.

Figure 10-21:
Viewing the
Entry List —
everything
you've ever
entered.

By Type

By Type view takes sorting one step further by grouping items according to their type. To view your entries by type, click the words By Type in the Current View section of the Navigation Pane. To view your entire list of items of a particular type, click the plus sign next to the name of that type. Click the icon next to the name of the Entry Type again to close the list of that type. Then you can click to open another list of entries by type.

By Contact

By Contact view shows your Journal items grouped by the name of the person associated with each item. To see your entries in By Contact view, click the words By Contact in the Current View section of the Navigation Pane (shown in Figure 10-22).

Click the plus sign next to the name of the person whose entries you want to see. You can see entries for more than one person at a time.

Figure 10-22:
Seeing your
entries
in the By
Contact
view.

By Category

If you've been assigning categories to your Journal items, By Category view collects all your entries into bunches of items of the same category. To see your entries by category, click the words By Category in the Current View section of the Navigation Pane. If you've assigned more than one category to an item, the item shows up under both categories you've assigned.

Last Seven Days

The items you're likely to need first are the ones you used last. That's why Last Seven Days view offers a quick way to see your most recent activities at a glance. To see a week's worth of Journal entries, click the words Last Seven Days in the Current View section of the Navigation Pane.

Documents you've created, phone calls, e-mail messages — anything you've done on your computer in the last seven days — you can see them all in Last Seven Days view. This view shows anything you've worked on during the last week — including documents you may have created a long time ago — that's why you may see some pretty old dates in this view.

Phone Calls

Because you can keep track of your phone calls in the Journal, the Journal enables you to see a list of the calls you've tracked. Simply choose Current View ⇨ Phone Calls in the Navigation Pane. To print a list of your phone calls, switch to Phone Calls view and press Ctrl+P.

It's All in the Journal

The Journal can be enormously helpful whether you choose to use it regularly or rarely. You don't have to limit yourself to recording documents or Outlook items. You can keep track of conversations or customer inquiries or any other transaction in which chronology matters. If you set the Journal for automatic entries, you can ignore it completely until you need to see what was recorded. You can also play starship captain and record everything you do. (I haven't tried Outlook in outer space yet, but I know I would enjoy the view.)

Part IV
Beyond the Basics: Tips and Tricks You Won't Want to Miss

The 5th Wave

By Rich Tennant

©RICHTENNANT

"My spam filter checks the recipient address, http links, and any writing that panders to postmodern English romanticism with conceits to 20th century graphic narrative."

In this part . . .

When you finally get ahead in the rat race, what do you find? Faster rats, of course. The people that I train and coach are often unsatisfied with just keeping up. They want to get ahead and stay ahead, so they want to learn to drive Outlook like a race car, not a minivan. In this part, I show you how to step into the high performance category with Outlook.

Chapter 11

Feeding on Blogs, Podcasts, and News with Outlook RSS

You can manage your whole life with Outlook. What could be more important than that? Blogs and podcasts, that's what! Now Outlook can help you explore the most exciting region of cyberspace: the world of blogs, podcasts, and other syndicated online media.

A system called RSS most often delivers blogs, podcasts, and newsfeeds to the people who subscribe to them. Lucky for us, you needn't know anything about RSS to enjoy its benefits — but it can't hurt!

Feeding Your Need for RSS

Everybody's heard about blogs. If you don't already write one, you probably know someone who does. People blog about anything and everything: their days, their kids, their hobbies (see Figure 11-1). Do you ever read your friends' blogs? Of course not — you're much to busy for such piffle.

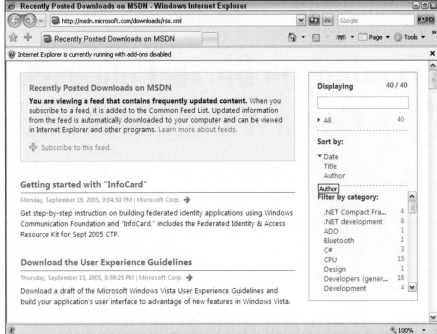

Figure 11-1:
You'll find blogs and RSS feeds on nearly any topic.

If you're so busy, what are you doing fiddling with your iPod? If you're one of those people who download songs from the Internet and listen on an iPod or other digital music player, you already know what I mean. If you're not, Outlook 2007 gives you an easy way to find out what all the fuss is about. But music isn't the only thing you can store and play on a digital music player; you can now download thousands of spoken-word programs in digital form. Many are taken from the radio programs that you already listen to over the air. Non-musical programs offered as digital downloads are usually called *podcasts.* Most of them are free, but some cost 99 cents or so.

Read up

The word *blog* comes from the phrase *Web log,* a kind of open diary in which people post regular entries to a Web site for the whole world to see. Tens of millions of people write blogs these days. Most of those blogs are silly or terrible or totally useless, or all of those things. But even if many of the blogs out there are useless, many

more are important sources of information you won't want to miss. *Business Week* magazine referred to blogs as "the most explosive outbreak in the information world since the Internet itself . . . blogs are not a business elective. They're a prerequisite."

You don't need an iPod to listen to podcasts. While podcasts are designed to be played on portable devices, most people actually listen to them on their computers. If your computer can run Outlook 2007, it can also run Windows Media Player, a program that plays podcasts. Podcasts are typically regular, recurring programs that come to you through a subscription. Outlook 2007 allows you to receive any podcasts to which you've subscribed and organize them with the same tools you use for organizing e-mail.

The common thread between blogs and podcasts is something called *RSS,* which stands for *Really Simple Syndication* or *Rich Site Summary* or Ringo Sings in the Shower. (Okay, that last one's fake, although maybe he does sing in the shower.) RSS technology lets you subscribe to information that changes frequently so that it automatically updates itself. For example, most news organizations such as the *Wall Street Journal* and MSNBC offer RSS feeds of their news stories. When you want to see the latest headlines, you don't need to open a Web site. Just check the RSS feed to look for any headlines that interest you. Every time a new story is posted to the respective Web site, the story shows up on the RSS feed as well.

RSS information is delivered in something called a *feed.* As appetizing as that sounds, it's not very filling. In fact it's not even edible. A feed is just a mechanism for updating information as it changes. Blogs and podcasts usually offer RSS feeds that allow you to keep track of new entries or episodes. Most news services also offer RSS feeds so you can read the latest news as it becomes available. *The New York Times,* the *Wall Street Journal,* the *Associated Press,* and lots of other news services include RSS feeds, and there's a good chance that your local newspaper offers one, too. Outlook 2007 has a separate folder for receiving RSS feeds so that you can organize the information in a way that you find useful. Generally, you don't need to know how RSS works, but it's good to know it's available when it's useful to you.

TIP

IE versus Outlook

You don't absolutely need to use Outlook for reading RSS feeds. You can sign up for RSS feeds in several popular Web browsers including Internet Explorer 7. If you have an earlier version of Internet Explorer, you can download the latest version for free from `www.microsoft.com/windows/ie` and get started with RSS. Internet Explorer is a good program for reading blogs and news feeds, but it doesn't offer any tools for managing the huge amount of information that RSS can deliver. That's where Outlook comes in. You can also buy a number of specialized programs for managing news feeds, but Outlook does a pretty good job if you're just getting started.

Setting Up an RSS Feed via Internet Explorer

Oddly enough, the simplest way to add an RSS feed to Outlook is to use Internet Explorer. You need the latest version of both Outlook and Internet Explorer to do that. When you subscribe to a feed in either Outlook or Internet Explorer, that feed becomes available in both programs.

Internet Explorer makes it much easier to subscribe to feeds than Outlook, so if you have a choice, Internet Explorer is the place to go to add a subscription to a feed.

To subscribe to an RSS feed in Internet Explorer, follow these steps:

1. **Click the Feeds button at the top of the screen.**

   A new page opens, as shown in Figure 11-2.

   When you open a Web site or blog that offers an RSS feed, the Feeds button at the top of the Internet Explorer screen changes from gray to orange.

2. **Click the Subscribe to This Feed link.**

   The Subscribe to This Feed dialog box appears; see Figure 11-3.

3. **Click the Subscribe button.**

   The Subscribe to This Feed dialog box closes.

Now you can view the feed in either Internet Explorer 7 or Outlook 2007.

Figure 11-2:
An RSS
page ready
for your sub-
scription.

Figure 11-3:
The
Subscribe to
This Feed
dialog box.

Setting Up an RSS Feed via Outlook

You can also set up an RSS feed directly in Outlook, although it usually requires several more steps (for those who like to deal with details).

Microsoft offers a collection of RSS feeds that you can add to Outlook pretty simply by just clicking the RSS folder under the Inbox folder, then clicking one of the orange buttons on the Web page that appears. But that page only includes a few dozen of the millions of available feeds. You need a different approach if you want to subscribe to feeds unlisted by Microsoft.

To set up an RSS feed through Outlook, follow along:

1. **Choose Tools ⇨ Account Settings.**

   The Account Settings dialog box appears; see Figure 11-4.

2. **Click the RSS Feeds tab.**

   The RSS sign-up page shows the list of feeds to which you've subscribed.

3. **Click New.**

   The New RSS Feed dialog box appears; see Figure 11-5.

Figure 11-4:
The
Account
Settings
dialog box.

4. Enter the URL of the RSS feed you want.

This typically looks like an unusually long URL: `http://www.
instantmovieblog.com/atom.xml`. If you enter the address
inaccurately, it won't work. Your best bet is to follow these steps:

1. Go to the site where the feed you want is hosted.

2. Right-click the XML, RSS, or Feed button. Different sites use different names for the same thing, but it's often an orange button.

3. Choose Copy Shortcut.

Once you've done that, you can follow the preceding steps and paste the
address into the New RSS Feed dialog box.

5. Click Add.

The RSS Feed Options dialog box (see Figure 11-6) shows a variety of
changes you can make to your subscription:

• **Feed Name:** You can change the name Outlook displays. Some
feeds have long, clumsy names.

- **Delivery Location:** Some feeds generate huge amounts of information every day, so you may want to send that information to a special folder or even to a totally separate data file. If you're on a big corporate network that limits the amount of e-mail messages you're allowed to store, you may want to send your RSS subscriptions to a separate Outlook data file to avoid running out of space.

- **Downloads:** Outlook automatically downloads only a brief summary of each item, which saves disk space but requires you to manually download full text of each item one by one. If you want Outlook to simply download the whole message, click the box labeled Download the Full Article as an .html Attachment to Each Item. Many blog entries also include attachments such as photos and sounds. Click the box labeled Automatically Download Enclosures for This Feed to do just that.

- **Update Limit:** Some RSS feed publishers don't let you update your information too frequently. If you try to update too often, they cancel your subscription. If there's a limit assigned to the feed you've chosen, this box will automatically be checked.

6. **Click OK.**

7. **Click Close.**

Figure 11-6:
The RSS
Feed
Options
dialog box.

As you can see, subscribing to an RSS feed takes three easy steps in Internet Explorer or six fairly complicated steps in Outlook. Outlook offers more options, but you can always subscribe to a feed through Internet Explorer, then go to Outlook's RSS page, select a feed, and click the Change button to modify your options.

Reading Feeds

Once you've subscribed to one or more RSS feeds, they appear in the RSS Feeds folder in the Outlook Folder List. You can read feeds as easily as you read e-mail.

The Navigation Bar has no button for RSS feeds, so you have to open the RSS folder to see what's inside. That means it takes a few more steps to read RSS feeds than to read e-mail, but once you find your way to the RSS folder, it's pretty easy.

Follow these instructions to read an RSS feed in Outlook 2007:

1. **Click the Mail button in the Navigation Bar.**

   The list of mail folders appears.

2. **Click the plus sign next to the RSS Feeds folder.**

   The folders containing RSS feeds appear. Each folder contains one feed. If the RSS Feeds folder is accompanied by a minus sign and no folders appear below it, no RSS feeds have been set up yet. You have to set up some feeds to make something appear there.

3. **Click the folder containing the feed you want to read.**

You can treat each item in a feed just as you'd treat individual e-mail messages. You can assign categories, move items to folders, and forward messages.

Chapter 12

What You Need to Know to Use Outlook at Home

In This Chapter

▶ Discovering and choosing ISPs

▶ Setting up an account

▶ Establishing directory services

▶ Preparing for multiple users

*W*orking at home is different from working in an office (but you knew that). Sure, working in your bathrobe is pretty unusual in big companies, but telecommuters have to do without the huge network, multiple phone lines, and standing army of computer gurus that many office workers take for granted. That's why Outlook works a bit differently for the home user than it does for the corporate user — and this chapter shows the home user how to get the most from those differences. (If you use Outlook in a large corporation, you may want to skip to Chapter 14, which focuses on using Outlook in big business.)

Investigating an ISP

If you use a computer at home, you probably send and receive e-mail through an outside service. It might be your cable company, your phone company, or a service that your computer dials up over the telephone. The general term for the kind of outfit that provides this service is *Internet service provider,* or *ISP.* ISPs do more than exchange e-mail messages for you; an ISP also provides the Internet connection that enables your browser to access and display pages from the World Wide Web and enables you to do nearly anything that you can do on the Internet.

Online services, such as America Online, EarthLink, and MSN (the Microsoft Network) function as ISPs, but they also offer a variety of other features, such as discussion forums and file libraries. If you belong to an online service, you don't need a separate ISP. On the other hand, if all you want to do is exchange e-mail and browse the Web, you may not want a full-featured online service; a basic ISP may be all you need.

Everything about the Internet and online services can — and does — change quickly. The best way to get and use an online service may change with the introduction of new technologies and services, but what I tell you here is how it is in 2006.

If you're working from home, using an online service to connect you to the Internet offers some big advantages:

- ✔ These services try to make the process of connecting as easy as possible.

- ✔ Most online services have plenty of staff to help you when things go wrong.

- ✔ If you want some assurance that you or your children won't run across scary people or nasty material while exploring cyberspace, online services are well equipped to screen out what you may find objectionable. If you're shopping for an online service, ask about features that protect you against nasty things that could pop up on your screen.

Keep your e-mail to yourself

Nearly every company that offers Internet connections also offers e-mail service. They often make their e-mail amazingly easy to set up and start using. Don't take the bait. Once you set up an address with AOL or MSN and send e-mail from that address for a year or more, it gets more and more difficult to change your ISP because you have to notify everyone you know of your new e-mail address. You can get your own e-mail address from lots of different services; many of them are free. You can even set up your name as an e-mail address. For example, if your name is Mordecai Roblevsky, you could get the address Mordecai@Roblevsky.com. If you have a more common name, such as John Smith, it might be too late to grab your name as an e-mail address. You could either choose a variation on your name, or change your name to Roblevsky. My favorite service for setting up custom Internet and e-mail addresses is Go Daddy at www.godaddy.com. They provide good service overall, no matter how weird their Super Bowl commercials get. If you want to check out one of the major online services, visit one of the following Web sites or call the phone number:

- ✔ AOL at www.aol.com and 1-800-392-5180

- ✔ MSN at www.msn.com and 1-800-386-5550

Picking a Provider

If you've never had Internet service, I have a question for you: Where have you been living? On Mars? Even Martians seem to be sending e-mail these days (although they all pretend to be from Nigeria). Anyway, you picked a good time to join the party. A fast, easy connection to the Internet is probably just a phone call away. I recently moved into a new apartment building that had high-speed Internet service built right into the walls like telephone service or electricity. I just had to plug one end of a computer network cable into the wall and the other end into my computer, make one phone call, and POOF! I had high-speed Internet service on the spot.

If your home didn't come equipped with Internet connections, check with your phone company or cable company to see what they offer. Maybe you can get the two companies to fight over you and give you a good deal.

You may live in an area without high-speed Internet service, which is sad, as well as unlikely in the continental United States. Unless you live 40 miles from Nowhere, some phone or cable company is looking for a way to get high-speed service to you as soon as possible. You have no idea how much time you can waste until you can log on to dozens of useless Web sites every day. If you have phone service, AOL and EarthLink still offer dial-up, but no broadband choices. There also might be a dial-up service in your community that can serve you. But if you have a choice, avoid dial-up Internet connections — even if it's cheaper. Most Web sites today are designed for high-speed Internet users. You'll be tearing your hair out after a few hours of surfing most of the popular sites by dial-up.

An extensive list of ISPs can be found at a Web site called www.thelist.com. There were once several companies that charged nothing for Internet access, but most went out of business. (For some reason, they couldn't make money by giving stuff away free. Imagine that!)

Setting Up Internet E-Mail Accounts

After you've signed up with an ISP, you can set up Outlook to send and receive e-mail from your account. Although any individual Internet e-mail account requires setup only once, you can set up many such accounts if you need them.

If you're a corporate user, your system administrators may not want you to mess around with account settings at all — and may have special arrangements and settings they want you to use when you work from home. Either way, it's best to ask first.

One catch with cable modems and DSL

If you have high-speed Internet access from your cable television operator or DSL through a telephone company, congratulations! You'll enjoy zippy Web surfing and your e-mail will come and go in a flash. You also don't need to deal with a separate ISP, because your cable company or DSL provider does that job for you.

You might run across one catch if you get your Internet connection from one company (such as your cable company) and your e-mail service from another. In that case you may need to enter your ISP's mail server name for outgoing e-mail and your e-mail service's server name for incoming e-mail. That's one method ISPs use to cut down on all that annoying junk e-mail that clutters up the Web. Whether that helps is hard to say, but be ready to deal with that in certain circumstances.

If you're on your own, you should probably call the tech support line from your online service or ISP to get all the proper spellings of the server names and passwords. (Don't forget to ask whether they're case sensitive!)

To set up an Internet e-mail account, follow these steps:

1. **Choose Tools ⇨ Account Settings.**

   The Account Settings dialog box appears (as seen in Figure 12-1).

2. **Click the E-mail tab.**

   The Email Accounts setup page appears.

3. **Click New.**

   The Add New Email Account dialog box appears.

4. **Fill in the blanks in the New Email Account dialog box.**

   Be careful to enter the information accurately — especially your e-mail address and password. Otherwise your e-mail won't work.

5. **Click Next.**

   A configuration screen appears and Outlook begins trying to automatically configure your e-mail account.

   - If it succeeds, the Congratulations screen appears and you can click Finish to complete the process.
   - If Outlook is unable to automatically configure your e-mail account, continue these steps.

6. **Click the check box labeled Manually Configure Server Settings.**

   The Server Type dialog box appears.

Figure 12-1:
The Account Settings screen is where you set up a new e-mail address.

7. **Click the radio button for the server type your e-mail provider requires.**

   Most home users choose E-mail, while people connecting to large office systems might choose Microsoft Exchange Server.

8. **Click Next.**

   A new configuration screen appears.

9. **Type the settings that your e-mail provider requires.**

   Again, each e-mail service differs, but most of them can tell you how to make their e-mail work with Outlook.

10. **Click the Test Account Settings button.**

    The Test Account Settings dialog box shows you what's happening while Outlook tests the entered settings to see if you got everything right.

    If you type one wrong letter in one of your e-mail settings, your messages won't go through. The computers that Outlook has to send messages through (called *servers*) are terribly literal, so it's good to find out whether your setup works while you're still tweaking your settings. If the test fails, try retyping some entries (and then clicking the Test Account Settings button) until you get a successful test. When the test is successful, the Test Account Settings dialog box says "Congratulations! All tests completed successfully. Click Close to continue." So that's what you should do.

Your Web site, your e-mail

If you have a Web site, you can probably get a free e-mail account in connection with your site. So if you have a site called www.your company.com (for example), you can also have an e-mail address that looks something like yourname@yourcompany.com. There's an even better chance that the mail service that you get in connection with your Web site is compatible with Outlook. Ask the tech-support people from the company that hosts your Web site what you have to do to set up Outlook with their e-mail service.

---

11. **Click Close.**

    The Test Account Settings dialog box closes.

12. **Click Next (or press Enter).**

    The Congratulations screen appears. Take a moment to feel the thrill of success.

13. **Click Finish.**

As I mention earlier in this section, you can set up more than one Internet e-mail account, so each member of the family can have a separate address. You also may want to have different accounts for business use and personal use. Perhaps you just want to set up separate accounts so you can send yourself messages. Whatever you like to do, the process is pretty much the same.

Dealing with Multiple Mail Accounts

It's possible to use Outlook to exchange e-mail through more than one e-mail address. For example, I have different e-mail addresses for business use and personal use. If you want to create a similar arrangement, all you have to do is set up a separate account for each address (using the method I describe in the previous section, "Setting Up Internet E-Mail Accounts").

Telling one Outlook account apart from another isn't too tough. Normally Outlook sends your reply to an e-mail message through the account in which you received the message. When you're replying, you don't have to think about which account you're using. When you're creating a message, however, Outlook sends the message through the account that you marked as the *default account* (the one it must use unless you specify otherwise). If you want to check which account a message will be sent through, click the Accounts button on the message form's toolbar and look at the box labeled *Send* Message Using.

If you use only the e-mail address provided by your ISP, you'll get along just fine. But if you want to set up a separate e-mail address for each member of your family, or keep your business e-mail separate from your personal messages, you can start up an account with any number of mailbox providers.

Mail.com (www.mail.com) is one of the more popular providers of electronic mailboxes. You can sign up for an address through Mail.com for free and check your e-mail messages through your Web browser. If you want to take advantage of Outlook's sophisticated mail-management features with your Mail.com account, you can pay an extra $18 per year for what they call a POP3 account. (I've been using Mail.com for about four years, and I think they do a good job.) Other companies that offer e-mail services include Microsoft's own Hotmail service (www.hotmail.com), Gmail from Google (http://gmail.google.com), and Yahoo! (www.yahoo.com).

Send, receive, whatever!

Just because you clicked Send on your outgoing message doesn't automatically mean that your message was sent. Some people who use Outlook at home connect to the Internet via the telephone line (the poor things). Each time you send messages over a dial-up connection, your computer must make a phone call to your ISP so Outlook can drop off the messages you created and pick up the messages that others have sent you. So, sometime after you've created a batch of messages, remember to choose Tools ⇨ Send/Receive (or press F9) to tell Outlook to dial up your ISP and actually send out the messages (if you're using Outlook at home).

Chapter 13

Supercharging Your Sales with Business Contact Manager

. . . .

In This Chapter

▶ Understanding the Business Contact Manager screen

▶ Adding contacts, accounts, and opportunities

▶ Checking reports

. . . .

*O*utlook is probably the world's second most popular business tool (right behind the ever-popular paycheck), because it's so good at dealing with all the little details of your daily work life. But as powerful as it is, Outlook has some limitations when it comes to connecting those details and using that information to move your business forward.

To help remedy that problem, Microsoft offers an add-on program for Outlook called Business Contact Manager. It's free if you buy Microsoft Office Professional and certain other bundles of Microsoft Office products.

Microsoft Office is offered in at least seven different bundles, so you need to make sure that your bundle includes Business Contact Manager if that interests you.

Understanding the Outlook Business Contact Manager

The purpose of Business Contact Manager is to organize and present your business information strategically, in a way that reflects the big picture. Where do you want your business to go? Outlook alone is a good tactical tool, but Business Contact Manager helps you look farther down the road.

The best reason for using Business Contact Manager is to manage a sales process, the system of keeping track of prospects to whom you might want to sell something. That means tracking the companies for whom they work, all the efforts you make on the way to closing a sale with that client, and the ongoing history of sales as your business relationship matures. Business Contact Manager can help you with other types of business processes, but most of the language you encounter when using the program relates to a sales process.

Bear in mind that sales-process management can be a fairly complex topic. If you look around, you'll find entire books on the subject. I can't cover the whole process in this chapter, but I can show you where to find the tools in the Outlook Business Contact Manager that can help you improve your sales process.

One oddity about using Business Contact Manager is that it appears as a part of Outlook, but doesn't work the same way in many respects. For example:

- ✔ If you drag an e-mail message to the Business Contact Manager folder, it doesn't automatically create a new contact record the way the Outlook Contacts module does.

- ✔ Business Contact Manager maintains a contacts database totally separate from your Outlook Contacts, and the two collections have nothing to do with each other.

The easiest place to begin exploring Business Contact Manager is on the home screen shown in Figure 13-1. There you can get an overview of all the program's parts as well as a quick view of how the parts interact.

There are two ways to open the home screen:

- ✔ Choose Business Contact Manager ➪ Business Contact Manager Home (or press Alt+M).

- ✔ Click the Business Contact Manager Home button on the toolbar.

Play nice

I've heard rumors that certain product development teams at Microsoft are jealous of one another and don't communicate or collaborate. It looks to me like the Outlook team and the Business Contact Manager team may be an example of that kind of rivalry. Perhaps someday Microsoft will develop an Interdepartmental Rivalry Manager to address this problem. In the meantime, Outlook and Business Contact Manager are offered as a system, but they don't cooperate as well as you might expect.

Figure 13-1:
The
Business
Contact
Manager
home
screen.

The home screen features four tabs:

- ✔ **Home** is the tab that shows you the big picture, offering a graph representing the value of the opportunities you have entered and an itemized list of those opportunities.

- ✔ **Sales** reveals nitty-gritty specifics about the sales you're trying to make and what you're doing to make those sales. It also offers buttons for adding new contacts, accounts, or opportunities (which are explained later in this chapter).

- ✔ **Marketing** offers a longer view than sales, with buttons for creating new campaigns and a list of campaigns in progress.

- ✔ **Projects** is the place for organizing specific actions that support your other sales efforts.

You can customize any of the four pages by clicking the Add/Remove Content link and clicking the check box next to the items you want; see Figure 13-2. To remove an item, just deselect a check box.

Figure 13-2:
The Add/
Remove
Content
dialog box.

Adding a Contact to Business Contact Manager

Before you manage contacts, you need some contacts to manage. As I mention earlier, Business Contact Manager appears as part of Outlook, but it doesn't really connect to Outlook.

You can import your Outlook contacts into Business Contact Manager by choosing File Í Import and Export Í Business Contact Manager for Outlook, but once you've done that, you have to add each new contact to Business Contact Manager individually.

Follow these steps to add a new contact to Business Contact Manager:

1. **Choose File ➪ New ➪ Business Contact.**

   The New Business Contact form appears; see Figure 13-3.

2. **Enter the appropriate information in the form.**

   The only required piece of information is a name. Everything else is optional, although the more information you enter, the more useful the entry will be. The other things you can enter are listed later in this section of the chapter.

3. **Click the Save & Close button when you've entered all the information you need.**

   The New Business Contact form closes.

The information you can enter includes the following:

- ✓ **Job Title:** The position held by the contact (such as Vice President, Marketing).

- ✓ **File As:** Outlook automatically fills this in. The File As name is normally the same name that you entered in the Name blank, except that this one appears with the last name first.

- ✔ **Account:** This is typically the person's employer. Set up an account for each company with which you do business. You can either set up accounts first, then click the Account button as you fill in each contact record (to link that contact with an account), or choose Account ➪ New to create an account while you fill in the contact information.

- ✔ **Phone Numbers:** This section has only four blanks, but you can choose from any of 19 different types of phone numbers by clicking the button next to the label. Your choices include Business, Home, Mobile, Fax, and others.

- ✔ **Address:** Type a street address here and Outlook automatically distinguishes city, state, and zip code.

- ✔ **Source Information:** Sometimes you may launch projects or campaigns just to acquire leads for future sales. Those projects can cost money, so after a while it's helpful to look back at which projects yielded the most leads for the money you spent. The Source Information section allows you to keep track of how you acquired each lead and what each lead found interesting about your company.

- ✔ **Source:** Enter the source of the lead in general terms (direct mail, trade show, employee referral, and so on).

- ✔ **Initiated By:** Lets you link the lead to a specific person or project.

- ✔ **Area of Interest:** Note the prospect's general interest.

- ✔ **Category:** Assign a custom category.

- ✔ **Internet:** Store the contact's e-mail address, URL, and other online contact information.

- ✔ **Business Card:** You don't need to enter information here because the information that you enter in other parts of the form is repeated here in an attractively formatted layout. However, you can rearrange the business card contents by clicking the Business Card button and choosing items from the Edit Business Card dialog box shown in Figure 13-4.

- ✔ **Classification:** Enter the contact's current status, whether it's a good lead, whether you're actively pursuing business with this person, which of your employees is responsible for following up, whether he or she is a likely customer, and if payment is up to date.

Figure 13-4:
The Edit
Business
Card dialog
box.

Adding an Account to Business Contact Manager

The steps you take to add an account are pretty much the same as those for adding a contact:

1. **Choose File ➪ New ➪ Account.**

   The New Account form appears.

2. **Enter the appropriate information in the form.**

3. **Click the Save and Close button when you've entered all the information you need.**

   The New Account form closes.

You can link a whole list of contacts to each account by clicking the Add button in the Business Contacts section.

You can see the Select the Business Contacts to Link to this Account dialog box in Figure 13-5. As you probably guessed, when you're doing business with a large organization, you may have to deal with several different people, either in different departments, different locations, or different job functions. The account list lets you deal with them as a group (if you like) or one by one (when that makes sense). Each contact can only be linked to one account, but each account can be linked to several different contacts.

Figure 13-5:
The Select
the
Business
Contacts to
Link to This
Account
dialog box.
(Snappy
name, eh?)

Adding a New Opportunity

As persuasive as you might be, you can't just run around selling to people randomly; you need to sell a specific thing to a specific person. Even bank robbers need a specific proposal ("Your money or your life!") if they want to be successful. If you follow up on each specific chance you get to sell a specific thing to a specific person, chances are you'll succeed at least once. The more often you follow up, the more often you'll succeed — unless you really are a bank robber, in which case you probably end up in jail. That tends to slow down business pretty dramatically.

To add an opportunity to Business Contact Manager, follow along:

1. **Choose File ⇨ New ⇨ Opportunity.**

   The Opportunity form appears, as shown in Figure 13-6.

2. **Enter a name in the Opportunity Title box.**

   Enter any name that makes sense to you. The text you enter appears as you type it.

3. **Click the Link To box.**

   The Link to an Account or Business Contact dialog box appears.

4. **Choose the specific person or company to which you want to sell something.**

   As the title of the dialog box suggests, you need to link the opportunity to either an account or a business contact.

   • To link your opportunity to an account, double-click an account. If Accounts appears in the Folder box, the dialog box lists the accounts you've created.

   • To link to a contact, click the Folder scroll button and choose Business Contacts, then double-click a name on the list.

   • If you're creating an opportunity for an entirely new contact or account, click the New button to enter information for that account or contact.

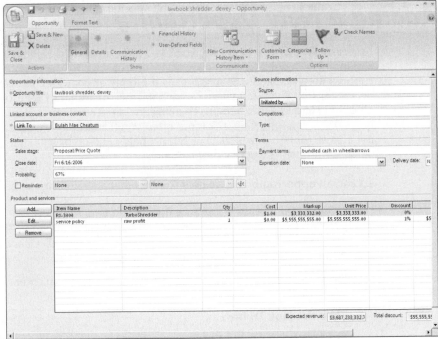

Figure 13-6:
The
Opportunity
form.

5. Enter as much of the remaining, optional information as you can.

Optional information you can enter in the Link to an Account or Business Contact dialog box includes the following:

✔ **Status:** How far into the sales process have you gone?

   • **Prospecting:** If you've just heard a name of someone who might be interested and you're about to call, that's the Prospecting stage.

   • **Proposal:** If you've already submitted a proposal, that's the Proposal stage.

✔ **Close Date:** When will the purchase decision be made? Outlook lets you enter either a specific date (June 17, for example) or an amount of time (in three weeks, for instance).

✔ **Probability:** You can enter a percentage to indicate the probability that the sales will go through, or Outlook will estimate one for you.

   If you want a reminder to pop up at a specific future time, click the Reminder box and enter the date when you want to be reminded.

✔ **Products and Services:** Define the specific thing you're offering to sell.

- Click the Add button to open the Add Product or Service dialog box and click the Item Name scroll button shown in Figure 13-7. The list of items you've entered appears, along with Edit This List.

- To add new items: Choose Edit This List ➪ Add. Enter the information (including Item Name, Description, Default Quantity, Unit Cost, and Unit Price) and click OK.

✔ **Source Information:** You might have added the same kind of information to a new contact or account the way I describe earlier in this chapter.

✔ **Terms:** Once you've closed a sale, you can enter information on the payment arrangements for future reference and for estimating cash flow.

Update opportunities regularly to reflect your ongoing efforts. If a contact starts out as a prospect, aim to get him or her to move ahead to the proposal and sale stage in a reasonable time. Otherwise, you need to adjust your opportunity record to show that the prospect didn't pay off and you can move on to more promising opportunities.

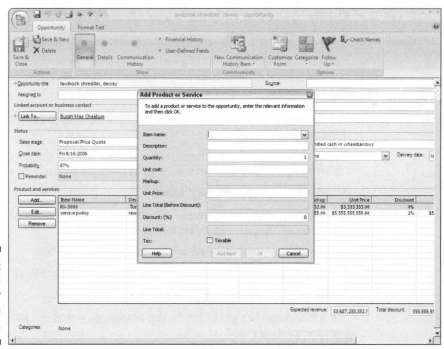

Figure 13-7:
The Add Product or Service dialog box.

Viewing and Using Reports

The whole reason for collecting all this information about your contacts, accounts, and opportunities is to get a clear picture about where your business stands at any minute. Reports give you that picture, and they also help you take action on the things that need to get done. For example, if you update all of your information every Friday, then go away for the weekend and forget about it completely, you can view a report first thing Monday morning to see what you need to do next and get right to it.

Business Contact Manager offers five general categories of reports:

- ✔ **Business Contacts** lists people according to status, location, or activity.
- ✔ **Accounts** lists accounts according to location or status.
- ✔ **Business Projects** lists projects you've entered according to what's being done and who's doing it.
- ✔ **Marketing Campaigns** gives detailed descriptions of the status of any launched campaigns.
- ✔ **Activity** has a full accounting of who's doing what, organized by contacts, accounts, or opportunities.

The Opportunity Funnel Report is good for starters, because it shows pending deals and who you need to contact to move those deals along. To view and use the Opportunity Funnel Report, follow these steps:

1. **Choose Business Contact Manager ➪ Reports ➪ Opportunities ➪ Opportunity Funnel.**

   The Opportunities Funnel Report appears, as shown in Figure 13-8. You can print it, but you may also want to explore it onscreen to save time.

2. **Double-click an opportunity name.**

   The Opportunity form appears, showing all current details; see Figure 13-9. You can update any information on this screen.

3. **Double-click a contact or an account in the Link To box.**

   The contact or account form to which you clicked the link appears.

4. **Contact that person to follow up.**

   The information is right there on the screen, so you don't have to spend any time looking it up.

5. Update any information about the opportunity, then click Save ⇨ Close.

The form closes.

The report is called the Opportunity Funnel Report because a sales process is like a funnel; you need to put a large number of prospects in the top of the funnel to get a small number of sales to come out of the bottom. It's essential to keep the funnel full and the prospects in motion to get a decent trickle of sales. That's what Business Contact Manager does for you: It helps you make sure that the funnel is full so that your sales keep flowing.

Figure 13-8: The Opportunities Funnel Report.

Figure 13-9:
The
Opportunity
form.

Part V
Outlook
at the Office

The 5th Wave · By Rich Tennant

"I hate when you bring 'Office' with you on camping trips."

In this part . . .

*L*ife is different when you work in a big organization from what it is when you work in a small one. My clients in large organization rely heavily on Outlook as a tool for improved teamwork and project management. Here I show you the parts of Outlook that work best in the big leagues (or for people with big ambitions).

Chapter 14

Big-Time Collaboration with Outlook

Microsoft is a big company that writes big programs for big companies with big bucks. So, as you'd expect, some parts of Outlook are intended for people at big companies. Big companies that use Outlook usually have a network that's running a program called Microsoft Exchange Server in the background. Exchange Server works as a team with Outlook to let you do what you can't do with Outlook alone. Outlook users on an Exchange Server can look at the calendar of another employee, or give someone else the power to answer e-mail messages on that person's behalf, or do any of a host of handy tasks right from a single desktop.

Many features of Microsoft Exchange Server look as if they're just a part of Outlook, so most Exchange Server users have no idea that any program other than Outlook is involved. In practical terms, it really doesn't matter whether you know the technical difference between Outlook and Exchange Server; what's important is that Outlook and Exchange together can tackle a lot of tasks that Outlook can't do as well alone.

Collaborating with Outlook's Help

If your company is like most others, then you spend a lot of time in meetings — and even more figuring out when to hold meetings and agreeing on what to do when you're not having meetings. Outlook has some tools for planning meetings and making decisions that are helpful for people who work in groups. Although some of these features are available to all Outlook 2002 users, they work much better when you're using Exchange as well.

Organizing a meeting

Suppose you want to set up a meeting with three coworkers. You call the first person to suggest a meeting time, and then call the second, only to find out that the second person isn't available when the first one wants to meet. So you agree on a time with the second person, only to discover that the third person can't make this new time. You might want to invite a fourth person, but heaven knows how long it'll take to come up with an appropriate time for that one.

If you use Outlook, you can check everyone's schedule, pick a time, and suggest a meeting time that everyone can work with in the first place — with a single message.

To invite several people to a meeting, follow these steps:

1. **Choose File ➪ New ➪ Meeting Request (or press Ctrl+Shift+Q).**

   The New Appointment form opens.

2. **Click the Scheduling button.**

   The Attendee Availability page appears (as shown in Figure 14-1).

Figure 14-1:
Use the Attendee Availability page to invite coworkers to a meeting.

3. **Click the Add Others button.**

   A drop-down list appears.

4. **Choose Add from Address Book.**

   The Select Attendees and Resources dialog box appears.

5. **Click the name of a person you want to invite to the meeting.**

   The name you click is highlighted to show you've selected it.

6. **Click either the Required or Optional button, depending on how important that person's attendance is to the meeting.**

   The name you select appears in either the Required or Optional box, depending on which button you click.

7. **Repeat Steps 5 and 6 until you've chosen everyone you want to add to the meeting.**

   The names you choose appear in the Select Attendees and Resources dialog box (as shown in Figure 14-2).

Figure 14-2:
You can pick your friends and you can pick your meetings.

8. **Click OK.**

   The Select Attendees and Resources dialog box closes and the names you chose appear in the Attendee Availability List. The Attendee Availability list also shows you a diagram of each person's schedule so you can see when everyone has free time.

9. **On the timeline at the top of the Attendee Availability list, click your preferred meeting time.**

   The time you pick appears in the Meeting Start Time box at the bottom of the Attendee Availability list. If you want, you can enter the Meeting start and end time in the boxes at the bottom of the Attendee Availability list instead of clicking the timeline. If you don't see a time when everyone you're inviting to your meeting is available, click the Autopick Next button and Outlook will find a meeting time that works for everyone.

10. **Click the Appointment button.**

    The Appointment page appears with the names of the people you invited to the meeting in the To box at the top of the form.

11. **Type the subject of the meeting in the Subject box.**

    The subject you enter appears in the Subject box.

12. **Enter any other information that you want attendees to know about your meeting.**

    You can include location or category.

13. **Click Send.**

    Your meeting request is sent to the people that you've invited.

If your system administrators see fit, they can set up Exchange Accounts for resources such as conference rooms. If they do, you can figure out a location for your meeting while you're figuring out who can attend.

Responding to a meeting request

Even if you don't organize meetings and send invitations, you may get invited to meetings now and then, so it's a good idea to know how to respond to a meeting request if you get one. ("Politely" is a good concept to start with.)

When you've been invited to a meeting, you get a special e-mail message that offers buttons labeled Accept, Decline, Tentative, Propose New Time, or Calendar. When you click either Accept or Tentative, Outlook automatically adds the meeting to your schedule and creates a new e-mail message to the person who organized the meeting, telling that person your decision. You can add an explanation to the message, or just click the Send button to deliver your message.

If you decline a meeting request, Outlook generates a message to the meeting organizer. (It's good form to add a business reason to explain why you're missing a meeting — "Sorry, I've got a deadline," rather than "I have to wash my aardvark" or "Sorry, I plan to be sane that day.") If you click the Calendar button, Outlook displays your calendar in a separate window so you can see whether you're free to attend the meeting at the suggested time.

Checking responses to your meeting request

Each time you organize a meeting with Outlook, you create a small flurry of e-mail messages inviting people to attend, and they respond with a flurry of messages either accepting or declining your invitation. You may have a good enough memory to recall who said Yes and No, but I usually need some help. Fortunately, Outlook keeps track of who said what.

To check the status of responses to your meeting request, follow these steps:

1. **Click the Calendar icon in the Navigation Pane.**

   The calendar appears.

2. **Double-click the item you want to check.**

   The meeting opens.

3. **Click the Tracking button.**

   The list of people you invited appears, listing each person's response to your invitation (as shown in Figure 14-3).

Sad to say, only the meeting organizer can find out who has agreed to attend a certain meeting. If you plan to attend a certain meeting only because that special someone you met in the elevator might also attend, you'll know whether that person accepted only if you organized the meeting yourself. You can tell who was invited to a meeting by checking the names on the meeting request that you got by e-mail.

Figure 14-3:
See the
RSVPs from
your VIPs.

Taking a vote

Management gurus constantly tell us about the importance of good team-work and decision-making. But how do you get a team to make a decision when you can't find most of the team members most of the time? You can use Outlook on an Exchange network as a decision-making tool if you take advantage of the Outlook Voting buttons.

Voting is a special feature of Outlook e-mail that adds buttons to an e-mail message sent to a group of people. When they get the message, recipients click a button to indicate their response. Outlook automatically tallies the responses so you can see which way the wind is blowing in your office.

To add voting buttons to an e-mail message you're creating, follow these steps while creating your message but before clicking the Send button. For more about creating messages, see Chapter 4.

1. **With a message open, click the Options tab.**

   The Message Options dialog box appears. You can click the Options button on the message toolbar instead. Either way, the Message Options dialog box appears.

2. **Click the Use Voting Button.**

   A list of suggested voting buttons appears. The suggested choices include the following, as shown in Figure 14-4:

   - Approve; Reject
   - Yes; No
   - Yes; No; Maybe
   - Custom

   If you choose Custom, type your own choices in the Message Options dialog box. Follow the pattern of the suggested choices; just separate your options with a semicolon. If you want to ask people to vote on the lunch menu, for example, include a range of choices such as Pizza;Burgers;Salad.

3. **Click the set of voting buttons that you want to use.**

   The set you choose (or enter) appears in the text box.

4. **Click Close.**

5. **Click Send.**

   And there you are! Democracy in action! Isn't that inspiring? When your recipients get your message, they can click the button of their choice and zoom their preference off to you.

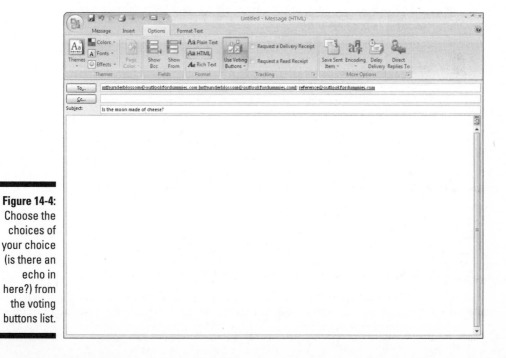

Figure 14-4:
Choose the choices of your choice (is there an echo in here?) from the voting buttons list.

Tallying votes

When the replies arrive, you'll see who chose what by looking at the subject of the replies. Messages from people who chose Approve, for example, start with the word *Approve;* rejection messages start with the word *Reject.*

You can also get a full tally of your vote by checking the Tracking tab on the copy of the message you send in your Sent Items folder. To do so, follow these steps:

1. **Click the Sent Items icon in the Navigation Pane.**

    Your list of sent messages appears.

2. **Double-click the message you sent to ask for a vote.**

    The message you chose opens.

3. **Click the Tracking tab.**

    The Tracking tab shows you the list of people you've asked for a vote — and how they voted. A banner at the top of the Tracking page tallies the votes (as shown in Figure 14-5).

Collaborating with Outlook and Exchange

One thing I've always found annoying about Outlook is the way certain features of Microsoft Exchange just show up in Outlook menus and tools even if you're not using Exchange. For example, the option to view another person's folder (which I explain in this chapter) shows up even if you're not using Outlook on an Exchange network. Without an Exchange Network, however, the feature doesn't work.

I focus the rest of this chapter on the features that work only if you have *both* Outlook and Exchange Server. Why confuse non-Exchange users by describing features they can't use?

If you use Outlook at home or in an office without Exchange Server, you won't be able to use the features I describe in the rest of this chapter. But take heart: little by little, Microsoft is finding ways to make Exchange-only features available to all Outlook users, so you can look over this section as a preview of things to come.

Giving delegate permissions

Good managers delegate authority. (That's what my assistant, Igor, says, anyway.) Extremely busy people sometimes give an assistant the job of managing the boss's calendar, schedule, and (sometimes) even e-mail. That way, the boss can concentrate on the big picture while the assistant dwells on the details.

When you designate a delegate in Outlook on an Exchange network, you give certain rights to the delegate you name — in particular, the right to look at whichever Outlook module you pick.

To name a delegate, follow these steps:

1. **Choose Tools ⇨ Options.**

   The Options dialog box appears.

2. **Click the Delegates tab.**

   The Delegates page appears.

3. **Click Add.**

   The Add Users dialog box appears.

4. **Double-click the name of each delegate you want to name.**

   The names you choose appear in the Add Users dialog box (as shown in Figure 14-6).

Figure 14-6:
Choose those you trust in the Add Users dialog box.

5. Click OK.

The Delegate Permissions dialog box appears (as shown in Figure 14-7) so you can choose exactly which permissions you want to give to your delegate(s).

6. Make any changes you want in the Delegate Permissions dialog box.

If you make no choices at all in the Delegate Permissions dialog box, then (by default) your delegate is granted Editor status in your calendar and Task List — which means that the delegate can read, create, and change items in those two Outlook modules.

7. Click OK.

The Delegate Permissions dialog box closes. The names you chose appear in the Options dialog box, as shown in Figure 14-8.

8. Click OK.

Figure 14-7:
Show how much trust you have in the Delegate Permissions dialog box.

Figure 14-8:
Check the Options dialog box to see who has permissions.

Opening someone else's folder

It's fairly common for a team of people who work closely together to share calendars or Task Lists so they not only can see what the other people are doing, but also enter appointments on behalf of a teammate (for example, if you work in a company that has sales and service people sitting side by side). As a service person, you may find it helpful if your partner on the sales side is allowed to enter appointments with a client on your calendar while you're out dealing with other clients. To do that, your partner needs to open your Calendar folder.

You can't open another person's Outlook folder unless that person has given you permission first, the way I describe in the preceding section. After you have permission, you can open the other person's folder by following these steps:

1. **Choose File ⇨ Open ⇨ Other User's Folder.**

   The Open Other User's Folder dialog box appears, as shown in Figure 14-9.

Figure 14-9:
Pick another person's folder to view.

2. **Click the Name button.**

   The Select Name dialog box appears. (It's really the Address Book.)

3. **Double-click the name of the person whose folder you want to open.**

   The Select Name dialog box closes; the name you double-clicked appears in the Open Other User's Folder dialog box.

4. **Click the triangle on the Folder box.**

   A list of the folders you can choose appears.

5. **Click the name of the folder you want to view.**

   The name of the folder you choose appears in the Folder box.

6. **Click OK.**

   The folder you pick appears in your Folder List.

Viewing Two Calendars Side by Side

It's pretty common for an executive to give an assistant the right to view the executive's calendar. That way the assistant can maintain the executive's schedule while the executive is busy doing other things. Sometimes, when you're working as someone's assistant, you need to see both the boss's calendar and your own calendar simultaneously. If you have the required rights (permissions), Outlook can display both calendars side by side — and you can compare schedules at a glance.

After you've gone through the steps to open someone else's calendar, you'll see a section near the top of the Navigation Pane labeled Other Calendars. There you'll see the names of people whose calendars you've opened. If you click the check box next to one of those names, that person's calendar appears on-screen right next to yours. (Your screen might look pretty cluttered when you put two busy schedules side by side, so you may need to switch to a one-day view to keep the screen comprehensible.) When you're done viewing two schedules, click the box in the Navigation Pane next to the other person's name to go back to viewing one calendar.

Setting access permissions

Many times, a busy executive gives his or her assistant the right to view and even edit the executive's entire Outlook account right from the assistant's desk. That way, the assistant organizes what the executive does, and the executive just goes out and does the job. This is known as granting access permissions, which is a lot like naming a delegate, as I describe in a prior section "Giving delegate permissions." When you grant access permissions, however, the power you're giving is broader; you're giving the assistant permission to use the entire account and even to make your Outlook folders a part of your Folder List.

Before people can open your schedule, you have to give them permission by following these steps:

1. **Right-click the Mailbox icon in the Navigation Pane.**

   A shortcut menu appears. If the Mailbox icon doesn't appear in the Navigation Pane, choose Go ➪ Folder List (or press Ctrl+6) to make it appear.

2. **Choose Properties.**

   The Properties dialog box appears.

3. **Click the Permissions tab.**

   The Permissions page appears (as shown in Figure 14-10).

Figure 14-10:
You can grant permission for viewing your folders to anyone on your network.

4. Click the Add button.

The Add Users dialog box, which is really the Global Address List, appears.

5. Double-click the name of the person to whom you want to give access.

The name you double-click appears in the Add Users box on the right side of the Add Users dialog box.

6. Click OK.

The Add Users dialog box closes and the name you chose appears in the Name box of the Properties page.

7. Click the name that you just added to the Name List in the Properties dialog box.

The name you click is highlighted to show you've selected it.

8. Click the scroll-down button (triangle) on the Permission Level List.

A list of available Permission Levels appears. Assigning a Permission Level gives a specific set of rights to the person to whom the level is assigned. For example, an editor can add, edit, change, or remove items from your Outlook folders, whereas a reviewer can only read items.

9. Pick the role you want to assign to the person you selected.

The role you chose appears in the Roles box. The check boxes following the Roles box change to reflect the tasks that the person is permitted to perform.

10. Click OK.

Now that you've given a person permission to see your account as a whole, you must give permission to see each folder in the account individually. You can either follow these steps for each icon on the Navigation Pane, or you can see the section "Giving delegate permissions" to grant access to another person.

However, you have no way of knowing whether people have given you permission to view their data unless you try to open one of their folders (or unless they tell you), which prevents nasty hackers from breaking into several people's data by stealing just one password.

Viewing two accounts

If your boss gives you permission to view his or her entire Outlook account, you can set up your copy of Outlook so both your folders and the boss's folders show up in your Outlook Folder List. When you want to see your calendar, click your calendar folder; when you want to see the boss's calendar, click the boss's calendar folder.

To add a second person's account to your view of Outlook, follow these steps:

1. **Right-click the Mailbox icon in the Navigation Pane.**

   A shortcut menu appears. If the Mailbox icon doesn't appear in the Navigation Pane, choose Go ➪ Folder List (or press Ctrl+6) to make it appear.

2. **Choose Properties.**

   The Properties dialog box appears.

3. **Click the Advanced button.**

   The Microsoft Exchange Server dialog box appears.

4. **Click the Advanced tab.**

   The Advanced page appears (as shown in Figure 14-11).

5. **Click Add.**

   The Add Mailbox dialog box appears.

6. **Type the name of the person whose account you want to add.**

   The name you type appears in the text box.

7. **Click OK.**

Figure 14-11:
Add someone else's folders to your Outlook collection.

If the person you chose didn't give you permission, you'll get an error message saying that the name you entered couldn't be matched to a name in the Address List. If that happens, make sure that the person you want to add really gave you the rights to his or her account.

After you add another person's account to Outlook, use the Folder List to see the new person's items. You'll see a new section in your Folder List called Mailbox, followed by the new person's name; that's where that person's Outlook items are located. When you click an icon in your Navigation Pane, you'll see your own Outlook items. If you like, you can create a new section in your Navigation Pane and add icons for the other person's items. See Chapter 2 for more about adding items to the Navigation Pane.

Assigning tasks

As Tom Sawyer could tell you, anything worth doing is worth getting someone else to do. Outlook on an Exchange network enables you to assign a task to another person in your company and keep track of that person's progress.

To assign a task to someone else, follow these steps:

1. **Right-click an item in your Task List.**

   A shortcut menu appears.

2. **Choose Assign Task.**

   A Task form appears.

3. **Type the name of the person to whom you're assigning the task in the To box just as you would on an e-mail message.**

   The person's name appears in the To box (as shown in Figure 14-12).

4. **Click Send.**

   The task is sent to the person to whom you've assigned it.

The person to whom you addressed the task will get an e-mail message with special buttons marked Accept and Decline, much like the special meeting request message that I discuss earlier in this chapter. When the person clicks Accept, the task is automatically added to his or her Task List in Outlook. If the person clicks Decline, that person is fired. Okay, just kidding, the person is not actually fired. Not yet, anyway.

Figure 14-12:
When in
doubt, send
it out.

Sending a status report

People who give out tasks really like the Assign Task feature. People who
have to do those tasks are much less enthusiastic. If you're a Task Getter
more often than you're a Task Giver, you have to look at the bright side:
Outlook on an Exchange network can also help the boss stay informed about
how much you're doing — and doing and doing!

You may have noticed that the task form has a box called Status and another
called % Complete. If you keep the information in those boxes up-to-date, you
can constantly remind the Big Cheese of your valuable contributions by sending status reports.

To send a status report, follow these steps:

1. **Double-click any task.**

   A Task form opens.

2. **Choose Actions ➪ Send Status Report.**

   A To box appears, as in an e-mail message, and the name of the person
   who assigned the task already appears in the To box.

3. **Enter any explanation you want to send about the task in the text box at the bottom of the form.**

   The text that you type appears in the form.

4. **Click Send.**

You can send status reports as often as you like — weekly, daily, hourly. It's probably a good idea to leave enough time between status reports to complete some tasks.

About Address Books

Outlook still uses several different Address Books that are really part of Microsoft Exchange Server. The Address Books involve several separate, independent lists of names and e-mail addresses — it's pretty confusing. Microsoft simplified the issue of dealing with Address Books in Outlook 2002 and later versions, but that doesn't help if you use Outlook on a large corporate network. I'll try to help you make sense of it all, anyway.

The Outlook Contacts List contains all kinds of personal information, whereas an Address Book focuses on just e-mail addresses. An Address Book can also deal with the nitty-gritty details of actually sending your message to people on your corporate e-mail system, especially if that system is Microsoft Exchange Server.

Here's the lowdown on your plethora of Address Books:

- **The Global Address List:** If you're using Outlook on a corporate network, the Global Address List, which your system administrator maintains, normally contains the names and e-mail addresses of all the people in your company. The Global Address List makes it possible to address an e-mail message to anybody in your company without having to look up the e-mail address.

- **The Outlook Address Book:** The Contacts Address Book is really the list of e-mail addresses from the Contacts List. Outlook automatically creates the Contacts Address Book to enable you to add the names of people in your Contacts List to a Personal Distribution List.

- **Additional Address Books:** If you create additional folders for Outlook contacts, those folders also become separate Address Books. Your system administrator can also create additional Address Books.

If you're lucky, you'll never see the Address Book. All the addresses of all the people you ever send e-mail to are listed in the Global Address List that somebody else maintains, such as on a corporate network. Under those circumstances, Outlook is a dream. You don't need to know what an Address

Book is most of the time — you just type the name of the person you're e-mailing in the To box of a message. Outlook checks the name for spelling and takes care of sending your message. You'd swear that a tiny psychic lives inside your computer who knows just what you need.

Under less-than-ideal conditions, when you try to send a message, Outlook either complains that it doesn't know how to send the message or can't figure out whom you're talking about. Then you have to mess with the address. That situation happens only when the address isn't listed in one of the Address Books or isn't in a form that Outlook understands. For these cases, you must either enter the full address manually or add your recipient's name and address to your Address Book.

Going Public with Public Folders

Another popular feature of Outlook on an Exchange network is the ability to use public folders. *Public folders* are places that a whole group of people can look at and add items to. You can have a public folder for tasks or contacts. You can also create a public folder that contains messages, a lot like your Inbox, except that everybody can add messages and read the same set of messages. Such an arrangement is often called a *bulletin board;* you post a message, someone replies to it, a third party then replies to both of you, and so on. It's a method of conducting a group conversation without having all the parties to the conversation available at the same time.

In Outlook, public folders look just like any other folders. A public folder may contain a Contacts List that the entire company shares or a Task List that an entire department uses. You can set up a public discussion folder for an ongoing group conference about topics of interest to everyone sharing the folder, such as current company news. You can also use a public discussion folder to collect opinions about decisions that have to be made or as an intracompany classified ad system. You can organize as a folder any kind of information that you'd like to exchange among groups of people on your network.

When you click a public folder, you see a list of items that looks like a list of e-mail messages, except that all the messages are addressed to the folder rather than to a person. In a public folder, you can change your view of the items, add items, or reply to items that someone else entered.

Viewing a public folder

Your company may maintain a public folder for an ongoing online discussion about important issues in your business or as a company bulletin board for announcements about activities, benefits, and other news.

To view a public folder, follow along:

1. **Choose Go ⇨ Folder List (or press Ctrl +6).**

   The Folder List appears.

2. **Click the name of the folder you want to see.**

   The list of items in the folder appears.

In public folders, you can double-click the title of any item that you see to view the contents of that item.

Adding new items

Many public folders are organized as open discussions in which anyone can put in his or her two cents' worth. All the messages can be read by anybody, so everybody reads and replies to everybody else. If you view a folder and find it's full of messages from different people all replying to one another, you're looking at a discussion folder.

To add new items to a public folder, follow these steps:

1. **Choose View ⇨ Folder List (or press Ctrl +6).**

   The Folder List appears.

2. **Click the name of the folder.**

   The list of messages in the folder appears.

3. **Choose File ⇨ New ⇨ Post in This Folder.**

   The New Item form appears.

4. **Type a subject and your message.**

5. **Click Post.**

Now your message is part of the list of items in the folder.

Replying to items in an existing public discussion folder

Good manners and good sense say that if you want to join a discussion, the best thing to do is respond to what the other members of the discussion are saying. But be nice — don't flame. Posting nasty responses to people in an online discussion group is called *flaming*. Flaming is not well regarded but also is not uncommon. Flaming creates online conversations that most people don't want to participate in. What good is a discussion when nobody talks? Besides, flaming in the workplace can get you fired. So cool down.

When you're participating in public folder discussions at work, assume that everyone in the company — from the top executives to the newest temp — will read what you've written. Check your spelling, DON'T WRITE IN CAPITAL LETTERS (IT LOOKS LIKE YOU'RE SHOUTING), and use discretion in what you say and how you say it. The same rules apply to interoffice e-mail; you don't know who reads what you send.

To reply to items in a public discussion folder, follow these steps:

1. **Double-click the item to which you want to reply.**

   The item opens so you can read it.

2. **Click the Post button in the toolbar.**

   The Discussion Reply form appears. The text of the message to which you're replying is already posted in the form.

3. **Type your subject and reply.**

   Your reply appears in a different color than the original text.

4. **Click Post.**

Your item joins the list of discussion items.

Moving items to a public folder

Not all public folders are discussion folders. Public folders can be designed to hold any type of item. You can share lists of tasks, calendars, or files of other types. You don't have to create a public folder item in the folder where you want the item to end up. You can create a task in your own Task List, for example, and then move it to a public task folder.

To move items to a public folder, follow these steps:

1. **Right-click the item that you want to move.**

   A menu appears.

2. **Click Move to Folder.**

   A Move Items dialog box that includes the Folder List appears.

3. **Click the folder to which you want to send the item.**

   The name of the folder you clicked is highlighted.

4. **Click OK.**

   Your item moves to its new folder.

Outsourcing Microsoft Exchange

Even if you're allergic to buzzwords, the term *outsourcing* still has its appeal. If you're an entrepreneur or freelancer, you know how distracted you can get with the details of running your business; you simply don't have time to fuss with the details of running an e-mail system such as Microsoft Exchange.

If you think you need the power of Microsoft Exchange but don't have time to deal with the details, plenty of companies out there are ready to provide Microsoft Exchange services to you

at the drop of the hat. These companies are known as ASPs (application service providers); lots of them are standing by with Microsoft Exchange servers you can log on to for as little as $10.00 per person per month. I used a company called www.mi8.com for all the examples in this book. I encourage you to check them out. If you'd like to shop around, you can search the Web for lists of other companies offering what they call *Hosted Exchange Service*.

For the public record

You may be using public folders without even knowing it. In Outlook, all folders look the same, whether you create them yourself on your own PC or they're on a corporate network or the Internet. All you really need to know about public folders is that they're public, so anybody who has access to the public folder can see whatever you post to that public folder. You can also create your own public folders; check with your system administrator to see whether you have the rights to create public folders and a place to put them.

Using SharePoint Team Services

Microsoft actually provides more than one method of using Outlook to collaborate with other people. I spend the first part of this chapter describing Microsoft Exchange, the most powerful collaboration tool you can connect to Outlook. But a second product, called SharePoint Team Services, also connects to Outlook and also helps you collaborate.

SharePoint is basically an Internet tool that helps you coordinate meetings, projects, and activities with other people. Most of the work you do through SharePoint can be done only through your Web browser, but the latest version of SharePoint can also set up folders in Outlook that enable you to view key information from a SharePoint Web site even when you're not online. SharePoint doesn't tie into Outlook nearly as closely as Microsoft Exchange, but it does provide some collaboration features that you could use with people outside your office.

In most cases, you won't have a choice about whether to use Microsoft Exchange or SharePoint Team Services; someone else (such as your system administrators) will have decided that for you. In fact, you may need to use both products; Outlook connects to Exchange and SharePoint at the same time without any problem. Chances are, if you ever get involved with SharePoint Team Services, you'll do so because someone asks you to join a shared team. If no one ever asks, you don't need to think about it, and you can skip this section.

Joining a SharePoint team

The first key to unlocking SharePoint is an e-mail that asks you to join a SharePoint team. The message is simply an ordinary e-mail containing your user name, password, and a link to the SharePoint site. Simply click the link and log in with the name and password you received in the e-mail. When you click the link that comes in the e-mail, your Web browser opens to a site devoted to the activities of the team you've been asked to join. Every SharePoint site looks different; click the links on the site to see what it has to offer.

Linking Outlook to SharePoint data

Certain parts of a SharePoint Web site can be tied into Outlook so the information from the site automatically appears in Outlook. If you see an icon on the SharePoint Web site labeled Link to Calendar or Link to Contacts, you can just click that icon to send the information from that page straight to Outlook.

Viewing SharePoint data from Outlook

Information that SharePoint sends to Outlook shows up in its own set of SharePoint folders. If you open your Folder List, you see SharePoint folders as part of the list. Just click any SharePoint folder to see what's inside. You can view SharePoint information in Outlook exactly the same way you view Outlook calendar and contact information. But you can't typically add new items to SharePoint folders through Outlook; you normally add information to SharePoint through your Web browser.

Updating SharePoint data from Outlook

Don't be deceived when you look at SharePoint folders in Outlook. The information you find in these folders is not automatically updated in Outlook; you have to link back to the SharePoint Web site to have updated data appear

So when are you most likely to run across SharePoint, and when will you use Exchange? In my opinion, Exchange is best suited for collaboration among people who share the same e-mail system, while SharePoint is better suited for people who need to collaborate but don't share the same e-mail system.

For example, suppose you work in a small law firm where everyone's e-mail comes to a similar-looking e-mail address, such as john.doe@smalllaw.com. In this situation, your best bet for working with people inside the firm is to collaborate via Exchange. If you're also a member of the local bar association, you might take advantage of SharePoint for organizing your chapter's meetings and other activities through the association's Web site.

Chapter 15

Keeping Secrets Safe with Outlook Security

*I*n the movies, computer hackers know everything — your credit card balance, Social Security number, what you ate for breakfast — everything. There doesn't seem to be a single scrap of personal information that a computer hacker in a movie can't find out.

Are real-life computer hackers just as brilliant and dangerous? Not really. Most crimes involving theft of personal information don't come from hackers sneaking into personal computers. More often than not, these losers dig credit-card slips out of a restaurant dumpster, or they just make a phone call and trick some poor slob into revealing a password.

Even though there isn't some hacker out there who knows what you bought at the Piggly Wiggly (or cares, for that matter), it may be wise to think about security when it comes to your e-mail and personal information. If you work in a corporation, you may be required by law to maintain certain standards of security over the messages you send and receive.

Outlook includes features that enable you to keep your secrets secret, to keep your identity secure, and to be sure that the messages you receive actually came from the people who seem to have sent them. In most cases, you'll need to add some small program to Outlook to enable these advanced security features, but once you've installed these features, you never have to fuss with them again.

If security is a really big deal to you (as it is to people in the finance, law-enforcement, and defense industries), you may want to look into the more sophisticated security systems starting to turn up. Several high-tech companies offer systems for confirming identity and ensuring message security, using fingerprint readers, eye scanners, and even gizmos that can recognize your face. Although many such systems can hook right into Outlook to make short work of message security, most of them cost quite a bit more than the average person needs to spend. In this chapter, I stick to discussing the security features that Outlook offers right out of the box.

Getting a Digital ID

You probably receive messages every day from people you've never met. And I'll bet you don't spend much time wondering whether the messages you receive actually come from the people they seem to be — but you might need to think about that from time to time. After all, it's possible for sneaky hackers to send out e-mail messages that appear to come from someone else. So how can you tell if the message actually came from the person who appears to have sent it? Of course, if you know the senders personally, you can simply phone them to verify that what you received is what they sent. But a quicker, high-tech approach is to use what's called a *digital signature* — a tiny piece of secret code mixed in with your message to prove three things:

- That the message really comes from the person who seems to have sent it.
- That the person who seems to have sent the message really is the person he claims to be.
- That the person who sent the message sent it intentionally. It's like putting your signature on a check; it shows that you really mean to send a specific message.

If you want to take advantage of Outlook's security features, the first step to take is to get yourself a Digital ID. If you work in a large organization, your employer may have obtained that for you — and your local computer gurus may have installed all the software — in which case, you can skip these steps. If you want to get a Digital ID for your own use, you can get one from one of the many companies that issue and maintain Digital ID services by following these steps:

1. **Click Tools ⇨ Trust Center.**

   The Trust Center screen appears.

2. **Click the words E-Mail Security.**

   The E-Mail Security page appears (as shown in Figure 15-1).

Figure 15-1:
The E-Mail
Security
page is
where you
can start
looking for
your Digital
ID.

3. Click the button labeled Get a Digital ID.

A Web site opens, offering a range of choices for obtaining a Digital ID.

Quite a few companies offer Digital IDs — some for free, others for a fee. The range of companies offering this service varies over time; your best bet is to check the Web site to see which you prefer. After you pick a provider for your Digital ID, you fill out a number of forms and pick a password for the ID. You'll also need to exchange several e-mails with a provider of the Digital ID; that's how you prove that your e-mail address is really yours.

Sending Digitally Signed Messages

Once you have a Digital ID, the simplest thing you can do is to send someone a message containing your Digital Signature. A Digitally Signed message does more than simply assure your recipient that you are really yourself — who else would you want to be, after all? Suppose you want to send an encrypted message that only your recipient can read. To do so, you have to send at least one Digitally Signed message first so Outlook can capture details about your Digital ID.

Once you've obtained a Digital ID, you can send a message with a Digital Signature by following these steps:

1. **While creating a message, click the Options tab at the top of the message screen.**

   The Options Ribbon appears.

2. **Click the icon to the right of More Options.**

   The Message Options dialog box appears.

3. **Click the Security Settings button.**

   The Security Properties dialog box appears (as shown in Figure 15-2).

4. **Click the Add Digital Signature to This Message check box.**

5. **Click Send.**

   The Signing Data with Your Private Exchange Key dialog box appears.

6. **Click OK.**

   Your message is sent.

Figure 15-2:
The Security
Properties
dialog box
enables you
to sign
messages
one at a
time.

Adding a digital signature slows down the process of sending a message somewhat because your computer has to check with the computer that issued your Digital ID to verify your signature. But because Outlook does check your Digital ID, your recipient can be sure that your message really came from you and that's the whole point of digital signatures.

You can also set up Microsoft Outlook to attach a digital signature to every message you send, if you like. Just choose Tools ⇨ Trust Center, choose the E-Mail Security tab, and then click Add Digital Signature to Outgoing Messages. In some industries, you may be required to add digital signatures to every outgoing message — but for most people, that's probably overkill.

Receiving Digitally Signed Messages

When you receive a message that contains a digital signature, you'll see a little icon in the upper-right corner of the message that looks like a little red prize ribbon you'd win at the county fair for the best peach preserves. Figure 15-3 shows it affixed to a message.

You don't really need to do anything when you get a message like that; the icon itself verifies that the message really came from the person it claims to have come from. But if you're unusually curious, you can find out more about the person who signed the message by clicking the icon and reading the dialog box that appears; see Figure 15-4. What you see should simply confirm what you already know: The person who sent the message is exactly who they say they are, the genuine article, the Real McCoy.

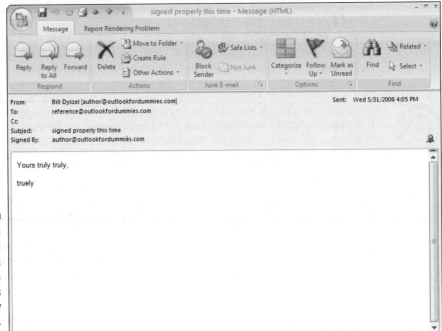

Figure 15-3:
That red
ribbon tells
you that the
message is
digitally
signed.

Figure 15-4:
To get the
lowdown on
someone's
digital
signature,
right-click
the red
ribbon icon.

Encrypting Messages

Back in the days of radio, millions of children loved to exchange "secret" messages that they encoded with Little Orphan Annie's Secret Decoder Ring. Outlook does something similar, using a feature called Encryption. Unfortunately, you don't get a colorful plastic ring with Outlook. On the other hand, you don't have to save your box tops to get one — the decoder is built right into Outlook. When you encrypt a message, your system scrambles the contents of your outgoing message so that only your intended recipient can read your message.

Before you can send someone an encrypted message using Outlook's encryption feature, both you and the person to whom you're sending your encrypted message need to have obtained a Digital Certificate, as I describe earlier in this chapter. Also, your intended recipient needs to have sent you at least one message with a Digital Signature, which I also describe earlier, so that Outlook recognizes that person as someone you can trust. Outlook can be pretty suspicious; even your mother can't send you an encrypted message unless you've sent her your Digital Signature first. Can you imagine? Your own mother! But I digress.

If you want to send an encrypted message to someone who meets all the requirements, follow these steps:

1. **While creating a message, click the Options tab at the top of the message screen.**

   The Options Ribbon appears.

2. **Click the icon to the right of More Options.**

   The Message Options dialog box appears.

3. **Click the Security Settings button.**

   The Security Properties dialog box appears.

4. **Click the Encrypt Message Contents and Attachments check box.**

5. **Click Send.**

   A Signing Data with Your Private Exchange Key dialog box appears.

6. **Click OK.**

   Your message is sent.

When you receive an encrypted message, the contents of the message don't appear in the Reading Pane; you have to double-click the message to open it. In fact, if you work in a big organization, your network may deliver the message to you as an attachment to a serious-sounding message warning you that encrypted messages can't be scanned for viruses.

Other Security Programs for Outlook

Lots of people are concerned about the security of the information they send by e-mail, so lots of companies offer products to help people feel more secure. Many of the products you can buy to secure and encrypt your messages are so powerful it's illegal to take them out of the United States. Some of the best-known vendors of add-on security products for Outlook include

- PGP Corporation at www.pgp.com
- RSA Corporation at www.rsa.com

Chapter 16

See It Your Way: Organizing and Customizing Outlook

. . . .

In This Chapter

▶ Using views

▶ Changing columns

▶ Sorting lists

▶ Grouping items in your table

▶ Saving your own views

▶ Customizing Outlook menus and toolbars

. . . .

*U*ser interface is a fancy term for the arrangement of screens, menus, and doodads on your computer. The people who write computer programs spend lots of time and money trying to figure out how best to arrange stuff on the screen to make a program like Outlook easy to use.

But one person's dream screen can be another person's nightmare. Some people like to read words on the screen that say what to do; other people like colorful icons with pictures to click. Other people prefer to see information in neat rows and columns; still others like to see their information arranged more (shall we say) informally.

Outlook enables you to display your information in an endless variety of arrangements and views. There's even a button labeled Organize that shows you what choices are available for slicing and dicing the information you've saved in Outlook. This chapter shows you many of the best steps you can take after you click the Organize button.

Organizing Outlook

You can get a feel for how many ways Outlook can help organize your information by choosing Tools ➪ Organize. (Wow. If only we had one of those buttons in real life.) If you can't figure out which icon in the toolbar is the Organize button, you'll see it pictured in the Tools menu next to the word Organize.

When you click the Organize button, a new section appears in Outlook's main screen, showing you which tools are available to organize the information in the module you're using. The tools that tidy up your e-mail, for example, are different from the tools you use to straighten out your calendar.

Two tools show up in the Organize window no matter what Outlook module you're using — Folders and Views. The most common way people use folders is for organizing e-mail, so I cover folders, along with other e-mail–management tools, in Chapter 6.

Enjoying the Views

Choosing a view is like renting a car. You can choose a model with the features you want, regardless of whether the car is a convertible, minivan, or luxury sedan. All cars are equipped with different features — radios, air conditioning, power cup holders, and so on — that you can use (or not use) as you please. Some rental agencies offer unlimited free mileage. Outlook views are much more economical, though. In fact, they're free.

Every Outlook module has its own selection of views. The calendar has (among others) a view that looks calendar-like. The Contacts module includes a view that looks like an address card. The Tasks module includes a Timeline view. All modules enable you to use at least one type of Table view, which organizes your data in the old-fashioned row-and-column arrangement.

Each type of view is organized to make something about your collection of information obvious at first glance. You can change the way that you view a view by sorting, filtering, or grouping. You can create an endless number of ways to organize and view the information that you save in Outlook. How you decide to view information depends on what kind of information you have and how you plan to use what you have. You can't go too wrong with views, because you can easily create new views if the old ones get messed up. So feel free to experiment.

You don't have to do anything to see a view; Outlook is *always* displaying a view. The *view* is the thing that takes up most of the screen most of the time. The view (or the Information Viewer, in official Microsoftese) is one of only two parts of Outlook that you can't turn off. (You also can't turn off the menu bar.) Most people don't even know that they have a choice of Outlook views; they just use the views that show up the first time they use Outlook. So now you're one step ahead of the game.

Each view has a name, which you can see in several different places:

- ✔ When you click the Organize button and choose Using Views, the current view's name is highlighted.
- ✔ Sometimes the list of available views also appears in the Navigation Pane, but not always.
- ✔ If all else fails, refer to the Current View menu, where a mark appears next to the current view's name.

To see the Current View menu, choose View ➪ Current View. The Current View menu lists all the views available in the current module.

Table/List view

All modules contain some version of the *Table view* — a rectangle made up of rows and columns. Some Outlook menus also refer to this arrangement as a *List view*. In either case, if you create a new item (by adding a new task to your Tasks List, for example), a new row turns up in the Table view. You see one row for each task in the Table view (as shown in Figure 16-1).

Figure 16-1:
The Tasks module in a Table view.

The names of Table views often contain the word *List,* as in Simple List, Phone List, or just List. The word *List* means they form a plain-vanilla table of items, just like a grocery list. Other Table view names start with the word *By,* which means that items in the view are grouped by a certain type of information, such as entry type or name of contact. I discuss grouped views later in the chapter and show you how to group items your own way.

Icons view

Icons view is the simplest view — just a bunch of icons with names thrown together on-screen (as shown in Figure 16-2). The only Icons views that come with Outlook are for viewing notes and file folders. Icons view doesn't show a great deal of information, and some people like it that way. I like to see more detailed information, so I stay with Table views. There's nothing wrong with using Icons view most of the time; you can easily switch to another view if you ever need to see more.

Figure 16-2:
The Notes
module in
Icons view.

Timeline view

Timeline views show you a set of small icons arranged across the screen. Icons higher on the screen represent created items or tasks that began earlier in the day. Icons farther to the left were created on an earlier date; see Figure 16-3.

The Timeline in the Tasks module also draws a line that represents the length of time needed to perform a task if its starting and ending times were specified previously.

A Timeline view includes four toolbar buttons that enable you to change the length of time you want to view:

- ✔ Today
- ✔ Day (not necessarily today)
- ✔ Week
- ✔ Month

As you can in all other view settings, you can click to move between one-day and seven-day views and back. (It's like changing television channels, but you don't have to argue over who gets the remote.)

Figure 16-3:
Tasks
arranged in
the Timeline
view.

Card views

Card views are designed for the Contacts module. Each contact item gets its own little block of information; see Figure 16-4. Each little block displays a little or a lot of information about the item, depending on what kind of card it is. (See Chapter 7 for more about the different views in the Contacts module.)

The Cards view shows you only a few items at a time because the cards are so big. To make it easier to find a name in your Contacts List, type the first letter of the name that your contact is filed under. Before you know it, you see that person's Address Card. Also, be consistent with name order: Always put the first name first (or last . . . whichever you think you might like best) when entering a contact.

Day/Week/Month view

Day/Week/Month view is designed particularly for the calendar. Like a Timeline view, this view adds Day, Work Week, Week, and Month buttons to the toolbar, enabling you to switch between views easily. All these views also display a monthly calendar. You can click any date in it to switch your view to that date (as shown in Figure 16-5).

Figure 16-4:
See your contacts in Card view.

Figure 16-5:
Starting a
day in the
life of your
calendar.

Playing with Columns in Table or List View

Table views (or List views) show you the most detailed information about the items that you've created; these views also enable you to organize the information in the greatest number of ways with the least effort. Okay, Table views look a little dull, but they get you where you need to go.

Table views are organized in columns and rows. Each row displays information for one item — one appointment in your calendar, one task in your Tasks List, or one person in your Contacts list. Adding a row is easy. Just add a new item by pressing Ctrl+N, and then fill in the information you want for that item. Getting rid of a row is easy, too. Just delete the item: Select the item by clicking it with your mouse, and then press the Delete key.

The columns in a Table view show you pieces of information about each item. Most Outlook modules can store far more data about an item than you can display on-screen in row-and-column format. The Contacts list, for example, holds more than 90 bits of information about every person in your list. If each person was represented by one row, you would need more than 90 columns to display everything.

Adding a column

Outlook starts you out with a limited number of columns in the Phone List view of your Contacts list. (Remember that the names of Table views usually have the word *List* in them somewhere.) If you want more columns, you can easily add some. You can display as many columns as you want in Outlook, but you may have to scroll across the screen to see the information that you want to see.

To add a column in any Table view, follow these steps:

1. **Right-click any column title in the gray header row of the column.**

   A shortcut menu appears.

2. **Pick Field Chooser from the shortcut menu.**

   The Field Chooser dialog box appears.

3. **Select the type of field that you want to add.**

   The words "Frequently-Used Fields" appear in the text box at the top of the Field Chooser. Those words mean that the types of fields most people like to add are already listed. If the name of the field you want isn't in one of the gray boxes at the bottom of the Field Chooser dialog box, you can pull down the menu that Frequently-Used Fields is part of and see what's available.

4. **Drag the field into the table.**

   Be sure to drag the new item to the table's top row, where the heading names are (as shown in Figure 16-6).

Notice that the names in the Field Chooser are in the same kind of gray box as the headers of each column. (If they look alike, they must belong together, like Michael and Lisa Marie. Right? Well, okay, maybe that's not the best example.) Two red arrows show you where your new field will end up when you drop it off.

Moving a column

Moving columns is even easier than adding columns. Just drag the column heading to where you want it; see Figure 16-7. Two little red arrows appear as you're dragging the heading to show you where the column will end up when you release the mouse button.

Figure 16-6:
The
Requested
By field
has been
dragged to
the top row
of the table.

Figure 16-7:
Moving the
Business
Phone
column.

Columns = fields

I promised to tell you how to add a column, and now I'm telling you about fields. What gives? Well, columns are fields, see? No? Well, think of it this way: In your checkbook, your check record has a column of the names of the people to whom you wrote checks and another column for the amounts of those checks. When you actually write a check, you write the name of the payee in a certain field on the check; the amount goes in a different field. So you enter tidbits of information as fields on the check, but you show them as columns in the check record. That's exactly how it works in Outlook. You enter somebody's name, address, and phone number in fields when you create a new item, but the Table view shows the same information to you in columns. When you're adding a column, you're adding a field. Same thing.

Formatting a column

Some fields contain too much information to fit in their columns. Dates are prime offenders. Outlook normally displays dates in this format: Sun 7/4/05 4:14 PM. I normally don't care which day of the week a date falls on, so I reformat the column to 7/4/05 4:14 PM and save the other space for something that I really want to know.

To change the formatting of a column, follow these steps:

1. **Right-click the heading of a column.**

   A menu appears.

2. **Choose Format Columns.**

   The Format Columns dialog box appears (as shown in Figure 16-8).

3. **Choose a format type from the Format menu.**

   Pick whatever suits your fancy. Some columns contain information that can be formatted only one way, such as names and categories. Information in number columns (especially dates) can be formatted in a variety of ways.

4. **Click OK.**

   Your column is reformatted.

Changing a column format affects only that column in that view of that module. If you want to change the formats of other views and modules, you have to change them one at a time.

Figure 16-8:
The Format
Columns
dialog box.

Widening or shrinking a column

Widening or shrinking a column is even easier than moving a column.
Here's how:

1. **Move the mouse pointer to the right edge of the column that you want
   to widen or shrink until the pointer becomes a two-headed arrow.**

   Making that mouse pointer turn into a two-headed arrow takes a bit of
   dexterity. If you find the procedure difficult, you can use the Format
   Column procedure that I describe in the preceding section. Type a
   number in the Width box — bigger numbers for wider boxes and smaller
   numbers for narrower boxes.

2. **Drag the edge of the column until it's the width that you desire.**

   The two-headed arrow creates a thin line that you can drag to resize the
   column. (Figure 16-9 shows a column being widened.) What you see is
   what you get.

If you're not really sure how wide a column needs to be, just double-click the
right edge of the column header. When you double-click that spot, Outlook
does a trick called *size-to-fit,* which widens or narrows a column to exactly the
size of the widest piece of data in the column.

Figure 16-9:
Widening
the Status
column.

Removing a column

You can remove columns that you don't want to look at. To remove a column, follow these steps:

1. **Right-click the heading of the column that you want to remove.**

   A menu appears.

2. **Choose Remove This Column.**

   Zap! It's gone!

Don't worry too much about deleting columns. When you zap a column, the field remains in the item. You can use the column-adding procedure (which I describe earlier in this chapter) to put it back. If you're confused by this whole notion of columns and fields, see the sidebar "Columns = fields" elsewhere in this chapter.

Sorting

Sorting just means putting your list in order. In fact, a list is always in some kind of order. Sorting just changes the order.

You can tell what order your list is sorted in by looking for triangles in headings. A heading with a triangle in it means that the entire list is sorted by the information in that column. If the column has numbers in it, and if the triangle's large side is at the top, the list goes from largest to smallest number. Columns that contain text get sorted in alphabetical order. *A* is the smallest letter, and *Z* is the largest.

From Table view

This is by far the easiest way: When sorting from Table view, click the heading of a column you want sorted. The entire table is sorted according to the column you clicked — by date, name, or whatever.

From the Sort dialog box

Although clicking a column is the easiest way to sort, doing so enables you to sort on only one column. You may want to sort on two or more columns.

To sort on two or more columns, follow these steps:

1. **Choose View ⇨ Current View ⇨ Customize Current View.**

   The Customize View dialog box appears.

2. **Click the Sort button.**

   The Sort dialog box appears.

3. **From the Sort Items By menu, choose the first field that you want to sort by.**

   Choose carefully; a much larger list of fields is in the list than is usually in the view. It's confusing.

4. **Choose Ascending or Descending sort order.**

   That means to choose whether to sort from smallest to largest (ascending) or vice versa (descending).

5. Repeat Steps 3 and 4 for each additional field that you want to sort.

As the dialog box implies, the first column that you select is the most important. The entire table is sorted according to that field — and then by the fields you pick later, in the order you select them. If you sort your phone list by company first and then by name, for example, your list begins with the names of the people who work for a certain company, displayed alphabetically, followed by the names of the people who work for another company, and so on.

6. Click OK.

Your list is sorted.

Grouping

Sorting and grouping are similar. Both procedures organize items in your table according to columns. *Grouping* is different from sorting, however; it creates bunches of similar items that you can open or close. You can look at only the bunches that interest you and ignore all the other bunches.

For example, when you balance your checkbook, you probably *sort* your checks by check number. At tax time, you *group* your checks; you make a pile of the checks for medical expenses, another pile of checks for charitable deductions, and another pile of checks for the money that you invested in *For Dummies* books. Then you can add up the amounts that you spent in each category and enter those figures in your tax return.

Grouping views with a few mouse clicks

The quickest way to group items is to right-click the heading of the column you want to group by, and then choose Group by This Field. The Group By box automatically appears, and the name of the field you chose automatically appears in the Group By box. Isn't that slick?

Grouping views with drag-and-drop

The next-simplest way to group items is to open the Group By box and drag a column heading into it (as shown in Figure 16-10).

Here's how you group items by dragging and dropping a column heading:

1. **Open the Advanced toolbar by choosing View ➪ Toolbars ➪ Advanced.**

   The Advanced toolbar displays the Group By Box button, normally the third button from the right. The Group By Box button contains an icon that looks like a box with some lines in it.

2. **Click the Group By Box button on the Advanced toolbar.**

   The table drops down slightly, and a box appears above the table, proclaiming Drag a Column Header Here to Group by That Column.

3. **Drag to the Group By box the header of the column that contains the data you want to group by.**

   You can drag several fields up to the Group By box to create groups based on more than one column. Figure 16-11 shows an example using two.

Figure 16-11:
Your
Contacts list
grouped
by two
headings —
State and
Category.

Using the Group By dialog box

Just as you have a second way to sort your listing, you have a second way to group your listing. Just use the Group By dialog box.

To group your list, follow these steps:

1. **Choose View ⇨ Current View ⇨ Customize Current View.**

   The Customize View dialog box appears. If you see the words Customize Current View in the Navigation Pane, you can also click those words to open the View Summary dialog box.

2. **Click the Group By button.**

   The Group By dialog box appears (as shown in Figure 16-12).

3. **Choose the first field that you want to group the view by.**

   The list has more fields than are showing in the table. If you choose to group by a field that's not showing in your table, you can check the Show Field in View check box, as shown in Figure 16-12.

You may also want to choose whether you want your groups to be sorted in Ascending or Descending alphabetical order, although that's less important when you're grouping.

4. Choose any other fields by which you want to group the view.

If you group by too many columns, your list will be harder rather than easier to use.

5. Click OK.

Your list is grouped by as many fields as you want to use for the purpose.

If you've ever used the Search and Replace feature in Microsoft Word, you might wish you could do the same trick in Outlook. Unfortunately, Outlook doesn't really have a search and replace function — but you can take advantage of Grouped views to change lots of information quickly. For example, if you know lots of people who work for a certain company and that company changes its name, you can change the company name for all your contacts at that company by using a grouped view. Just go to your Contacts list, change one person's record to reflect the new company name, then choose the By Company view. The person whose record you changed will be in a different group than all the others. Drag the names of people grouped under the old company name to the new company section, and they'll all get changed automatically.

Figure 16-12:
The Group By dialog box with the Show Field in View box checked.

Viewing grouped items

A grouped view shows you the names of the columns that you used to create the grouped view. If you click the Contacts icon and choose By Company view (which is a grouped view), you see gray bars with an icon at the right. The word *Company* appears next to the icon because that's the column that the view is grouped on. A company name appears next to the word Company; the grouped view includes a gray bar for each company in the list.

The icon at the left end of the gray bar is either a plus sign or a minus sign. A plus sign means that there's more to be seen. Click the plus sign, and the group opens, revealing the other items that belong to the group. A minus sign means that there's nothing more to see; what you see is what you get in that group.

If you click the gray bar itself but not the icon, you select the entire group. You can delete the group if you select the gray bar and press the Delete key. When a group bar is selected, it's dark gray rather than light gray, like all the others.

Viewing headings only

You can click the plus and minus signs one at a time to open and close individual groups, or you can open or close all the groups simultaneously.

To open or close groups, follow these steps:

1. **Simply choose View ⇨ Expand/Collapse Groups.**

   I think expanding and collapsing are dramatic words for what you're doing with these groups. It's not like Scarlett O'Hara getting the vapors; it's just revealing (expanding) or hiding (collapsing) the contents.

2. **To open a single selected group, choose Collapse This Group or Expand This Group.**

3. **To expand or collapse all the groups, choose Expand All or Collapse All.**

What could be easier?

Saving Custom Views

If you're used to saving documents in your word processor, you're familiar with the idea of saving views. When you make any of the changes to a view that I describe earlier in this chapter, you can save the changes as a new view, or make the changes the new way to see the current view. If you plan to use a certain view repeatedly, it's worth saving.

You can save any view you like by using the Define Views dialog box. Choose View ➪ Current View ➪ Define Views and follow the prompts. When you're comfortable with Outlook, you may want to give the Define Views method a try, but I think that you can do almost anything you want just by changing the views you already have.

Using Categories

There's a lot of value in a good collection of information. However, you can't squeeze full value from a list of contacts or tasks if you can't get a quick handle on which items are important and which aren't. The Categories feature in Outlook is designed to help you distinguish what's urgent from what can wait.

Assigning a category

When you first set up Outlook 2007, you can find out what categories are available by clicking the Categorize button at the top of the Inbox screen, just to the right of the Forward button, or by choosing Actions ➪ Categorize. The Categorize button looks like a small, multicolored tic-tac-toe square. Several other Outlook modules also display the Categorize button; it does the same job wherever you find it. Clicking the Categorize button brings up a list of (surprise!) categories, each named after a color. If you simply want to color code your items from the default, the process is pretty simple.

Follow these steps to assign a category to an item:

1. **Click the item you want to categorize.**

   The item is highlighted.

2. **Click the Categorize button and choose from the list.**

   A colored block appears in the item to indicate which category you chose.

You can assign multiple categories to each item, although putting too many on an item may be more confusing than assigning no categories at all.

Renaming a category

You can memorize what each Outlook category color means if you like, but I think that's rather difficult. I would rather have a name associated with each color so I know why I'm assigning a certain category to a certain item.

To rename a category, follow along:

1. **Click the Categories button and choose All Categories.**

   The Color Categories dialog box appears.

2. **Click the category you want to rename.**

   The category you select is highlighted.

3. **Click the Rename button.**

   The category you chose is surrounded by a box to show that you can edit it.

4. **Type the new name you want to assign to that category.**

   The name you type appears in place of the old name.

5. **Click OK.**

   The Color Categories dialog box closes.

If you change the name of a category that you had already assigned to some Outlook items, that category name changes on those items automatically.

Changing a category color

You can change the color of a category as well as its name. Assigning memorable colors can give important clues about how your work is going or how well you're keeping up with current projects.

Follow the steps to change the color of a category:

1. **Click the Categories button and choose All Categories.**

   The Color Categories dialog box appears.

2. **Click the category to which you want to assign a new color.**

   The category you select is highlighted.

3. **Click the Color button.**

   A drop-down box appears, showing the colors you can choose.

4. **Click the color you want to assign.**

   The color you chose appears in place of the old color.

5. **Click OK.**

   The Color Categories dialog box closes.

 You can also choose None and create a colorless category. That's kind of drab, but if it fits your mood, goes for it. One possible reason for creating colorless categories is because Outlook only offers 25 colors, and you may have more than 25 categories. But once you get past 25 categories, you might consider cutting down on the number of categories to reduce confusion.

Assigning a category shortcut key

You can give each category a shortcut key, which allows you to assign a category without touching your mouse. That's very handy when you want to zoom through a screen full of e-mail messages or tasks and set everything into some kind of order.

To assign a shortcut key to a category, follow these steps:

1. **Click the Categories button and choose All Categories.**

   The Color Categories dialog box appears.

2. **Click the category to which you want to assign a shortcut key.**

   The category you select is highlighted to show that you selected it.

3. **Click the Shortcut Key menu.**

   The list of shortcut keys appears.

4. **Click the shortcut key you want to assign.**

   The name of the shortcut key you chose appears to the right of the category.

5. **Click OK.**

   You can't assign more than one shortcut key to a category; that would be confusing. However, you can assign more than one category to an item.

Customizing Outlook Menus and Toolbars

You can customize Outlook's menus and toolbars to display a button for nearly any task that you use Outlook to do repeatedly. You also may want to make the Standard toolbar a little more advanced by adding one or two of your favorite tools from the Advanced toolbar. Customizing the toolbar is as easy as dragging and dropping, if you know where to start dragging. Here's what to do:

1. **Choose View ➪ Toolbars ➪ Customize.**

   The Customize dialog box appears.

2. **Click the Commands tab.**

   A list of command categories appears at the left side of the dialog box, and the commands in each category appear on the right.

3. **Click the name of the category of the command you want to add from the category column.**

   The commands in the selected category appear on the right.

4. **Select the command you want to add from the list on the right by clicking it once.**

   A heavy black border appears around the command you select.

5. **Drag the selected command to the menu or toolbar in which you want it to appear.**

   The command you dragged appears in the spot where you dragged it.

6. **Click Close.**

   Your command is now part of the toolbar.

Another trick you may want to try is changing the way toolbar buttons look. For example, although some buttons contain both an icon and text, the Organize button contains only an icon. If you want the Organize button to display both text and an icon, right click the Organize button (while the Customize dialog box is open) and then choose Image and Text from the menu that drops down from the Organize button.

 When the Customize dialog box is open, you can drag tools and menu commands to and from the Outlook toolbars and menus. Messing up Outlook's controls this way is amazingly easy, so be careful. If you do make a mess of things, choose View ➪ Toolbars ➪ Customize, and then click the Reset button to set everything right.

Chapter 17

Work from Anywhere with Outlook Web Access

- -

In This Chapter

▶ Logging in

▶ Reading and sending e-mail

▶ Viewing and entering appointments

▶ Organizing a meeting

▶ Posting to public folders

- -

Some jokers claim that WWW stands for World Wide Waste of time. Well, it's certainly easy to find Web pages devoted to goofing off, lollygagging, and just plain messing around, that's for sure! But one kind of Web page, called Outlook Web Access, can help you become super productive by giving you access to all your Outlook data from any Web-connected computer. If you take advantage of Outlook Web Access to get your work done sooner, you'll have extra time to fritter away as you please.

Outlook Web Access is part of a program called Microsoft Exchange, which many large and not-so-large organizations run to power advanced Outlook features such as public folders, shared calendars, and assigned tasks. Not every company that uses Microsoft Exchange offers Outlook Web Access, but if yours does, you can log on to Outlook nearly anywhere: from a computer at your local public library, an Internet café, or any old photocopy parlor. There's nothing difficult about Outlook Web Access; it's really nothing more than a special Web page that looks and acts quite a bit like the version of Outlook you have on your desk. If your company uses an older version of Microsoft Exchange, Outlook Web Access will look different than what I show in this chapter, but the essential features should be the same.

Outlook everywhere

Now that everyone is on the Internet and everyone carries a cell phone (or the like), it's possible to have your Outlook information everywhere at all times. You can access your Outlook information three main ways:

- ✔ Outlook on your desktop

- ✔ Outlook Web Access

- ✔ A mobile device (such as a Treo or Blackberry)

Why would you want three different ways to see the same information? The desktop approach offers more power and flexibility, Outlook Web Access gives you access from other people's computers, and a mobile device gives up-to-the-minute information and allows you to respond on the run.

The desktop version of Outlook is much more powerful than Outlook Web Access, but you many find it enormously convenient to get access to your Outlook data when you find yourself in certain situations, such as

- ✔ When you don't want to lug a laptop on a very short business trip just to check your e-mail.

- ✔ When you really *do* have to work from home now and then, and you don't want to fuss with getting your home computer connected to the office network.

- ✔ When you want to do some simple planning and collaborating with your office colleagues from someone else's computer.

- ✔ When you get an e-mail on a mobile device (such as a Blackberry or Treo phone) and want to compose a more detailed response than you'd attempt on the tiny thumb-keyboard built into those devices.

- ✔ When you need access to your e-mail and other Outlook data from a Mac (or another kind of computer that won't run Outlook).

Also, some organizations only offer Outlook Web Access to certain mobile employees who share a computer. That way the company can keep these people connected to the corporate e-mail system without purchasing a separate computer for every single employee.

Getting Started with Outlook Web Access

You don't need special software or equipment to use Outlook Web Access. If you can find your way to a page on the Internet, you have everything you need to use Outlook Web Access. You need to know only a few bits of information, such as your login name and password.

Logging on and off

You log in to Outlook Web Access the same way you sign on to any number of Web sites; go to the Internet, enter the address of the page that your organization has set up for logging on to Outlook Web Access and enter your user name and password. The exact steps of the process will differ between organizations, so you'll need to ask your system administrators for the details.

When you finish your Outlook Web Access session, you should log off by clicking the Log Off icon on the right side of the screen. If you're using a computer in a public place such as an Internet cafe, you don't want the next person using that computer to see your private information.

The Outlook screen

Outlook Web Access is designed to look a lot like the desktop version of Outlook, so you can switch between the two versions without having to learn a whole new bunch of tricks and techniques. You'll probably notice that the two programs feature a lot of the same icons, designs, and screen parts, including the following:

✔ The **Navigation Bar** is a stripe along the left side of the screen containing buttons labeled Inbox, Calendar, Contacts, Tasks, Public Folders, Rules, and Options; see Figure 17-1. When you click the Inbox, Calendar, Contacts, or Tasks button, the main screen reveals the items each of those icons describe: The Inbox displays e-mail messages, the calendar shows your appointments, and so on. The top half of the Navigation Bar displays all the folders you can see in your desktop version of Outlook, including Sent Items, Deleted Items, Tasks, and Notes.

✔ **Toolbars** in Outlook Web Access include fewer tools than the desktop version of Outlook, but they contain all the icons to do what you need to get done. You can get a description of what a toolbar button does by hovering your mouse pointer over the button until a little yellow message box pops up to give you details.

When you're using Outlook Web Access, you see many of the buttons and screens you may recognize from the regular version of Outlook, but you're still really using a Web browser. That means that the menus at the top of the screen, the ones labeled File, Edit, and so on, are part of the Browser program, not Outlook. So you can't click a menu and get the results you might expect. For example, if you're reading your e-mail and you choose File ➪ New, you won't see a New Message form (as you would in Outlook); instead, you automatically open a new window in Internet Explorer. Only the screens, toolbars, and buttons do the same in Outlook Web Access that they do in the desktop version of Outlook.

Figure 17-1:
The Outlook
Web
Access
screen
offers
toolbars and
buttons to
help you get
around.

Exchanging E-Mail

Whether you're reading messages from management or deleting get-rich-quick spams, you can log on to Outlook Web View from any browser to keep yourself in the loop.

Reading messages

If you're stuck out on the road without a company laptop, you still have many ways to catch up on your e-mail, but Outlook Web Access enables you to see the exact collection of messages that you have sitting in your Inbox at the office. Lots of people use the Inbox as a kind of to-do list; Outlook Web Access makes that possible from any computer connected to the Internet.

To read your messages, follow these steps:

1. **Click the Inbox icon.**

   Your list of messages appears.

2. Click the message you want to read.

The message text appears in the Reading Pane on the right side of the screen. As you click each message in the Message List, the contents show up in the Reading Pane.

Just use the arrow keys to move from one e-mail message to the next. An icon on the toolbar looks like a little message box split in half. Click that icon to see a list of Reading Pane options. You can choose to have the pane open on the right, on the bottom, or closed entirely. If you'd rather leave the Reading Pane closed, double-click any message to view its contents in a separate window.

Sending a message

When you feel the urge to dash off a quick e-mail from your favorite Internet cafe, you can do that with Outlook Web Access in a jiffy. You'll probably have your message finished before your barista finishes mixing that High-Octane Mocha Latte Supremo. Just follow these steps:

1. Click the Inbox icon in the Navigation Bar.

Your list of messages appears.

2. Click the New button in the toolbar.

The New Message screen opens (shown in Figure 17-2).

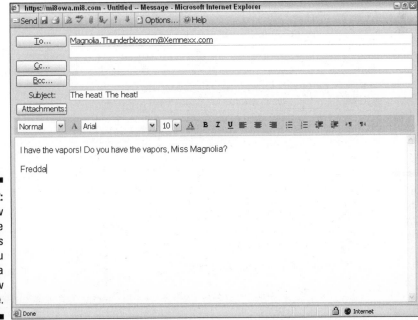

Figure 17-2:
The New Message form is where you create a new message.

3. **Fill out the New Message screen.**

   Put your recipient's address in the To box, a subject in the Subject box, and the message in the main box.

4. **Click the Send button at the top of the New Message screen.**

   Your message is on its way.

If you're not ready to send your message right away, you can click the Save button and resume work on your message later by clicking the Drafts folder to find your unfinished message. Clicking the message opens it for further editing.

Flagging messages

Outlook Web Access messages have the same flag feature that you know from the desktop version of Outlook. (However, when you set message flags on the desktop, you can add extra tricks such as dated reminders; you can't do that in Outlook Web Access. But the ability to flag a message for future reference can make you more efficient, no matter whether you do it on the Web or at your desktop. To flag a message in your Inbox, click the little outlined flag to the right of the message title. You can also right-click the outlined flag to open a shortcut menu that offers a variety of flag colors as well as the ability to clear a flag when you don't need it anymore; see Figure 17-3.

Figure 17-3:
Choose from a variety of flag colors in Outlook Web Access.

Setting individual message options

You can't set as many options for an individual message in Outlook Web Access as you can in the regular version of Outlook, but you can set priority and sensitivity levels or request delivery notifications and read receipts. Just follow these steps:

1. **Click the Inbox icon in the Navigation Bar.**

2. **Click the New button in the toolbar.**

3. **Fill out the New Message screen.**

   Put your recipient's address in the To box, a subject in the Subject box, and the message in the main box.

4. **Click the Options button on the toolbar.**

   The Message Options Web Page dialog box opens, showing the options you can choose from (as shown in Figure 17-4).

5. **Choose the options you want; then click Close.**

6. **Click Send.**

Figure 17-4: You can set your message to high priority in the Message Options screen.

It's a good idea not to overuse the message options available in Outlook Web Access. Setting all your messages to high priority, for example, eventually leads people to ignore your priority markings ("Oh, she thinks everything is urgent; just ignore her."). For a full explanation of message options, see Chapter 4.

An easy way to assign high priority to your message is to click the red exclamation point in the Message Form toolbar while you're creating your message.

Using Your Calendar

The beauty (and horror) of using Outlook is that it enables other people to add appointments to your calendar. That means sometimes you won't know what appointments are in your calendar, because you didn't put them there. (Some senior executives have assistants to enter Outlook calendar appointments on their behalf.)

So a word to the wise: Check your calendar regularly just to be sure you're in the right place at the right time.

Entering an appointment

If you're a heavy-duty road warrior, you probably keep your calendar on a handheld computer for your own reference — but your colleagues often need that information too. It's a good idea to keep your appointments posted in Outlook so other people at the office know when you're available for meetings, lunches, and random tongue-lashings.

To enter an appointment, follow these steps:

1. **Click the Calendar icon in the Outlook Bar.**

   The calendar appears, showing your appointments (as shown in Figure 17-5).

2. **Click the New button in the toolbar at the top of the screen.**

   The New Appointment form appears.

3. **Click the Subject box and enter a name for your appointment.**

   Enter something that describes your appointment, such as "Meeting with Bambi and Godzilla."

4. **Click the triangle next to the Start Time box.**

   A small calendar appears (as shown in Figure 17-6).

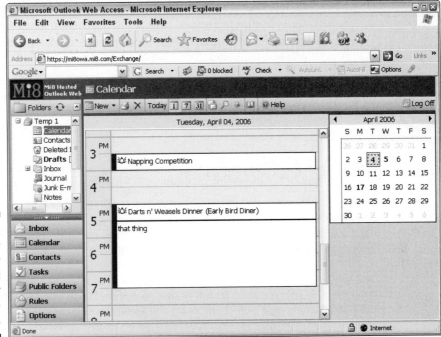

Figure 17-5:
Your calendar displays your appointments.

Figure 17-6:
Choose a start time for your appointment in the Start Time box.

5. **Click the date of your appointment.**

   If the pop-up calendar doesn't contain the date you have in mind, click the arrows next to the name of the month in the small calendar until the month you want appears.

6. **Click the box to the right of the box where you entered the date; then type in the time of your appointment.**

   The time you entered appears.

7. **Click Save & Close.**

While you're entering appointment information, you can enter the location, end time, and other information about your appointment in the appropriately labeled boxes.

Changing an appointment

You can change the hour of your appointment (but not the date) by simply dragging the appointment to the hour you desire. If you need to change the date or anything else about your appointment, double-click the appointment, select the information you want to change, enter the updated information, then click Save and Close. To delete an appointment, click the appointment to select it, and then click the black X in the toolbar to zap it completely. (You can find out more about the power of the Outlook calendar in Chapter 8.)

Viewing the Calendar

Time-management gurus insist that you manage your schedule for the long term, medium term, and short term. The Outlook Web Access calendar lets you view your appointments in different ways depending on what you want to see (or avoid seeing). The buttons at the top of the Calendar screen are for changing your view:

- ✔ Today shows today's appointments.
- ✔ 1 shows one day.
- ✔ 7 shows a week.
- ✔ 31 shows a month. Yes, even February. Don't quibble.

You can't view your schedule in Outlook Web Access at the level of detail that you can with the desktop version of Outlook, but you can add and change items to get the "big picture," then deal with the details back at your desk.

Managing Contacts

The whole point of Outlook Web Access is to let you see your collection of information from anywhere — and what's more important than keeping track of the people on your Contacts List? Practically nothing, so look at the basics.

Viewing your contacts

Some people see their Contacts List as pure gold. They ogle and admire it whenever they're not busy playing Solitaire. If you'd like to get a different view of your Contacts List, click the words in parentheses just to the right of the word Contacts at the top of the screen. That reveals a list of ways you can view your contacts; see Figure 17-7. For your viewing pleasure

- Address Cards
- Detailed Address Cards
- Phone List
- By Company
- By Location
- By Follow Up Flag

And now for the fine print . . .

Although Outlook Web Access can offer some pretty powerful capabilities to authorized users, it isn't for everybody. Here's why:

- Outlook Web Access works best when viewed with Microsoft's own Web browser, Internet Explorer. If you use another browser, such as Firefox or AOL, the program may look quite different from the way I describe it in this chapter. The basic functions are the same, but the exact locations of the buttons differ.

- Outlook Web Access is not actually a part of the Outlook program; it's built into the Microsoft Exchange program. You may run across a version that looks and acts quite different from the version I describe in this chapter (which is the one most widely available as I write this book).

- Outlook Web Access has to be set up by a network administrator through your organization's main computer network. Do-it-yourself setup isn't an option.

- If you work for a security-conscious organization that isn't comfortable letting confidential information show up on just any computer anywhere — aw, where's their sense of adventure? — you have to be understanding about that. In that case, stick to using Outlook on your regular desktop computer.

You can do much more powerful things with your list of contacts in the desktop version of Outlook, but seeing your contacts when you're away from your desk is mighty convenient.

Adding contacts

A good Contacts List is precious; it's even more valuable than that snazzy office chair you covet, or even that enviable cubicle near the coffee pot. Outlook Web Access can help you keep your Contacts List up to date from wherever you are. For example, if you go to a conference or convention and exchange business cards with lots of people, you probably want to get those names into your Contacts List as soon as possible. If your office has Outlook Web Access, you might want to stop at the nearest public library or Internet café, log in to your account remotely, and enter all those new addresses before you go home.

Figure 17-7:
You can choose among several views of your contacts.

To add a new contact through Outlook Web Access, follow these steps:

1. **Click the Contacts icon in the Navigation Bar.**

   Your list of contacts appears.

2. **Click the New button in the toolbar.**

   The Contact form appears (as shown in Figure 17-8).

3. **Fill in the blanks in the Contact form.**

   The information you type appears in the Contact form.

4. **Click Save and Close.**

   The Contact form closes and the name you entered appears in your list of contacts.

If you want to edit the contacts you've entered, just open a contact record and follow the same steps you use to enter information about a new contact. (For a fuller explanation of Outlook contact entries, see Chapter 7.)

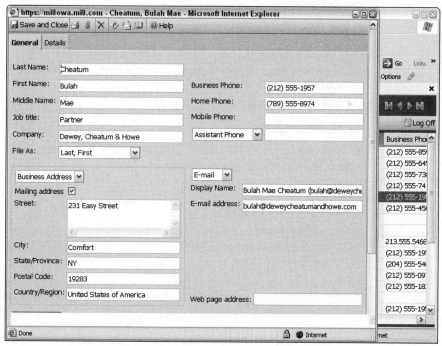

Figure 17-8:
Fill in the blanks in the Contact form to save information about the people you know.

Collaborating with Outlook Web Access

If you work in an organization where people hold lots and lots of meetings, you have my sympathy. To help you keep track of all those fascinating confabs, Outlook gives you the tools to stay current on who's meeting when and with whom. Otherwise you might miss that next meeting, and (horrors!) they could be talking about you.

Inviting attendees to a meeting

The only thing that seems to take more time than an office meeting is *planning* one. Although Outlook can't quiet the blowhard who bores everyone at weekly staff meetings (gotta let the boss have *some* fun), it can reduce the time you spend planning them. If you're charged with that duty, you can get a boost from Outlook Web Access by following these steps:

1. **With your calendar open, double-click the appointment to which you want to invite others.**

   The appointment form opens.

2. **Click the Invite Attendees button at the top of the form.**

   Three new lines appear at the top of the form, labeled Required, Optional, and Resources.

3. **Click the Required button.**

   The Find Names dialog box appears (as shown in Figure 17-9).

4. **Click the box labeled Last Name and enter the last name of a person you want to invite to the meeting.**

   The name you type appears.

5. **Click the Find button.**

   - If the name you entered is listed in your Global Address List, the name appears at the bottom of the dialog box (as shown in Figure 17-10).

   - If you just want to see the names of everyone at your company, don't enter any text in the Last Name box before searching; just press the spacebar once. If you search for a single blank space, the Find box shows the whole address list; then you can just start clicking names to add them to your meeting.

Figure 17-9:
The Find
Names
dialog box
searches for
people to
invite to
your
meeting.

Figure 17-10:
Search and
you will
find — at
the bottom
of the Find
screen.

6. **Click a name to select it; then click one of the three boxes at the bottom of the screen.**

   You can choose either Required or Optional, depending on how crucial that person's attendance is to the meeting. When you click Required, the name of the person you chose appears as a link in the Find Names dialog box.

   The third choice, Resource, is where you request something you may need for the meeting, such as a conference room or a projector. Some organizations don't set up this option, but the resource box appears anyway.

7. **Repeat Steps 5 and 6 until you've chosen everyone you want to add to the meeting.**

   The names you select appear as underlined text on the appointment form.

8. **Click the Close button in the Find Names dialog box.**

   At this point, you can click the Send button to send off your invitation, but you might want to check everyone's availability first. No use inviting people to a meeting they can't attend.

9. **Click the Availability tab.**

   The Availability page appears, showing a diagram of everyone's schedule. If you've picked a time that doesn't fit all attendees' schedules, use the Start Time and End Time boxes at the bottom of the screen to pick workable times.

10. **Click Send.**

    Your meeting request goes to the people you've invited.

Although the regular version of Outlook offers slicker planning tools than you'll find in Outlook Web Access, the Web version is a big help when you need a quick-and-dirty way to plan a meeting while you're away from the office.

Respond to a meeting request

If you travel a lot, you may need to check in frequently to see whether other people in your organization have summoned you to attend meetings when you return. Outlook Web Access enables other people to send you a special e-mail that invites you to a meeting. You can then accept that request to be automatically included in the meeting. To respond to a meeting request, follow these steps:

1. **Click the Inbox icon in the Navigation Bar.**

   Your list of messages appears.

2. **Click the message that includes a meeting request.**

   The message you click opens, displaying a special toolbar with buttons labeled Accept, Tentative, and Decline; see Figure 17-11. Meeting requests appear in your Inbox (as with any other e-mail message), but the icon in front of a meeting request looks different from the icon in front of other messages. (Normal e-mail messages have an icon that looks like a tiny envelope; the meeting request icon is an envelope with two faces in front of it.)

3. **Click one of the buttons in the toolbar; then click Send.**

   Your response is sent to the meeting organizer.

When you accept a meeting request, the meeting is automatically added to your calendar and the meeting organizer's calendar reflects the fact that you've agreed to attend the meeting. (To find out more about sending and responding to meeting requests, see Chapter 14.)

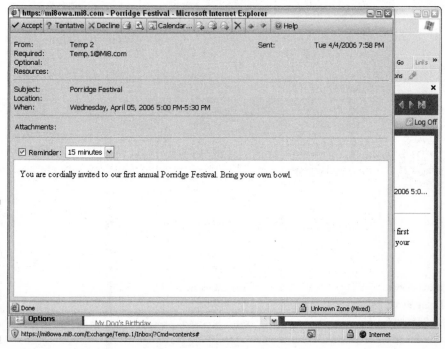

Figure 17-11:
A meeting request has special buttons for accepting or declining a meeting.

Using Public Folders

Many organizations set up a system called public folders — a forum for sharing information and for conducting ongoing group discussions. You can use Outlook Web Access to see your group's public folders and participate in the group discussion even when you're out of the office.

Viewing public folders

Before you jump into a conversation, you probably ought to find out what's being discussed. If the conversation is being held in a public folder, you can do that by following these steps:

1. **Click the Public Folders button in the Navigation Bar.**

   Your list of public folders appears (as shown in Figure 17-12).

2. **Click the name of the public folder you want to view.**

   A list of messages appears.

3. **Click the message you want to view.**

   The text of the message you click appears in the Reading Pane.

Figure 17-12:
The Folder List includes your collection of public folders.

The Reading Pane is normally on, allowing you to zoom through the messages in the folder you've selected by pressing the up and down arrow keys on your keyboard.

Adding items to a public folder

When you read a discussion in a public folder and you just can't resist putting your two cents in, don't (resist, that is). You can post your words of wisdom for all to see by following these steps:

1. **Click the Public Folders button in the Navigation Bar.**

   Your list of public folders appears.

2. **Click the name of the public folder to which you want to post a new message.**

   A list of messages appears.

3. **Click the New button in the toolbar.**

   The new message form appears.

4. **Enter the subject and text of your message, then click the Post button.**

   Your message is posted to the public folder you chose.

Bear in mind, public folders can be set up so most people can only read messages but not write messages to that folder. Don't be offended if your masterpiece doesn't get posted to a certain public folder; just ask your system administrator to tell you who owns the folder and ask them to give you rights to post to that folder. (For more about public folders, see Chapter 14.)

Exploring Your Options

You can adjust a limited number of options through Outlook Web Access. To see what options are available, click the Options icon in the Outlook Bar. You may want to adjust the e-mail notification options or the way dates are displayed. For the most part, however, you won't miss much if you leave the options alone.

Out of Office

If you have to call in sick, remember these two important rules:

- ✔ Don't come back from your "Sick Day" with a glorious new suntan.
- ✔ Turn on your Outlook Out of Office message so people don't think you're avoiding them (even if you are).

Of course, it's pretty silly to come into the office just to turn on your Outlook Out of Office message. With Web view, you can just log on from home (or Tahiti, or wherever you are) and set up an Out of Office message — which automatically sends a response to all incoming e-mail messages saying that you're not immediately available.

The option you're most likely to use is the Out of Office notice. After all, if you have to take a sick day, you don't want to have to drag into the office to turn on that pesky Out of Office message. Spare yourself the hassle (and your colleagues the germs) by following these steps:

1. **Click the Options icon in the Outlook Bar.**

   The Options page appears.

2. **Click the words I'm Currently Out of the Office.**

   The circle next to the words you clicked darkens, to show you've selected them. You can also add a detailed message, describing all the gory details of why you're absent. (Figure 17-13 shows a typical piteous example.)

3. **Click Save and Close.**

   The Options page closes.

Now you can stop feeling guilty about not coming in. (Well, okay, maybe you'll still feel a teeny bit guilty, but you've done your part.) Try to remember to turn your Out of Office message off when you get back to the office, otherwise your co-workers will think you're still at home lounging around and not at the office lounging around.

Ruling the school

Outlook lets you make the rules! Isn't that great? Well, okay, you only get to make rules about what happens to your incoming e-mail messages. Rules about washing the dishes or taking out the trash are made by someone else — usually your spouse or your mother. But you can still create an Outlook rule to ignore messages about trash and dishes. That's progress!

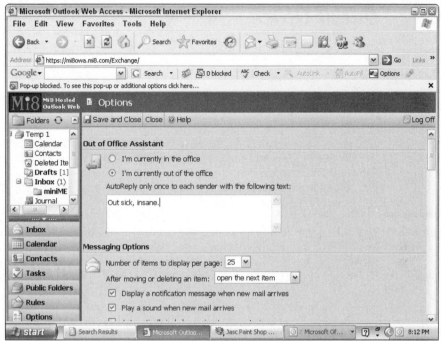

Figure 17-13:
If you're out
of the office,
let people
know.

Outlook Web Access only lets you make a few teeny-weeny rules, mostly about moving messages from certain people to certain folders. To create a new rule in Outlook Web Access, follow along:

1. **Click the Rules button in the Navigation Bar.**

   The Rules screen appears.

2. **Click the New button.**

   The Edit Rule screen appears, as shown in Figure 17-14.

3. **Fill out the Edit Rule screen.**

   For example, if you want to move messages that you get from a certain person into a certain folder, enter that person's e-mail address in the From Field Contains box, then click the underlined word specified in Move It to the Specified Folder. That opens the Move/Copy Item screen, where you can click a folder, and then click OK.

4. **Click Save and Close.**

You can only create fairly simple rules from Outlook Web Access, but any elaborate rules you created earlier in your desktop version still work when you're working in the Web version.

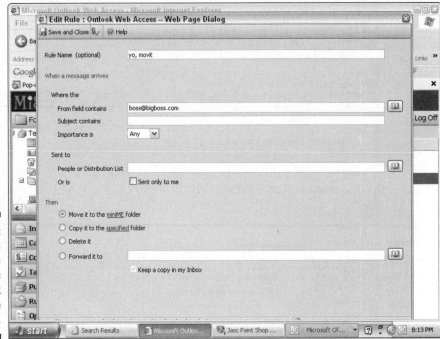

Figure 17-14:
You can
create
simple rules
in Outlook
Web
Access.

Creating a signature

You get to decide when to include the one signature you're allowed to create in Outlook Web Access. Your signature for business might be very grand and official, the better to impress lackeys and sycophants as well as to intimidate rivals. In that case, you might prefer to leave it off the messages you send to your friends. Unless, of course, your only friends are lackeys and sycophants; then, lay it on thick, Your Royal Highness!

Create a signature in Outlook Web Access with these steps:

1. **Click the Options button in the Navigation Bar.**

   The Options screen appears.

2. **Click the Edit Signature button.**

   You might have to scroll down a bit to see the button. When you click it, the Signature screen appears; see Figure 17-15.

Figure 17-15:
Create a
signature
for Outlook
Web
Access.

3. **Type your signature text.**

   You can stylize the text using the formatting buttons at the top of the screen.

4. **Click Save and Close.**

   The Signature screen closes.

If you click the Automatically Include My Signature on Outgoing Messages check box, you can guess what happens. That's right: Your signature is automatically included on all outgoing messages. What a coincidence! If you don't check the box, you can just click the signature button at the top of the message form when you want to add the signature to an e-mail.

Part VI
The Part of Tens

The 5th Wave   By Rich Tennant

"Roger! Check the sewing machine's connection to the PC. I'm getting e-mails stitched across my curtains again."

In this part . . .

Top-ten lists are everybody's favorite. They're short. They're easy to read. And they're the perfect spot for writers like me to toss in useful stuff that doesn't easily fit into the main chapters of the book. Flip through my top-ten list for tips you'll want to use, including a timesaving look at things you *can't* do with Outlook (so you don't have to waste your time trying).

Chapter 18

Top Ten Accessories for Outlook

*O*utlook can do plenty for you without any outside help, but a few well-considered accessories can make your life even easier. Some of my favorite accessories make up for capabilities that Outlook ought to have (in my humble opinion) but doesn't. Some of my other favorite accessories help me use my Outlook data anywhere, anytime.

Smartphones

A Treo smartphone is far and away my favorite "accessory" for Outlook. If you haven't shopped for a new cell phone lately, *smartphones* are cell phones with built-in personal organizing software. Although I can enter and manage data in a snap with Outlook, I can carry my most important Outlook info in my pocket on my Treo. I can even read my e-mail on the subway using the Treo (something I wouldn't try with a laptop).

Several types of smartphones and handheld computers are on the market today. I generally find it easier to utilize those that use the Palm operating system, although lately I've switched to a Treo that uses Windows Mobile, and I'm pretty happy with it. Other products worth considering include the Palm-brand devices, Hewlett-Packard handheld computers, and certain phones by Kyocera and Samsung. Some new handheld computers use the Pocket PC system that Microsoft makes.

Migo

Smartphones and handheld computers are only two of many ways to make your Outlook information portable. Another favorite of mine is Migo, a program that lets you synchronize your e-mail messages, contacts, calendar, tasks, notes, and even your recent documents to a Smartdrive, memory card, or iPod. You can then plug that device into a second computer and work as if you were sitting at your own computer. Not only is Migo handy when you're traveling, it's a slick way to keep a backup of your most recent work. You can find out more at www.migosoftware.com.

Microsoft Office

When Outlook was first released, it was a part of the Microsoft Office 97 suite. Now that you can buy Outlook as a stand-alone product (or in a package with Internet Explorer), you may not have the benefits of using Microsoft Office and Outlook in concert. Office enables you to do all sorts of tricks with outgoing e-mail and graphics, while Outlook makes it a snap to exchange the work you've created in Office via e-mail. I recommend using both, if possible.

A Business-Card Scanner

You can use several brands of business-card scanners to copy contact information into Outlook from the business cards you collect at conferences and trade shows. Of course, you *can* enter all the info manually, but if you collect more than a few dozen cards per week, a business-card scanner can save you lots of work. (Personally, I use a business-card scanner from Corex because I find it connects to Outlook seamlessly.)

A Large, Removable Disk Drive

The second most common question I hear is, "How do I back up my Outlook data for safekeeping?" Again, because the Outlook data file is much too big to save on a floppy disk, you may want a large-capacity device. You can pick up a large, external hard drive for as little as $100 or so. Hook one up to your Universal Service Bus (USB) port and add lots of extra space.

You might also consider a CD or DVD burner for backing up your Outlook data. Many new computers come with a burner already installed, so if you have one, take advantage of it.

Nelson E-mail Organizer

Lots of people are deluged with e-mail; it's not uncommon to meet someone who gets over 1,000 e-mail messages a week. If you live and die by e-mail, the Nelson E-mail Organizer (NEO) is designed to help you sort, organize, and manage e-mail collections with blazing speed. NEO uses a technique called *indexing,* which enables it to display any message you search for almost instantly. For more information about NEO, go to www.caelo.com.

Address Grabber

The quickest way I know of to fill up your Address Book is to capture addresses from the Internet by using a product called Address Grabber, which is available as a free download from www.eGrabber.com. If you've installed Address Grabber on your computer, just highlight any address that appears on-screen — from a Web page, a document, or an e-mail message — and the address is automatically sorted out and transferred to your Outlook Contacts List. It's a wonderful timesaver.

Microsoft Exchange

Many of the features that appear built into Outlook actually require you to run a program called Microsoft Exchange. Exchange lets you share your Outlook information with other people in your office and coordinate meetings and tasks. The program is pretty expensive and quite hairy to manage, but you can find outside companies to host it for you over the Internet. See Chapter 14 to find out more about Microsoft Exchange.

MindManager

The tasks you save in Outlook appear in nice, tidy rows and columns. In real life, your tasks probably come at you from all angles: up, down, and sideways. That's why I was happy to discover that of my favorite planning and brainstorming programs, MindManager now connects with Outlook. When you view your Outlook tasks in MindManager, you get an elaborate, weblike arrangement that helps you visualize the relationships among the many things you do. You can find out more about MindManager from the developer's site at www.mindjet.com.

Dymo LabelWriter

The people who designed Outlook got so excited about e-mail that they completely forgot about that old-fashioned stamp-and-paper system that some people still prefer. (How quaint!) Outlook alone can store zillions of mailing addresses, but it doesn't do a very good job of putting an address on an envelope. I use a Dymo LabelWriter to bridge that gap, printing any address from Outlook to a convenient gummed label that you can stick on a package or envelope faster than you can say "United States Postal Service."

Chapter 19

Ten (Or So) Things You Can't Do with Outlook

....

In This Chapter

▶ Put a phone number in your calendar

▶ Drag and drop many items

▶ Print on two sides

▶ Search phone numbers in reverse

▶ Search and replace area codes

▶ Nix AutoPreview

▶ Put pictures in notes

▶ Record all contact info in the Journal

▶ Do math with Journal phone call entries

▶ Cross-reference items

▶ Prevent people from nitpicking

....

Maybe I sound crabby listing the things that Outlook can't do, considering all the things it *can* do. But it takes only a few minutes to find out something that a program can do, and you can spend all day trying to figure out something that a program *can't* do. I could easily list *more* than ten things that Outlook can't do (walk the dog, deflect incoming asteroids — the usual). This chapter lists just the first big ones that I've run into.

The Top Ten (or so) List

Bear in mind that Outlook can't do these ten things when you first get it. Because you can reprogram Outlook with Visual Basic, however, a clever person could make Outlook do many of these things.

Change the Inbox color

You can color the individual items that you create in Outlook, but you can't do anything about the overall, plain-vanilla color scheme of the Inbox or any of the other modules. If you need more color in your life, dig out those rose-colored glasses.

Insert a phone number into your calendar

When you're entering an appointment, it would be nice if Outlook could look up the phone number of the person you're meeting and insert the number into the appointment record. If you have a Palm organizer, you may be used to doing just that with the Address Lookup feature, but you can't get Outlook to follow suit. Maybe some other time.

Drag and drop multiple items

You can drag an e-mail message to the Contact module to create a new contact record, but if the message has multiple recipients in the Cc field, you can't automatically turn that collection of addresses into a Distribution List. You have to type each one into a Distribution List one by one. What a drag!

Perform two-sided printing

Some people like to print their schedule and keep it in a binder to look just like one of those old-fashioned planner books. I guess they're just sentimental for the good ol' paper-and-pencil days. The only problem with that is that Outlook doesn't know how to reorganize printed pages according to whether the page is on the left side or the right side of the book when you look at it. This is a very small quibble, but if it's important to you, sorry — you'll have to live with one-sided printing.

Search and replace area codes

It seems like the people at the phone company change area codes more often than they change their socks these days. If you need to change all your 312s to 708s, Outlook can't do that automatically; you'll have to change them one by one.

Turn off AutoPreview globally

Sometimes the AutoPreview feature is pretty handy, but other times you want to save screen space with a simple list, sans preview. Your view of each folder is controlled separately, so if you want to turn off AutoPreview in all your folders, you need to go to each folder and turn off the feature one folder at a time.

Embed pictures in notes

You can copy and paste a picture, file, or other item into the text box at the bottom of any Outlook record when you open nearly any Outlook form. You can paste a photo of a person in the text box of the person's Contact record, for example, but those little, yellow stick-on notes don't let you do that; they accept only text.

Automatically record all contact stuff in the Journal

You can open the Tools ⇨ Options dialog box and check off all the names of contacts you want to record, but you can't click a single button that checks 'em all. When you click the Activities tab for a contact, Outlook searches for all items related to that contact so you can see where you stand with your important clients.

Calculate expenses with Journal phone call entries

You can keep track of how much time you spend talking to any person, but you can't calculate the total call time or total call cost for billing purposes.

Create a Distribution List from a single e-mail

When you get an e-mail message addressed to a whole group of people, it would be nice to be able to create a Distribution List directly from that message. That way you can send messages to that whole group by sending to a single Distribution List address. You can turn a message from a single person into an individual contact record by dragging the message to the Contact icon, but you can't do that to create a group: You have to add every single person individually to the Distribution List.

Back up Outlook data

Many people store their most critical business information in Outlook — information that is so valuable that losing it could practically close a business or end a career. It's no joke. But after more than ten years in the marketplace, Outlook has never been given a decent tool for safeguarding its own data from loss. Besides, Outlook is well known for corrupting its own data files, which means that the biggest threat to your Outlook data might be Outlook itself.

Yes, everyone knows that you should back up all the data on your computer regularly, and you can make copies of your critical Outlook data (some of those tiny memory keys can do the job, and you can save Outlook data to a handheld computer if need be), but it's a little bit disturbing that no such feature has ever been added to Outlook itself.

Ten More Things Outlook Can't Do for You

Alas, Outlook is also deficient in some other ways, though you may prefer to do these things for yourself, anyway.

Outlook can't

- ✔ Do the Electric Slide.
- ✔ Play "Melancholy Baby" for you.
- ✔ Tattoo the name of you-know-who on your you-know-what.
- ✔ Catch the Energizer Bunny.
- ✔ Stop tooth decay.
- ✔ Take the *Jeopardy!* Challenge.
- ✔ Refresh your breath while you scream.
- ✔ Fight City Hall.
- ✔ Make millions while you sleep.
- ✔ Find Mr. Right (unless you send e-mail to me).

Oh, well. Aside from all that, it's a pretty neat program. You can save scads of time and work more smoothly by mastering all the things Outlook *can* do for you.

Chapter 20

Ten Things You Can Do After You're Comfy

*I*f Outlook is an iceberg's worth of capabilities, I can only show you the tip in this book. You can already do some formidable tasks with Outlook. Time will tell (and pretty quickly at that) how much more you'll be able to do with future versions of Outlook, Internet Explorer, and all the other powerful technology associated with those applications.

You can't do much to really mess up Outlook, so feel free to experiment. Add new fields, new views, new icons — go wild. This chapter describes a few Outlook adventures to try out.

Customizing the Quick Access Toolbar

Office 2007 features an arrangement of controls (a *user interface,* as geeks like to say) that eliminates menus in favor of big ribbons, tabs, and buttons. The new scheme is much more colorful, but I have trouble figuring out how to do many of the things I want to do. With an old-fashioned menu system, you know that everything you want to do is on a menu somewhere. In the new arrangement . . . who knows? If you find the new system confusing, don't feel bad; I've been writing books about Outlook for over ten years now, and I'm often baffled by this new scheme.

There is hope, however. Once you've found the tool you need, you can right-click the tool and choose Add to Quick Access toolbar. That adds a tiny icon to that thin strip of icons that sits just above the ribbon of buttons (or below the ribbon, if you move it there). If you've ever bookmarked a Web site, you know how this works. If you right-click the Quick Access toolbar and choose Move the Quick Access Toolbar below the Ribbon, that's exactly what happens.

The main Outlook screens haven't been affected by this new arrangement, thank goodness, so the Quick Access toolbar isn't necessary there. However, many of the forms you use to compose e-mail messages and enter appointments have gone to the dark side.

Embellishing E-Mail with Word Art

Now you can spiff up your e-mail messages with all kinds of colorful graphics and individual designs. You may have already seen the Word Art tool, a feature that's been available in Microsoft Word for years. Now the tool is built right into Outlook.

Follow these steps to add Word Art:

1. **Create a new e-mail.**

2. **Click the Insert tab.**

3. **Click the Word Art button.**

4. **Click one of the examples in the gallery of available text styles.**

5. **Type some text.**

6. **Click OK.**

Try to use Word Art sparingly, at least in business situations, lest your business colleagues begin to see you as slightly insane.

Wising Up Your Messages with Smart Art

I don't know if art makes you smart, but design can make you look smart if you know what you're doing. If you don't know what you're doing, you can fall back on Smart Art, another intriguing feature on the Insert Ribbon. Smart Art helps you create colorful, annotated designs to add to your e-mail. To get a better picture of what Smart Art can do, click the Insert tab, click the Smart Art button, and try a few designs on for size.

Adding Charts for Impact

Just a few doors down from the Word Art button on the Insert Ribbon is the Chart tool, which can make the thoughts you express in your e-mail look positively orderly (no matter how disordered you mind may be).

Chart it up with these steps:

1. **Click the Chart tool.**

   You see a two-part gallery: a list of general chart types on the left and specific examples of each type on the right.

2. **Choose a general type from the list on the left.**

3. **Choose a specific type from the list on the right.**

4. **Click OK.**

   A grid opens, allowing you to enter numbers.

The mechanics of creating an Outlook chart are very similar to those for creating an Excel chart. If you need more detailed information about creating charts, pick up a copy of *Office 2007 All-in-One Desk Reference For Dummies* (Wiley).

Opening Multiple Calendars

You can create more than one calendar in Outlook. You might want to do so to track the activities of more than one person, or to keep your business life separate from your personal life (which is always a good idea). The tricky part of keeping multiple calendars is dealing with schedule conflicts between the two. To see two calendars at a time, click the check box next to each calendar name in the Navigation Pane to view both calendars.

Superimposing Calendars

An even slicker way to avoid conflicts on multiple calendars is to superimpose one calendar on top of another. When you have two calendars open, a small arrow appears next to the name of one. When you click that arrow, both calendars appear, one atop the other, with both sets of appointments showing. The appointments in the bottom calendar appear slightly opaque, while the top calendar items look clearer and bolder than the bottom ones. When calendars are superimposed, you can see right away when there's time available on both.

Viewing Unusual Numbers of Days

When you're viewing your calendar, you can decide to view only three days or eight days or, for that matter, any number between one and ten days by holding down the Alt key and typing the number of days you want to see. Press Alt+2 for two days, Alt+3 for three days, and so on. Pressing Alt+0 (zero) gives you ten days.

Selecting Dates as a Group

When you're viewing a range of dates, you don't have to limit yourself to fixed days, weeks, or months. Suppose you want to look at a range of dates from September 25 to October 5. In the To-Do Bar, click September 25, and then (while pressing the Shift key) click October 5. All the dates in between are selected, appearing in the Information Viewer.

Turning on Additional Toolbars

Outlook has several toolbars to choose from if the mood strikes you. The Standard toolbar is the one that shows up when you first start Outlook. You can only see the Advanced toolbar if you turn it on by choosing View ➪ Toolbars ➪ Advanced. You don't have to be advanced to use the Advanced toolbar, so give it a try. You can also flip on the Web toolbar by choosing View ➪ Toolbars ➪ Web.

Opening a Web Page from Outlook

If you like to surf the Net, your best bet is to use a Web browser, such as Internet Explorer, which was made for the job. If you want to browse a page now and then from Outlook, that's possible, too.

To open a Web page from Outlook, follow these steps:

1. **Choose View ⇨ Toolbars ⇨ Web.**

    The Web toolbar appears, along with any other toolbars you have open.

2. **Click the Address box on the Web toolbar.**

    The Address box contains strange-looking text, something like `outlook:\\personal%20Folders\Inbox`. When you click that text, it turns blue.

3. **Type the Web page URL you want to view.**

    You've seen Web addresses everywhere: those odd strings of letters that begin with *www,* such as `www.outlookfordummies.com`.

4. **Press Enter.**

    The address of the page you've entered appears in Outlook's main screen.

The Web toolbar also contains some of the same browser buttons Internet Explorer has to help you navigate.

Index

Notes

BUSINESS, CAREERS & PERSONAL FINANCE

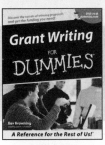

Grant Writing FOR DUMMIES
0-7645-5307-0

Home Buying FOR DUMMIES
0-7645-5331-3 *†

Also available:

- Accounting For Dummies †
  0-7645-5314-3
- Business Plans Kit For Dummies †
  0-7645-5365-8
- Cover Letters For Dummies
  0-7645-5224-4
- Frugal Living For Dummies
  0-7645-5403-4
- Leadership For Dummies
  0-7645-5176-0
- Managing For Dummies
  0-7645-1771-6

- Marketing For Dummies
  0-7645-5600-2
- Personal Finance For Dummies *
  0-7645-2590-5
- Project Management For Dummies
  0-7645-5283-X
- Resumes For Dummies †
  0-7645-5471-9
- Selling For Dummies
  0-7645-5363-1
- Small Business Kit For Dummies *†
  0-7645-5093-4

HOME & BUSINESS COMPUTER BASICS

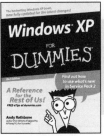

Windows XP FOR DUMMIES
0-7645-4074-2

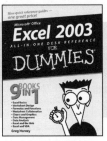

Excel 2003 FOR DUMMIES
0-7645-3758-X

Also available:

- ACT! 6 For Dummies
  0-7645-2645-6
- iLife '04 All-in-One Desk Reference
  For Dummies
  0-7645-7347-0
- iPAQ For Dummies
  0-7645-6769-1
- Mac OS X Panther Timesaving
  Techniques For Dummies
  0-7645-5812-9
- Macs For Dummies
  0-7645-5656-8

- Microsoft Money 2004 For Dummies
  0-7645-4195-1
- Office 2003 All-in-One Desk Reference
  For Dummies
  0-7645-3883-7
- Outlook 2003 For Dummies
  0-7645-3759-8
- PCs For Dummies
  0-7645-4074-2
- TiVo For Dummies
  0-7645-6923-6
- Upgrading and Fixing PCs For Dummies
  0-7645-1665-5
- Windows XP Timesaving Techniques
  For Dummies
  0-7645-3748-2

FOOD, HOME, GARDEN, HOBBIES, MUSIC & PETS

Feng Shui FOR DUMMIES
0-7645-5295-3

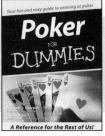

Poker FOR DUMMIES
0-7645-5232-5

Also available:

- Bass Guitar For Dummies
  0-7645-2487-9
- Diabetes Cookbook For Dummies
  0-7645-5230-9
- Gardening For Dummies *
  0-7645-5130-2
- Guitar For Dummies
  0-7645-5106-X
- Holiday Decorating For Dummies
  0-7645-2570-0
- Home Improvement All-in-One
  For Dummies
  0-7645-5680-0

- Knitting For Dummies
  0-7645-5395-X
- Piano For Dummies
  0-7645-5105-1
- Puppies For Dummies
  0-7645-5255-4
- Scrapbooking For Dummies
  0-7645-7208-3
- Senior Dogs For Dummies
  0-7645-5818-8
- Singing For Dummies
  0-7645-2475-5
- 30-Minute Meals For Dummies
  0-7645-2589-1

INTERNET & DIGITAL MEDIA

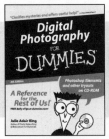

Digital Photography FOR DUMMIES
0-7645-1664-7

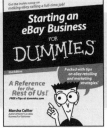

Starting an eBay Business FOR DUMMIES
0-7645-6924-4

Also available:

- 2005 Online Shopping Directory
  For Dummies
  0-7645-7495-7
- CD & DVD Recording For Dummies
  0-7645-5956-7
- eBay For Dummies
  0-7645-5654-1
- Fighting Spam For Dummies
  0-7645-5965-6
- Genealogy Online For Dummies
  0-7645-5964-8
- Google For Dummies
  0-7645-4420-9

- Home Recording For Musicians
  For Dummies
  0-7645-1634-5
- The Internet For Dummies
  0-7645-4173-0
- iPod & iTunes For Dummies
  0-7645-7772-7
- Preventing Identity Theft For Dummies
  0-7645-7336-5
- Pro Tools All-in-One Desk Reference
  For Dummies
  0-7645-5714-9
- Roxio Easy Media Creator For Dummies
  0-7645-7131-1

* Separate Canadian edition also available

† Separate U.K. edition also available

Available wherever books are sold. For more information or to order direct: U.S. customers visit www.dummies.com or call 1-877-762-2974.
U.K. customers visit www.wileyeurope.com or call 0800 243407. Canadian customers visit www.wiley.ca or call 1-800-567-4797.

SPORTS, FITNESS, PARENTING, RELIGION & SPIRITUALITY

0-7645-5146-9

0-7645-5418-2

Also available:
- Adoption For Dummies
  0-7645-5488-3
- Basketball For Dummies
  0-7645-5248-1
- The Bible For Dummies
  0-7645-5296-1
- Buddhism For Dummies
  0-7645-5359-3
- Catholicism For Dummies
  0-7645-5391-7
- Hockey For Dummies
  0-7645-5228-7

- Judaism For Dummies
  0-7645-5299-6
- Martial Arts For Dummies
  0-7645-5358-5
- Pilates For Dummies
  0-7645-5397-6
- Religion For Dummies
  0-7645-5264-3
- Teaching Kids to Read For Dummies
  0-7645-4043-2
- Weight Training For Dummies
  0-7645-5168-X
- Yoga For Dummies
  0-7645-5117-5

TRAVEL

0-7645-5438-7

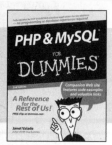

0-7645-5453-0

Also available:
- Alaska For Dummies
  0-7645-1761-9
- Arizona For Dummies
  0-7645-6938-4
- Cancún and the Yucatán For Dummies
  0-7645-2437-2
- Cruise Vacations For Dummies
  0-7645-6941-4
- Europe For Dummies
  0-7645-5456-5
- Ireland For Dummies
  0-7645-5455-7

- Las Vegas For Dummies
  0-7645-5448-4
- London For Dummies
  0-7645-4277-X
- New York City For Dummies
  0-7645-6945-7
- Paris For Dummies
  0-7645-5494-8
- RV Vacations For Dummies
  0-7645-5443-3
- Walt Disney World & Orlando For Dummies
  0-7645-6943-0

GRAPHICS, DESIGN & WEB DEVELOPMENT

0-7645-4345-8

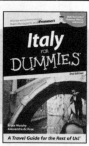

0-7645-5589-8

Also available:
- Adobe Acrobat 6 PDF For Dummies
  0-7645-3760-1
- Building a Web Site For Dummies
  0-7645-7144-3
- Dreamweaver MX 2004 For Dummies
  0-7645-4342-3
- FrontPage 2003 For Dummies
  0-7645-3882-9
- HTML 4 For Dummies
  0-7645-1995-6
- Illustrator CS For Dummies
  0-7645-4084-X

- Macromedia Flash MX 2004 For Dummies
  0-7645-4358-X
- Photoshop 7 All-in-One Desk Reference For Dummies
  0-7645-1667-1
- Photoshop CS Timesaving Techniques For Dummies
  0-7645-6782-9
- PHP 5 For Dummies
  0-7645-4166-8
- PowerPoint 2003 For Dummies
  0-7645-3908-6
- QuarkXPress 6 For Dummies
  0-7645-2593-X

NETWORKING, SECURITY, PROGRAMMING & DATABASES

0-7645-6852-3

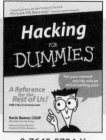

0-7645-5784-X

Also available:
- A+ Certification For Dummies
  0-7645-4187-0
- Access 2003 All-in-One Desk Reference For Dummies
  0-7645-3988-4
- Beginning Programming For Dummies
  0-7645-4997-9
- C For Dummies
  0-7645-7068-4
- Firewalls For Dummies
  0-7645-4048-3
- Home Networking For Dummies
  0-7645-42796

- Network Security For Dummies
  0-7645-1679-5
- Networking For Dummies
  0-7645-1677-9
- TCP/IP For Dummies
  0-7645-1760-0
- VBA For Dummies
  0-7645-3989-2
- Wireless All-in-One Desk Reference For Dummies
  0-7645-7496-5
- Wireless Home Networking For Dummies
  0-7645-3910-8